Edco Drama for Schools

William Shakespeare's

Hamlet

for Leaving Certificate

with annotations, analysis and commentary by
Patrick Murray

Edco
The Educational Company of Ireland

First published 2015

The Educational Company of Ireland
Ballymount Road
Walkinstown
Dublin 12

www.edco.ie

A member of the Smurfit Kappa Group plc

ISBN: 978-1-84536-641-4

The paper used in this book comes from Managed Forests in Northern Europe For every tree felled, at least one new tree is planted

Editor: Jennifer Armstrong

Design, layout and cover: Liz White Designs

Cover photography: Karl Hugh, courtesy of the Utah Shakespeare Festival, 2006

Photograph acknowledgements:

Pages 6, 16, 54, 83, 116, 120, 122, 131, 134, 136, 141, 142, 152, 162, 163, 166, 173, 174, 177, 185, 230, 232, 233, 244, 250, 282, 283: Brian Stethem, courtesy of the Kingsmen Shakespeare Company

Pages 29, 41, 42, 49, 51, 61, 69, 76, 87, 97, 103, 151, 190, 222, 223, 227, 229, 234, 237, 242, 243, 251, 254, 272, 273, 275, 278, 279, 280: New American Shakespeare Tavern

Pages 53, 86, 133, 147, 165, 176, 211, 217, 218, 219, 220, 255, 256, 257, 258, 259, 260, 261: Shutterstock

Pages 212, 215: TopFoto

Pages iv, 5, 14, 20, 36, 60, 115, 138, 191, 192, 224, 225, 235, 239, 240, 241, 248, 252, 263, 276, 277: Karl Hugh, courtesy of the Utah Shakespeare Festival, 2006

While every care has been taken to trace and acknowledge copyright, the publishers tender their apologies for any accidental infringement where copyright has proved untraceable. They would be pleased to come to a suitable arrangement with the rightful owner in each case.

Preface

All modern students of Shakespeare's plays struggle with the difference between his language, particularly his diction, and present-day English. Some of the words in *Hamlet* are no longer in common use, and some have different meanings from those they had when the play was written over four hundred years ago. The syntax, or ordering of words, can also be complex, even puzzling.

In response, this edition of *Hamlet* seeks to enlighten the reader by providing useful explanatory notes in the margins of the text, summaries for each scene and detailed commentary on the play. These features will ensure that students have a good understanding of the text.

To appreciate a play, we must think about what is happening to and within the characters, as revealed by their actions, dialogue with other characters, soliloquies and asides. Questions at the end of each scene and activities at the end of each Act should stimulate such thinking. They are designed to suit both Ordinary and Higher Level students. Detailed accounts of the characters are given at the back of the book.

It is also important to be aware of the kind of world in which *Hamlet* was written (Elizabethan England). This edition therefore includes contextual information on the type of theatre and audience for which Shakespeare wrote the play.

All the major areas prescribed for study in the Leaving Certificate syllabus in relation to *Hamlet* are extensively covered. These include literary genre (i.e. revenge tragedy); themes; imagery; general vision and viewpoint; roles of hero and villain; character change and development; and relationships between characters.

Colour photographs from various theatre productions of *Hamlet* are displayed throughout the book. These images remind students that they are dealing with a play and provide a chance to consider different casting and staging decisions.

To assist with revision and exam preparation, key moments in the play and useful quotations are identified. A final section is devoted to typical exam questions, accompanied by some tips and sample answers.

The approach taken to *Hamlet* in this edition will help students to:

- develop an appreciation of Shakespeare's use of language
- acquire a sound knowledge of the meaning of the text
- understand the workings of the plot
- recognise the play's tragic elements, themes and imagery
- study the characters, their motives and their interactions with each other
- learn about the social, cultural and intellectual background to the play
- remember that *Hamlet* was written for performance rather than reading
- learn about Shakespeare's theatre and audience
- consider how the play might be performed and produced today.

Teachers can access the *Hamlet* e-book at **www.edcodigital.ie**.

Contents

Introduction

About William Shakespeare

LITTLE IS KNOWN FOR certain about William Shakespeare. His father, John, moved to Stratford-upon-Avon in Warwickshire in the 1550s, practised a variety of trades, achieved prosperity, owned property and became a leading citizen of the town, which then had a population of about 1,000. William Shakespeare was christened in the parish church in Stratford on 26 April 1564.

It seems likely that Shakespeare went to the local grammar school until he was aged sixteen. However, the attendance records of the school have not been preserved. At that time a grammar school education focused on the Latin language, its grammar and its literature, and on rhetoric, which is the art of public speaking. Ancient Roman history was also studied. Such knowledge is evident in Shakespeare's plays.

In 1582 Shakespeare married Anne Hathaway. She was twenty-six years of age; he was eighteen. They had three children: Susanna and twins, Judith and Hamnet. Hamnet died in 1596, aged eleven. No record of Anne exists between the baptisms of her children and the drafting of her husband's will in 1616, when he left her his second-best bed.

By the 1590s Shakespeare was an established actor and a promising dramatist, based in London. We do not know how he became a man of the theatre or when he left Stratford. By 1595 he was a shareholder in an acting company. Two years later he was able to buy New Place, the second-largest property in Stratford. He retired to Stratford in 1611, and died there in 1616.

Shakespeare combined his creativity and mastery of language with an impressive business sense. He wrote at least thirty-seven plays, including five tragic masterpieces: *Hamlet*, *Othello*, *King Lear*, *Macbeth* and *Anthony and Cleopatra*. He also wrote poetry and he contributed hundreds of new words and phrases to the English language.

Records show him acquiring considerable property and shrewdly protecting his legal interests. He also purchased farmland and an interest in tithes (church taxes), which guaranteed a substantial income. When debts owing to him were unpaid, he was quick to sue the defaulters, even in petty cases.

About *Hamlet*

SHAKESPEARE DID NOT OVERSEE the printing of those editions of his plays published during his lifetime. Much of his work was still in manuscript form when he died, and remained so until two of his friends and colleagues published his plays in 1623 in an edition now known as the First Folio.

MR. WILLIAM
SHAKESPEARES
COMEDIES,
HISTORIES, &
TRAGEDIES.
Published according to the True Originall Copies.

LONDON
Printed by Isaac Iaggard, and Ed. Blount. 1623.

Hamlet was written between 1600 and 1601. It first appeared in print in 1603 in what became known as the 'bad' Quarto edition as many lines were missing or incorrect. A second Quarto edition in 1604 was described by its publishers as a 'true and perfect copy'.

About Shakespeare's theatre

THE THEATRES THAT hosted most of the early performances of Shakespeare's plays were public ones, such as the Globe theatre. Shakespeare was a shareholder in the Globe, which was situated close to the River Thames in Southwark, London. It opened in 1599.

A Dutch traveller called Johannes de Witt made a drawing around 1596 of London's Swan theatre. A copy of de Witt's drawing is shown here. It is the only surviving sketch of the interior of the kind of playhouse in which Shakespeare's plays were first performed. The Swan was quite a large theatre and de Witt estimated that it could hold 3,000 spectators.

The drawing, labelled in Latin, shows a round, open-air playhouse. The main feature is the large stage (*proscaenium*) with its overhead canopy known as 'the heavens'. The stage extends into an open yard, described as level ground without sand (*planities sine arena*).

For the price of a penny, spectators (called 'groundlings') stood in the yard looking up at the actors. There were also three tiers of galleries, where, for an extra penny or two, people could sit and avail of some shelter under the roof (*tectum*).

The wealthiest members of the audience wanted to see and also to be seen and therefore availed of a private box in a gallery above the stage. This gallery was part of the tiring-house (*mimorum ades*) building at the back of the stage. It housed a dressing area where actors changed their costumes or attire (hence the term 'tiring-house') and stored props.

The tiring-house was topped by a storage loft and a flagpole. A banner was hoisted to indicate that a play would be performed that afternoon. Different flags may have been used for different types of play, for example comedy or tragedy. The man shown outside the loft in the drawing appears to be sounding a trumpet.

Actors entered and exited the stage through two sets of large doors in the tiring-house façade. There was no painted scenery to indicate where the action was taking place. The audience members suspended their disbelief and understood the stage to be any place required by the action.

Trapdoors permitted action below the stage, such as can be seen in the scenes involving the ghost and the gravediggers in *Hamlet*.

Women were not permitted to take part in dramatic performances and female characters were played by specially trained boy-actors.

Dramatists were experts in using language to set a scene. For example, the opening scene of *Hamlet* is a night scene, but performances in the playhouse took place in daylight. To overcome this problem, the language spoken by the actors gives the impression of a cold, dark night: "Tis now struck twelve, get thee to bed . . . 'tis bitter cold . . . '.

The relative absence of scenery and stage props meant that productions depended on descriptions of scenery and stage-effects rather than on the use of these. Such references drew attention to the permanent structure of the theatre. For example, an actor making a reference to the stars is likely to have gestured towards the underside of 'the heavens', which was painted to represent the sky and the heavenly bodies.

The physical shape of Shakespeare's theatre, particularly the projecting stage and canopy and the watching audience become part of the meaning of *Hamlet* at various points in the play. See, for example, Act 1, Scene 5, lines 96–7; Act 2, Scene 2, lines 286–90; Act 5, Scene 2, lines 325–6. In this way, Shakespeare breaks down the barrier between illusion and reality, and reminds the members of his audience that they are attending a play, even giving them a sense that they are participating in it.

Audience members were trained listeners, and much better equipped than modern audiences to cope with Shakespeare's blank (unrhymed) verse and complex word order. The majority enjoyed listening to and learning from very long church sermons. Such sermons featured magnificent passages of rhetoric, subtle argument and splendid imagery.

Sketch of the interior of the Swan Theatre, by Johannes de Witt,
as copied by Aernout van Buchel, c. 1596.

KEY

1 Playhouse flag
2 Storage loft
3 The heavens
4 Gallery over stage
5 Tiring-house
6 Stage doors
7 Upper gallery
8 Middle gallery
9 Entrance to lower gallery
10 Stage
11 Hell (under stage)
12 Yard

HAMLET

Dramatis personae

HAMLET	Prince of Denmark
KING CLAUDIUS	of Denmark, brother of the late King Hamlet
QUEEN GERTRUDE	of Denmark, Hamlet's mother
GHOST	of the late King Hamlet of Denmark, Hamlet's father
HORATIO	friend of Hamlet
POLONIUS	chief counsellor to King Claudius
LAERTES	son of Polonius
OPHELIA	daughter of Polonius
REYNALDO	servant of Polonius
VOLTEMAND	courtier, Ambassador to Norway
CORNELIUS	courtier, Ambassador to Norway
ROSENCRANTZ	courtier
GUILDENSTERN	courtier
OSRIC	courtier
MARCELLUS	officer of the Royal Guard
BARNARDO	officer of the Royal Guard
FRANCISCO	officer of the Royal Guard
FORTINBRAS	Prince of Norway

LORDS, ENGLISH AMBASSADORS, GENTLEMEN, ATTENDANTS, A MESSENGER, PLAYERS, MUSICIANS, A PRIEST, GRAVEDIGGERS, A CAPTAIN, SOLDIERS, SAILORS, AND FOLLOWERS OF LAERTES

ACT 1 † Scene 1

Plot summary

The play opens with a solitary soldier, Francisco, on guard on the battlements of Elsinore Castle, the residence of the newly married King Claudius and Queen Gertrude of Denmark. Gertrude is the widow of King Hamlet, who died recently. Claudius was King Hamlet's brother.

The scene is played out in the cold, dark hours between midnight and dawn. Barnardo arrives to take over the watch from Francisco. The men are tense and anxious. Horatio and Marcellus join Barnardo and they discuss recent events. A ghostly figure, resembling the late King Hamlet, appears. Horatio (who is a scholar, not a soldier) challenges the ghost, which stalks away. The men talk about Denmark's war preparations and fear of a Norwegian attack. The ghost returns, but leaves on hearing a cock crow, which signals the arrival of dawn. The men agree to tell Prince Hamlet what they have seen.

Before my God, I might not this believe
Without the sensible and true avouch
Of mine own eyes.

HORATIO, Act 1, Scene 1, 59–61

Elsinore. The guard-platform of the castle.

FRANCISCO at his post. Enter BARNARDO.

BARNARDO
Who's there?

FRANCISCO
Nay, answer me. Stand and unfold yourself.

[handwritten: This introduces the idea that the world is upside down]

BARNARDO
Long live the king!

FRANCISCO
Barnardo?

BARNARDO
He.   5

FRANCISCO
You come most carefully upon your hour.

BARNARDO
'Tis now struck twelve; get thee to bed, Francisco.

FRANCISCO
For this relief much thanks: 'tis bitter cold,
And I am sick at heart.

BARNARDO
Have you had quiet guard?   10

FRANCISCO
Not a mouse stirring.

BARNARDO
Well, good night.
If you do meet Horatio and Marcellus,
The rivals of my watch, bid them make haste.

Enter HORATIO and MARCELLUS.

FRANCISCO
I think I hear them. Stand, ho! Who's there?   15

HORATIO
Friends to this ground.

MARCELLUS
                         And liegemen to the Dane.

FRANCISCO
Give you good night.

---

2   *Nay . . . yourself:* no, you must answer to *me*. Stop there and tell me who *you* are. Barnardo has no business making the first challenge, since he is the one coming on guard. It is clear from this opening exchange that the men are uneasy

6   *You . . . hour:* Francisco notes Barnardo's punctual arrival on duty, and commends him for being considerate

7   *'Tis . . . twelve:* it is midnight (the hour when ghosts were said to appear)

8   *For this relief:* for relieving me of my duty

10   *quiet guard:* a peaceful time on duty

14   *The . . . haste:* my partners on guard duty, tell them to hurry up. Barnardo does not want to be left alone for long

16   *this ground:* Denmark

16   *And . . . Dane:* and loyal soldiers of its king

17   *Give . . . night:* may God give you good night

MARCELLUS

O, farewell, honest soldier: who hath relieved you?

FRANCISCO

Barnardo hath my place. Give you good night.

Exit.

MARCELLUS

20 Holla, Barnardo!

BARNARDO

Say, what, is Horatio there?

HORATIO

                    A piece of him.

BARNARDO

Welcome, Horatio. Welcome, good Marcellus.

MARCELLUS

What, has this thing appeared again tonight?

BARNARDO

I have seen nothing.

MARCELLUS

25 Horatio says 'tis but our fantasy,

And will not let belief take hold of him

Touching this dreaded sight twice seen of us.

Therefore I have entreated him along

With us to watch the minutes of this night,

30 That, if again this apparition come,

He may approve our eyes, and speak to it.

HORATIO

Tush, tush, 'twill not appear.

BARNARDO

                    Sit down a while,

And let us once again assail your ears,

That are so fortified against our story,

35 What we have two nights seen.

HORATIO

Well, sit we down,

And let us hear Barnardo speak of this.

BARNARDO

Last night of all,

When yond same star that's westward from the pole

---

19 *Give . . . night:* Francisco's repetition of this farewell, spoken only two lines earlier, shows his anxiety to get away quickly

21 *is Horatio there:* Barnardo cannot see Horatio in the darkness

21 *A . . . him:* perhaps Horatio offers his hand to Barnardo

25 *fantasy:* imagination

27 *Touching . . . us:* concerning the fearful apparition that we have seen two times
28 *entreated him:* asked him to come

31 *approve our eyes:* support or confirm what we have seen
speak to it: it was thought that ghosts should be spoken to in Latin, a language known to the scholar Horatio, but not, presumably, to the soldiers

33–4 *assail . . . story:* try to conquer your disbelief by repeating our story. Barnardo is a soldier and uses military images

38–9 *Last . . . pole:* only last night, when that star to the west of the pole-star

[handwritten note:] The changing of the guard represents the change of the King in Denmark

Had made his course t'illume that part of heaven 40

Where now it burns, Marcellus and myself,

The bell then beating one—

Enter GHOST.

MARCELLUS

Peace, break thee off.

Look, where it comes again!

BARNARDO

In the same figure like the king that's dead.

MARCELLUS

Thou art a scholar; speak to it, Horatio. 45

BARNARDO

Looks it not like the king? Mark it, Horatio.

HORATIO

Most like. It harrows me with fear and wonder.

BARNARDO

It would be spoke to.

MARCELLUS

Question it, Horatio.

HORATIO

What art thou that usurp'st this time of night,

Together with that fair and warlike form 50

In which the majesty of buried Denmark

Did sometimes march? By heaven I charge thee, speak!

MARCELLUS

It is offended.

BARNARDO

See, it stalks away.

HORATIO

Stay! Speak, speak! I charge thee, speak!

Exit GHOST.

MARCELLUS

'Tis gone, and will not answer. 55

BARNARDO

How now, Horatio? You tremble and look pale.

Is not this something more than fantasy?

What think you on't?

40–41 *made ... burns:* moved to the position it now holds. Barnardo is about to refer to what happened at this time the night before

42 *Peace ... off:* be silent, stop talking

44 *In ... dead:* the apparition is the same as on previous occasions, and resembles the late King Hamlet

45 *speak to it:* Horatio is being asked to speak to the ghost in order to discover its identity and its purpose

46 *Mark:* take close note of, observe

47 *harrows:* alarms, distresses

48 *It ... to:* it was thought that ghosts were not able to speak unless they were first spoken to

49–52 *What ... march?* What right do you have to take over this time of night and to take on the appearance of the dead King of Denmark?

52 *charge:* order, command

55 *will not answer:* it was thought that ghosts would speak only to those for whom they had news or some request

58 *on't:* of it

Glossary

59 *Before:* I swear before

60 *sensible . . . avouch:* proof or assurance provided by the senses, in this case the eyes

64 *Norway:* old Fortinbras, King of Norway *combated:* fought

65–6 *So . . . ice:* Horatio seems to be describing a failed negotiation between old Hamlet and some Polish soldiers that led to a battle in which old Hamlet defeated the Poles

68 *jump:* exactly, precisely

69 *martial stalk:* military stride

70–72 *In . . . state:* I do not know what exactly I should think of this, but my general feeling is that it foreshadows some violent disturbance in our country's affairs

73–82 *Good . . . inform me?* Please sit down and let anyone who knows tell me why soldiers and civilians are obliged to give up their nights, the former to guard duty, the latter to the manufacture of arms and shipbuilding? Why the daily manufacture of cannons, and the purchase of weapons abroad? Why are shipbuilders being conscripted to work day and night, seven days a week? Who can tell me?

75 *toils . . . land:* imposes hard work on the people of Denmark

80 *toward:* about to happen, imminent

83 *whisper:* rumour

83–9 *our . . . this Fortinbras:* King Hamlet, whose likeness we have just seen, was challenged to armed combat by King Fortinbras of Norway, who was motivated by pride and jealous rivalry. In this combat, Hamlet, by common consent a brave warrior, killed Fortinbras

HORATIO

Before my God, I might not this believe

60 Without the sensible and true avouch

Of mine own eyes.

MARCELLUS

                              Is it not like the king?

HORATIO

As thou art to thyself.

Such was the very armour he had on

When he the ambitious Norway combated;

65 So frowned he once, when, in an angry parle,

He smote the sledded Polacks on the ice.

'Tis strange.

MARCELLUS

Thus twice before, and jump at this dead hour,

With martial stalk hath he gone by our watch.

HORATIO

70 In what particular thought to work I know not,

But, in the gross and scope of my opinion,

This bodes some strange eruption to our state.

MARCELLUS

Good now, sit down, and tell me, he that knows,

Why this same strict and most observant watch

75 So nightly toils the subject of the land;

And why such daily cast of brazen cannon

And foreign mart for implements of war;

Why such impress of shipwrights, whose sore task

Does not divide the Sunday from the week;

80 What might be toward that this sweaty haste

Doth make the night joint-labourer with the day:

Who is't that can inform me?

HORATIO

                              That can I.

At least the whisper goes so: our last king,

Whose image even but now appeared to us,

85 Was, as you know, by Fortinbras of Norway,

Thereto pricked on by a most emulate pride,

Dared to the combat; in which our valiant Hamlet

(For so this side of our known world esteemed him)

Did slay this Fortinbras, who, by a sealed compact,

Well ratified by law and heraldry,   90

Did forfeit, with his life, all those his lands

Which he stood seized of, to the conqueror;

Against the which a moiety competent

Was gagèd by our king, which had returned

To the inheritance of Fortinbras,   95

Had he been vanquisher, as, by the same covenant

And carriage of the article designed,

His fell to Hamlet. Now, sir, young Fortinbras,

Of unimprovèd mettle hot and full,

Hath in the skirts of Norway here and there   100

Sharked up a list of lawless resolutes,

For food and diet, to some enterprise

That hath a stomach in't; which is no other,

As it doth well appear unto our state,

But to recover of us, by strong hand   105

And terms compulsatory, those foresaid lands

So by his father lost. And this, I take it,

Is the main motive of our preparations,

The source of this our watch and the chief head

Of this post-haste and romage in the land.   110

BARNARDO

I think it be no other but e'en so:

Well may it sort that this portentous figure

Comes armèd through our watch, so like the king

That was and is the question of these wars.

HORATIO

A mote it is to trouble the mind's eye.   115

In the most high and palmy state of Rome,

A little ere the mightiest Julius fell,

The graves stood tenantless, and the sheeted dead

Did squeak and gibber in the Roman streets,

As stars with trains of fire and dews of blood,   120

Disasters in the sun; and the moist star,

Upon whose influence Neptune's empire stands,

Was sick almost to doomsday with eclipse.

And even the like precurse of feared events,

As harbingers preceding still the fates   125

89–98 *by ... Hamlet:* under a legally binding agreement, his personal property in land would fall to King Hamlet if he, King Fortinbras, died; Hamlet would have lost land of equal value to Fortinbras had *he* been the loser

93 *moiety competent:* portion sufficient to match that wagered by old Fortinbras

94 *gagèd:* wagered
had returned: would have gone to (*not* gone back to)

96–7 *same ... designed:* terms of the agreement and particularly of the article of that agreement already mentioned

97 *designed:* designated

98 *young Fortinbras:* son of the late King Fortinbras and nephew of the present King of Norway

99 *Of ... full:* lively and energetic, but lacking in self-control and restraint

100 *skirts:* remote parts, outskirts

101–3 *Sharked ... in't:* gathered up, without discrimination, a troop of desperate adventurers, whose purpose will be to serve some cause that demands courage and daring ('stomach')

105 *recover of:* take from

106 *terms compulsatory:* by force
foresaid lands: lands I've been talking about

109–10 *source ... land:* reason for us being on guard, and the main origin of this frantic activity and turmoil in Denmark

111 *e'en:* even

112–14 *Well ... wars:* it is indeed appropriate that a figure resembling King Hamlet, who was the cause of these wars, should be wearing armour, given this threat from Norway

115 *A ... eye:* the ghost puzzles and irritates the minds of the beholders, like a piece of dust or grit in an eye

116 *most ... palmy:* flourishing and victorious

117 *ere:* before

118 *tenantless:* empty
sheeted dead: dead people dressed in shrouds

120 *As stars:* like comets

121 *Disasters ... sun:* eclipses or sun-spots, signs of ill omen
moist star: moon

122 *Neptune's empire:* the sea (whose tides depend on the power of the moon)

123 *sick ... eclipse:* eclipsed almost to the point of total darkness

124 *like ... events:* similar ominous warnings of fearful happenings about to come

125 *harbingers ... fates:* signs that always herald certain calamities

126 *prologue . . . on:* are an introduction to the bad fortune about to come

128 *climatures:* regions, part of the world

129 *soft:* wait a moment, be quiet

130 *cross . . . me:* stand in its way even if by doing so I may suffer fearful consequences

133–42 *If . . . it:* in trying to discover why the ghost has appeared, Horatio puts forward three common explanations for such apparitions. They may: (a) require some earthly deed to be done before they can rest; (b) want to warn of some impending national disaster; or (c) be unable to find rest because in their lifetime they secreted ill-gotten treasure

136 *privy to:* in possession of secret information concerning

137 *foreknowing:* advance warning

144 *partisan:* long-handled spear

145 *stand:* stop

149 *being so majestical:* because it is so regal in bearing

151–2 *For . . . mockery:* since the ghost is unable to feel, our futile blows cannot harm him

And prologue to the omen coming on,

Have heaven and earth together demonstrated

Unto our climatures and countrymen—

Enter GHOST.

But soft, behold, lo, where it comes again!

130 I'll cross it, though it blast me. Stay, illusion!

If thou hast any sound, or use of voice,

Speak to me.

If there be any good thing to be done,

That may to thee do ease and grace to me,

135 Speak to me.

If thou art privy to thy country's fate,

Which, happily, foreknowing may avoid,

O speak!

Or if thou hast uphoarded in thy life

140 Extorted treasure in the womb of earth,

For which, they say, you spirits oft walk in death,

Speak of it.

A cock crows. GHOST turns away.

Stay, and speak! Stop it, Marcellus.

MARCELLUS
Shall I strike at it with my partisan?

HORATIO
145 Do, if it will not stand.

BARNARDO
'Tis here!

HORATIO
'Tis here!

Exit GHOST.

MARCELLUS
'Tis gone!

We do it wrong, being so majestical,

150 To offer it the show of violence;

For it is as the air, invulnerable,

And our vain blows malicious mockery.

BARNARDO
It was about to speak, when the cock crew.

HORATIO

And then it started, like a guilty thing

Upon a fearful summons. I have heard   155

The cock, that is the trumpet to the morn,

Doth with his lofty and shrill-sounding throat

Awake the god of day, and, at his warning,

Whether in sea or fire, in earth or air,

Th'extravagant and erring spirit hies   160

To his confine; and of the truth herein

This present object made probation.

MARCELLUS

It faded on the crowing of the cock.

Some say that ever 'gainst that season comes

Wherein our Saviour's birth is celebrated,   165

The bird of dawning singeth all night long.

And then, they say, no spirit dares stir abroad,

The nights are wholesome, then no planets strike,

No fairy takes, nor witch hath power to charm,

So hallowed and so gracious is the time.   170

HORATIO

So have I heard and do in part believe it.

But look, the morn, in russet mantle clad,

Walks o'er the dew of yon high eastward hill.

Break we our watch up; and by my advice

Let us impart what we have seen tonight   175

Unto young Hamlet; for, upon my life,

This spirit, dumb to us, will speak to him.

Do you consent we shall acquaint him with it,

As needful in our loves, fitting our duty?

MARCELLUS

Let's do't, I pray; and I this morning know   180

Where we shall find him most conveniently.

Exeunt.

---

154 *started:* jumped, hurried away

156 *trumpet . . . morn:* trumpeter or announcer of the morning

158 *the god of day:* Phoebus Apollo, the sun-god

160–61 *Th'extravagant . . . confine:* the ghost, who has wandered beyond his proper boundaries, hurries off to the place where he should be contained

161–2 *of . . . probation:* the ghost we have seen affords proof of the truth of this belief

164–5 *ever . . . celebrated:* always just before Christmas

166 *bird of dawning:* cock

167 *abroad:* outside

168 *nights . . . strike:* night air is healthy at Christmas time because the planets do not exert an evil influence

169 *takes:* enchants, bewitches
charm: weave magic spells

170 *hallowed . . . gracious:* holy and full of heavenly grace

171 *in part believe:* Horatio is often sceptical

172 *russet mantle clad:* wearing a cloak of a reddish or grey colour; here, either or both colours would be appropriate

173 *o'er:* over
yon: that . . . over there

174 *by my advice:* I advise, I suggest

175 *impart:* tell, make known

176 *young Hamlet:* the use of 'young' distinguishes the prince, here mentioned for the first time, from old Hamlet, his father, the late King of Denmark

179 *As . . . duty:* as befits our love for him and our sense of duty

Exeunt: exit of more than one character

Given important background information about the play

Pathetic fallacy is a literary device in which nature reflects the actions of man and has feelings for humanity

Key points

This scene provides some useful background information and creates an atmosphere of unease and foreboding. It also introduces Horatio and indicates the kind of man he is.

- The opening exchanges establish an air of tension. The soldiers are nervous and jumpy. Francisco can hardly wait to get away; he feels 'sick at heart' (line 9). Barnardo is anxious that his colleagues join him quickly.

- Horatio is a scholar and a sceptic. He did not believe the soldiers when they reported that they had seen a ghost, and so he agreed to join them on their watch. He is shocked when the ghost appears. He suggests that the ghost 'bodes some strange eruption to our state' (line 72) and recalls some portents or signs of coming disaster from ancient history.

- Horatio can speak Latin, the language of exorcism, which was believed to be the appropriate language in which to address a ghost. The soldiers urge him to speak with the ghost in order to discover what the ghost's visit means.

- The men fear that the return from the dead of King Hamlet's spirit is a sign that some calamity is about to occur. Horatio (reflecting common beliefs of Shakespeare's time) speculates on the possible reasons for this ghostly visit: (a) he wants something done; (b) he has come to warn about a danger facing the country; (c) he had hoarded up ill-gotten treasure and is now returning to confess. It later turns out that (a) is the best explanation.

- The fact that the ghost is that of King Hamlet, and is dressed in armour as if for war, causes both Barnardo and Horatio to believe that the apparition has something to do with the military threat to Denmark posed by young Prince Fortinbras of Norway.

- We learn about the urgent preparations for war in Denmark. This conversation also reveals details about an earlier war that King Fortinbras of Norway waged against King Hamlet, in which the latter killed old Fortinbras and seized some of his territory. This has given young Fortinbras, son of the slain king, two motives for attacking Denmark: to avenge the death of his father and to recapture lost Norwegian territory.

- The references to the late King Hamlet are flattering and encourage admiration. Horatio talks of 'that fair and warlike form' (line 50) and describes him as 'our valiant Hamlet' (line 87). This anticipates the way in which young Hamlet will soon emphasise the differences between his superior father and his degenerate uncle, King Claudius.

Useful quotes

> Horatio says 'tis but our fantasy,
> And will not let belief take hold of him
> Touching this dreaded sight twice seen of us.
>
> (Marcellus, lines 25–7)

> Such was the very armour he had on
> When he the ambitious Norway combated
>
> (Horatio, lines 63–4)

> Thou art a scholar; speak to it, Horatio.
>
> (Marcellus, line 45)

> Now, sir, young Fortinbras,
> Of unimprovèd mettle hot and full,
> Hath in the skirts of Norway here and there
> Sharked up a list of lawless resolutes
>
> (Horatio, lines 98–101)

> What art thou that usurp'st this time of night,
> Together with that fair and warlike form
> In which the majesty of buried Denmark
> Did sometimes march?
>
> (Horatio, lines 49–52)

> Let us impart what we have seen tonight
> Unto young Hamlet; for, upon my life,
> This spirit, dumb to us, will speak to him.
>
> (Horatio, lines 175–7)

Questions ?

1 What is the mood of the characters on the battlements before the ghost appears? How does Shakespeare convey this mood?

2 Why is Horatio the one chosen to question the ghost?

3 What is there about Horatio that sets him apart from the other characters in this scene? For example, what do his speeches tell us about the kind of person he is, about his background, his education, his outlook?

4 How does Horatio's attitude to the ghost differ from the attitudes of the other characters?

5 What is the purpose of the men's conversation about the preparations for war against Norway? What do we learn from it?

6 Explain Horatio's comments on events in ancient Rome before the assassination of Julius Caesar (lines 116–23).

7 Having read this scene, have you any idea of what might happen next? Explain.

8 If you were directing a theatre production of Hamlet, how would you portray the ghost on stage? For example, would you use an actor or some sort of special effect?

9 How might costumes be used in this scene to help the audience understand what is taking place?

10 The action of this fairly short scene spans the hours from midnight to dawn. Shakespeare uses language and a sound effect to indicate the passing of time. In modern theatres, what other methods might be used?

ACT 1 † Scene 2

Plot summary

King Claudius addresses his court. He justifies his marriage and his accession to the throne. He sends ambassadors to Norway to deal with the threat posed by young Fortinbras. He confirms Hamlet as his successor. He permits Laertes, son of Polonius (his chief counsellor or minister), to return to France. He then turns to the more difficult family matter that is troubling both him and Queen Gertrude: Hamlet's hostility to Claudius and resentment that his mother married again so soon after his father's death. Claudius and Gertrude urge Hamlet to accept their marriage. However, Hamlet's first soliloquy is a passionate condemnation of both of them. Horatio and Marcellus tell Hamlet that they have seen his father's spirit in armour. Hamlet is determined to confront the ghost.

Let not thy mother lose her prayers, Hamlet.
I pray thee stay with us; go not to Wittenberg.

GERTRUDE, Act 1, Scene 2, 118–19

Elsinore. A room of state in the castle.

Enter KING CLAUDIUS, QUEEN GERTRUDE, HAMLET, POLONIUS, LAERTES, VOLTEMAND, CORNELIUS, LORDS, and ATTENDANTS.

KING CLAUDIUS

Though yet of Hamlet our dear brother's death

The memory be green, and that it us befitted

To bear our hearts in grief, and our whole kingdom

To be contracted in one brow of woe,

Yet so far hath discretion fought with nature 5

That we with wisest sorrow think on him,

Together with remembrance of ourselves.

Therefore, our sometime sister, now our queen,

The imperial jointress to this warlike state,

Have we, as 'twere with a defeated joy, 10

With an auspicious and a dropping eye,

With mirth in funeral, and with dirge in marriage,

In equal scale weighing delight and dole,

Taken to wife; nor have we herein barred

Your better wisdoms, which have freely gone 15

With this affair along. For all, our thanks.

Now follows that you know: young Fortinbras,

Holding a weak supposal of our worth,

Or thinking by our late dear brother's death

Our state to be disjoint and out of frame, 20

Colleagued with the dream of his advantage,

He hath not failed to pester us with message

Importing the surrender of those lands

Lost by his father, with all bands of law,

To our most valiant brother. So much for him. 25

Now for ourself and for this time of meeting.

Thus much the business is: we have here writ

To Norway, uncle of young Fortinbras —

Who, impotent and bed-rid, scarcely hears

Of this his nephew's purpose — to suppress 30

His further gait herein; in that the levies,

The lists, and full proportions are all made

Out of his subject. And we here dispatch

You, good Cornelius, and you, Voltemand,

For bearers of this greeting to old Norway; 35

1–7 *Though ... ourselves:* although my brother's death is still fresh in my memory, and although it was only proper ('befitted') that all of us in Denmark should be united in mourning for him, reason and common sense ('discretion') have not allowed natural sorrow to exclude concern for myself and my subjects

6 *wisest sorrow:* grief, tempered by wisdom. This paradox is an example of the spurious balancing of opposites that is a feature of this and other speeches in the play

8 *our sometime sister:* my former sister-in-law

9 *imperial ... state:* royal heiress to the throne

10 *defeated:* subdued, spoiled (by sorrow)

11 *With ... eye:* with one eye happy and the other shedding tears

12 *With ... marriage:* with merry-making at the funeral and funeral songs at the wedding

13 *dole:* grief, sorrow

14–16 *nor ... along:* I have not excluded your wise advice in all of this, which has willingly supported the marriage and accession to the throne

18 *Holding ... worth:* thinking that I am not likely to be a strong ruler

20 *disjoint ... frame:* disordered and disorganised

21 *Colleagued ... advantage:* allied to his feelings of imaginary superiority

23 *Importing:* signifying

24 *with ... law:* in a perfectly legal manner

25 *our ... brother:* my brave brother, the late King Hamlet

28 *Norway:* the King of Norway (as in Denmark, the brother, and not the son, of the late king has taken the throne)

29 *impotent and bed-rid:* a powerless invalid

30 *suppress:* prevent

31–3 *His ... subject:* his nephew from proceeding any further against Denmark; this is something he can do, since the soldiers and all their supplies are from Norway

36–8 *Giving . . . allow:* I am giving you no authority in your dealings with the king beyond what is specified in these detailed instructions

38 *delated:* carefully set out

41 *We . . . nothing:* I do not doubt it

42–50 *And . . . Laertes?* Claudius's desire to please Laertes is emphasised by the repetition of his name. The speech is fulsome and wheedling in tone

43 *suit:* formal request, petition

44–6 *You . . . asking:* if you ask the King of Denmark for anything within reason, you will not ask in vain: anything you want will be freely given by me, without your needing to ask for it

47 *native:* connected by nature

48 *instrumental:* useful

50 *dread:* respected, honoured

51 *leave and favour:* gracious permission. Laertes, being a courtier, requires the king's permission to leave the country

52 *whence:* where

56 *pardon:* permission to go

59 *laboursome petition:* constant pleading

60 *Upon . . . consent:* I reluctantly approved of his request

61 *beseech:* ask, beg

62 *Take . . . hour:* this is the best time of your life; enjoy it

62–3 *time . . . will:* you have all the time you need; may your good qualities enable you to spend it with pleasure

64 *cousin:* here, nephew; as well as its modern sense, 'cousin' was used in Shakespeare's day to mean uncle, aunt, nephew or niece

---

Giving to you no further personal power

To business with the king, more than the scope

Of these delated articles allow.

Farewell, and let your haste commend your duty.

CORNELIUS, VOLTEMAND

40   In that, and all things, will we show our duty.

KING CLAUDIUS

We doubt it nothing; heartily farewell.

Exeunt VOLTEMAND and CORNELIUS.

And now, Laertes, what's the news with you?

You told us of some suit; what is't, Laertes?

You cannot speak of reason to the Dane

45   And lose your voice: what wouldst thou beg, Laertes,

That shall not be my offer, not thy asking?

The head is not more native to the heart,

The hand more instrumental to the mouth,

Than is the throne of Denmark to thy father.

What wouldst thou have, Laertes?

LAERTES

50   My dread lord,

Your leave and favour to return to France;

From whence though willingly I came to Denmark

To show my duty in your coronation,

Yet now, I must confess, that duty done,

55   My thoughts and wishes bend again towards France

And bow them to your gracious leave and pardon.

KING CLAUDIUS

Have you your father's leave? What says Polonius?

POLONIUS

He hath, my lord, wrung from me my slow leave

By laboursome petition, and at last

60   Upon his will I sealed my hard consent.

I do beseech you, give him leave to go.

KING CLAUDIUS

Take thy fair hour, Laertes; time be thine,

And thy best graces spend it at thy will.

But now, my cousin Hamlet, and my son—

HAMLET [*aside*]

A little more than kin, and less than kind. 65

KING CLAUDIUS

How is it that the clouds still hang on you?

HAMLET

Not so, my lord; I am too much in the sun.

QUEEN GERTRUDE

Good Hamlet, cast thy nighted colour off,

And let thine eye look like a friend on Denmark.

Do not forever with thy vailèd lids 70

Seek for thy noble father in the dust:

Thou know'st 'tis common, all that lives must die,

Passing through nature to eternity.

HAMLET

Ay, madam, it is common.

QUEEN GERTRUDE

　　　　　　　　If it be,

Why seems it so particular with thee? 75

HAMLET

'Seems', madam! Nay it is. I know not 'seems'.

'Tis not alone my inky cloak, good mother,

Nor customary suits of solemn black,

Nor windy suspiration of forced breath,

No, nor the fruitful river in the eye, 80

Nor the dejected haviour of the visage,

Together with all forms, moods, shapes of grief,

That can denote me truly. These indeed 'seem',

For they are actions that a man might play.

But I have that within which passeth show; 85

These, but the trappings and the suits of woe.

KING CLAUDIUS

'Tis sweet and commendable in your nature, Hamlet,

To give these mourning duties to your father,

But you must know your father lost a father;

That father lost, lost his; and the survivor bound 90

In filial obligation for some term

To do obsequious sorrow. But to persever

In obstinate condolement is a course

---

aside: a speech that is not heard by the other characters on stage

65 *A . . . kind*: you are more than a mere kinsman (being his uncle and stepfather), but you are still not close to me in natural family feeling. Hamlet, who often plays on words, implies a lack of mutual kindness

66 *How . . . you?* Why are you so melancholy (gloomy, depressed)?

67 *I . . . sun*: this is a bitter pun: he is offended at being called 'son' by Claudius (line 64) and may be saying that he is too much in the sunshine of his uncle's favour. Also, melancholy people were supposed to dislike sunlight

68 *nighted colour*: black mourning garments

69 *Denmark*: the King of Denmark, Claudius

70 *vailèd lids*: downcast eyes

72 *common*: universal

73 *nature*: natural life, life on earth

75 *Why . . . thee?* Why are you behaving as if you are the only person ever to have suffered a bereavement?

76–86 *'Seems' . . . woe*: Hamlet angrily picks up his mother's use of 'seems', as if she meant that his grief only seems genuine, but is really false. He tells her that his outward signs of grief (dark clothes, mournful face, tears, sighs) might be adopted by any man, but that the grief he feels within is too deep to be properly expressed

79 *windy . . . breath*: sighing

81 *haviour*: aspect, demeanour; here, facial appearance

83 *denote*: describe, characterise

84 *play*: perform, act, put on

85 *passeth show*: goes beyond appearance

86 *trappings*: ornaments

87–8 *'Tis . . . your father*: your mourning for your father is admirable in its way

90–92 *and . . . sorrow*: and every person who has lost a father is obliged to mourn him for a while with appropriate rituals ('obsequious sorrow')

92–3 *But . . . condolement'*: but grief that persists too long

94 *impious stubbornness:* wicked resistance

95–106 *It . . . so:* it offends God, is contrary to the Christian virtue of patience, defies common sense, wrongs the dead and flies in the face of the inevitable

99 *any . . . sense:* something familiar to everyday observation
100 *peevish:* foolishly perverse

101 *Fie!* an expression of disgust or disapproval *fault:* sin

107 *unprevailing woe:* useless, futile sorrow

109 *most immediate:* next in line. Claudius is here publicly proclaiming that Hamlet is to be his successor as king

112 *intent:* intention
113 *Wittenberg:* a university town in Germany
114 *retrograde:* contrary

Of impious stubbornness. 'Tis unmanly grief.

95 It shows a will most incorrect to heaven,

A heart unfortified, a mind impatient,

An understanding simple and unschooled.

For what we know must be, and is as common

As any the most vulgar thing to sense,

100 Why should we in our peevish opposition

Take it to heart? Fie! 'Tis a fault to heaven,

A fault against the dead, a fault to nature,

To reason most absurd, whose common theme

Is death of fathers, and who still hath cried,

105 From the first corpse till he that died today,

'This must be so.' We pray you throw to earth

This unprevailing woe, and think of us

As of a father. For let the world take note,

You are the most immediate to our throne;

110 And with no less nobility of love

Than that which dearest father bears his son,

Do I impart towards you. For your intent

In going back to school in Wittenberg,

It is most retrograde to our desire;

For let the world take note,
You are the most immediate to our throne

CLAUDIUS, Act 1, Scene 2, 108–9

And we beseech you, bend you to remain   115

Here, in the cheer and comfort of our eye,

Our chiefest courtier, cousin, and our son.

QUEEN GERTRUDE

Let not thy mother lose her prayers, Hamlet.

I pray thee stay with us; go not to Wittenberg.

HAMLET

I shall in all my best obey you, madam.   120

KING CLAUDIUS

Why, 'tis a loving and a fair reply.

Be as ourself in Denmark. Madam, come.

This gentle and unforced accord of Hamlet

Sits smiling to my heart, in grace whereof

No jocund health that Denmark drinks today,   125

But the great cannon to the clouds shall tell,

And the king's rouse the heavens shall bruit again,

Re-speaking earthly thunder. Come away.

Flourish. Exeunt all but HAMLET.

HAMLET

O that this too too solid flesh would melt,

Thaw, and resolve itself into a dew.   *soliloquy*   130

Or that the Everlasting had not fixed

His canon 'gainst self-slaughter. O God! God!

How weary, stale, flat and unprofitable

Seem to me all the uses of this world!

Fie on't! Ah fie! 'Tis an unweeded garden   135

That grows to seed; things rank and gross in nature

Possess it merely. That it should come to this!

But two months dead; nay, not so much, not two.   *very depressed*

So excellent a king that was, to this,

Hyperion to a satyr; so loving to my mother   140

That he might not beteem the winds of heaven

Visit her face too roughly. Heaven and earth!

Must I remember? Why, she would hang on him,

As if increase of appetite had grown

By what it fed on. And yet, within a month —   145

Let me not think on't: frailty, thy name is woman! —

A little month, or ere those shoes were old

With which she followed my poor father's body,

---

115 *we ... remain:* I implore you, give way to my request and stay

118 *lose her prayers:* beg in vain

120 *I ... madam:* Hamlet has pointedly refrained from answering Claudius — even his reply to Gertrude is not enthusiastic ('madam' is a formal, distant greeting) — and if he puts the emphasis on 'you' in this line, he is further insulting the king

122 *Be ... Denmark:* act as if you had all the rights and privileges of the King of Denmark

123 *unforced accord:* agreement or consent freely given. Claudius exaggerates

124–8 *in grace ... thunder:* in celebration of Hamlet's decision to remain, every joyful ('jocund') toast and drinking bout ('rouse') indulged in by me ('Denmark') today will be accompanied by the firing of the big cannon, which the heavens will echo

127 *bruit again:* re-echo noisily

Flourish: fanfare of trumpets

129–59 *O ... tongue:* Hamlet's first soliloquy is a cry of despair and disgust at his mother's hasty marriage to a man who, in Hamlet's eyes, is totally inferior to his own father. His revulsion is intensified by the incestuous character of the marriage (her two husbands were brothers)

130 *resolve:* dissolve

131–2 *Or ... self-slaughter:* or that God had not prohibited suicide. The 'canon' (religious law) is the commandment 'Thou shalt not kill'

134 *uses:* customs, activities

136–7 *things ... merely:* completely overgrown with coarse, rotting weeds

137 *merely:* entirely, totally

139–40 *So ... satyr:* compared with the base, brutish Claudius, the late King Hamlet was like a god

140 *Hyperion:* the beautiful Greek god of light
satyr: a creature of Greek mythology, half-man half-goat, ugly, lustful and repulsive in behaviour

141 *might not beteem:* would not permit

143–5 *hang ... fed on:* cling to him as if the more she had of him, the more she wanted

146 *frailty ... woman:* women are fundamentally fickle; they personify moral weakness. This was a common view in Shakespeare's time

147 *A ... old:* a short month, before those shoes were worn out

149 *Niobe:* the legendary Greek mother who wept so much at the loss of her fourteen children that she was turned to stone

150 *wants . . . reason:* lacks the power of reason

153 *Hercules:* an ancient Greek hero and son of Zeus. Hamlet is implying here that he is no hero, able to put things right as Hercules did

154–6 *Ere . . . married:* before her insincere ('unrighteous') tears had stopped causing redness ('flushing') in her eyes, she remarried

155 *gallèd:* sore from weeping

156–7 *post . . . sheets:* rush to her brother-in-law's bed. Hamlet is saying that, in marrying her close relative, Gertrude's behaviour is outside the law and morality

160 *Hail:* a greeting to royalty

161–2 *Horatio . . . myself:* the depressed, tearful Hamlet fails at first to recognise Horatio

164 *Sir . . . you:* Hamlet wants Horatio to think of himself as his friend; each can regard himself as both friend and servant to the other

165 *make you:* brings you here

168 *even:* evening

170 *A truant disposition:* an idle temperament has caused me to stay away from university

171–4 *I . . . truant:* Hamlet is saying that he cannot possibly believe that Horatio is a truant, even if Horatio himself claims he is

173 *truster:* believer

175 *affair:* business
Elsinore: Helsingor in eastern Denmark

176 *We'll . . . depart:* a sarcastic reference to the drinking habits of the Danish court

---

Like Niobe, all tears: why she, even she —

150 O God! A beast, that wants discourse of reason,
Would have mourned longer — married with my uncle,
My father's brother, but no more like my father
Than I to Hercules. Within a month?
Ere yet the salt of most unrighteous tears

155 Had left the flushing in her gallèd eyes,
She married. O most wicked speed, to post
With such dexterity to incestuous sheets!
It is not, nor it cannot come to good,
But break my heart, for I must hold my tongue.

Enter HORATIO, MARCELLUS and BARNARDO.

HORATIO

160 Hail to your lordship!

HAMLET

I am glad to see you well. Horatio —
Or I do forget myself!

HORATIO

The same, my lord, and your poor servant ever.

HAMLET

Sir, my good friend; I'll change that name with you.

165 And what make you from Wittenberg, Horatio?
Marcellus?

MARCELLUS

My good lord!

HAMLET

I am very glad to see you. [*to BARNARDO*] Good even, sir.
[*to HORATIO*] But what, in faith, make you from Wittenberg?

HORATIO

170 A truant disposition, good my lord.

HAMLET

I would not hear your enemy say so,
Nor shall you do mine ear that violence,
To make it truster of your own report
Against yourself. I know you are no truant.

175 But what is your affair in Elsinore?
We'll teach you to drink deep ere you depart.

HORATIO

My lord, I came to see your father's funeral.

HAMLET

I prithee, do not mock me, fellow-student.

I think it was to see my mother's wedding.

HORATIO

Indeed, my lord, it followed hard upon.   180

HAMLET

Thrift, thrift, Horatio; the funeral baked meats

Did coldly furnish forth the marriage tables.

Would I had met my dearest foe in heaven

Or ever I had seen that day, Horatio —

My father, methinks I see my father.   185

HORATIO

Where, my lord?

HAMLET

                    In my mind's eye, Horatio.

HORATIO

I saw him once; he was a goodly king—

HAMLET

He was a man, take him for all in all,

I shall not look upon his like again.

HORATIO

My lord, I think I saw him yesternight.   190

HAMLET

Saw who?

HORATIO

My lord, the king your father.

HAMLET

                    The king my father!

HORATIO

Season your admiration for a while

With an attent ear, till I may deliver,

Upon the witness of these gentlemen,   195

This marvel to you.

HAMLET

                    For God's love, let me hear.

178 *I prithee:* I pray you, please

180 *followed hard upon:* happened soon after

181–2 *Thrift . . . tables:* Hamlet, bitterly sarcastic, remarks that the wedding and funeral ceremonies were arranged to save expense; the food cooked for the funeral was served cold at the wedding
181 *baked meats:* pies
183 *Would . . . foe:* I would prefer to see my greatest enemy (i.e. the one I hate most)
185 *methinks:* it seems to me

186 *mind's eye:* memory

187 *once:* Horatio's detailed account of old Hamlet in Act 1, Scene 1 suggests that he saw him more than once

190 *yesternight:* last night

193 *Season your admiration:* curb your astonishment

194 *attent:* attentive
     deliver: relate, describe

199 *dead waste:* gloomy desolation

201 *Armèd . . . cap-a-pe:* fully armed from head to foot

204 *oppressed:* troubled

205 *his truncheon's length:* the length of the short staff or baton that a king carries as a sign of his authority

205–6 *distilled . . . fear:* almost melted with fear

207–8 *This . . . did:* they confided this to me as a fearful secret

210–12 *Where . . . comes:* on the watch, what Marcellus and Barnardo had reported about the ghost was confirmed, as to the time of its arrival and its outward appearance

212 *knew:* recognised

213 *These . . . like:* the ghost resembled the king as closely as one of my hands resembles the other

214 *platform:* guard-platform, battlements

217–18 *did . . . speak:* began to move as though it wished to speak

219 *even:* just

223 *writ down in:* part of

HORATIO
Two nights together had these gentlemen,
Marcellus and Barnardo, on their watch,
In the dead waste and middle of the night,
200 Been thus encountered: a figure like your father,
Armèd at point exactly, cap-a-pe,
Appears before them, and with solemn march
Goes slow and stately by them; thrice he walked
By their oppressed and fear-surprisèd eyes,
205 Within his truncheon's length, whilst they, distilled
Almost to jelly with the act of fear,
Stand dumb and speak not to him. This to me
In dreadful secrecy impart they did;
And I with them the third night kept the watch;
210 Where, as they had delivered, both in time,
Form of the thing, each word made true and good,
The apparition comes. I knew your father;
These hands are not more like.

HAMLET
                                            But where was this?

MARCELLUS
My lord, upon the platform where we watched.

HAMLET
Did you not speak to it?

HORATIO
215   My lord, I did;
But answer made it none. Yet once methought
It lifted up its head and did address
Itself to motion, like as it would speak;
But even then the morning cock crew loud,
220 And at the sound it shrunk in haste away
And vanished from our sight.

HAMLET
                                            'Tis very strange.

HORATIO
As I do live, my honoured lord, 'tis true.
And we did think it writ down in our duty
To let you know of it.

HAMLET

Indeed, indeed, sirs. But this troubles me.   225

Hold you the watch tonight?

MARCELLUS, BARNARDO

We do, my lord.

HAMLET

Armed, say you?

MARCELLUS, BARNARDO

Armed, my lord.

HAMLET

From top to toe?

MARCELLUS, BARNARDO

My lord, from head to foot.

HAMLET

Then saw you not his face?   230

HORATIO

O yes, my lord; he wore his beaver up.

HAMLET

What, looked he frowningly?

HORATIO

A countenance more in sorrow than in anger.

HAMLET

Pale or red?

HORATIO

Nay, very pale.   235

HAMLET

And fixed his eyes upon you?

HORATIO

Most constantly.

HAMLET

I would I had been there.

HORATIO

It would have much amazed you.

HAMLET

Very like.

Very like. Stayed it long?

226 *Hold . . . watch:* are you on guard duty

231 *beaver:* visor of his helmet

233 *countenance:* facial expression

237 *constantly:* steadily, firmly

238 *would:* wish

238 *like:* likely

240   *tell:* count to

242   *grizzled:* grey

244   *sable silvered:* black tinged with grey

244   *watch:* keep the watch, stay on guard

245   *Perchance:* perhaps

245   *warrant:* guarantee

247   *gape:* Hamlet sees hell as a mouth, open to receive the damned, and suspects that the ghost may be a devil disguised as his father

249   *hitherto:* until now

250   *Let . . . still:* continue to keep it secret

251–2   *whatsoever . . . tongue:* whatever happens tonight, observe it with a view to understanding it, but do not speak about it

253   *requite your loves:* reward your loyalty and affection

256   *Your loves:* Horatio and the others have pledged their duty to Hamlet; he is prepared to pledge his love to them as well, and he expects their love in return

258   *doubt:* suspect, fear

259–60   *Foul . . . eyes:* however carefully evil deeds are concealed, they will eventually come to light

---

HORATIO

240   While one with moderate haste might tell a hundred.

MARCELLUS, BARNARDO

Longer, longer.

HORATIO

Not when I saw't.

HAMLET

        His beard was grizzled, no?

HORATIO

It was, as I have seen it in his life,

A sable silvered.

HAMLET

       I will watch tonight;

Perchance 'twill walk again.

HORATIO

245   I warrant it will.

HAMLET

If it assume my noble father's person,

I'll speak to it, though hell itself should gape

And bid me hold my peace. I pray you all,

If you have hitherto concealed this sight,

250   Let it be tenable in your silence still;

And whatsoever else shall hap tonight,

Give it an understanding, but no tongue.

I will requite your loves, so fare you well.

Upon the platform, 'twixt eleven and twelve,

I'll visit you.

ALL

255   Our duty to your honour.

HAMLET

Your loves, as mine to you. Farewell.

Exeunt all but HAMLET.

My father's spirit in arms? All is not well.

I doubt some foul play. Would the night were come!

Till then sit still, my soul. Foul deeds will rise,

260   Though all the earth o'erwhelm them, to men's eyes.

Exit.

Key points

This scene presents the royal Danish court and introduces many of the play's main characters. In particular, we are given an insight into the characters of Claudius and Hamlet.

- Notice that Shakespeare does not introduce Claudius as a villain. He appears instead as a kindly monarch, husband and uncle, anxious to please everybody, saying the proper things about his 'dear brother's death' (line 1), thanking his counsellors, flattering Polonius and being charming to Laertes.

- Claudius is shown to be a confident ruler. He appears in full control and uses the royal 'we' to indicate his power. He announces that Hamlet, who also had a claim to the throne following his father's death, will be his heir.

- Claudius is shown to be an efficient monarch. He deals with the threat posed by young Fortinbras in a brisk, diplomatic way. He will not confront Fortinbras. Instead, he will make peace with the King of Norway, uncle of Fortinbras, who will discipline his unruly nephew and end the threat to Denmark. He is courteous and pleasant to Cornelius and Voltemand, the two ambassadors he is sending to Norway to bring about peace.

- Claudius casually explains that he did not want to submit entirely to grief for his brother, and, therefore, enlivened the funeral ceremonies with a wedding festival. Since Gertrude was the 'imperial jointress' (line 9; sharer of the throne with her late husband), it was more convenient to marry her than to marry anyone else, because this marriage made it easier for him to become king.

- Shakespeare's audience would have seen the marriage of Claudius and Gertrude, formerly brother and sister-in-law, as immoral.

- The really awkward aspect of the scene for Claudius is that his appeal to Hamlet to accept him as a father is met with a boorish silence: Hamlet ignores Claudius and everything he has said. The embarrassed Gertrude has to intervene to save the situation, but she meets with only a grudging response: 'I shall in all my best obey you, madam' (line 120). This is a calculated insult to Claudius, who shows skill in making the best of it, pretending to regard the snub as 'a loving and a fair reply' (line 121), and then, cheerfully, but dishonestly, talking of 'This gentle and unforced accord of Hamlet' (line 123).

- The first of Hamlet's soliloquies in the play reveals that Gertrude married Claudius 'within a month' (line 145) of King Hamlet's funeral.

- Hamlet is sullen and grim in public, but manages to maintain his self-control. Alone on stage, he speaks out in soliloquy with fierce passion. Through the soliloquy we discover the true reasons for Hamlet's depressive state: his ill-concealed hostility towards his mother, and his hatred and resentment of his uncle. He is outraged that his mother could marry such a man as Claudius, having been the wife of King Hamlet, whose devotion to her was complete.

- The joy of life is gone for Hamlet and he wishes that suicide was not a sin.

- A soliloquy is a dramatic convention where a character alone on stage speaks to himself or herself. It enables the audience to gain an insight into that character's true thoughts and feelings.

- When Hamlet learns of the appearance of his father's ghost he feels, unlike Horatio and the others, that the ghost has come to disclose some evil deed done in the past. He arranges to join the watch and confront the ghost himself.

- We get our first glimpse of Polonius and Laertes in this scene. They are suitably deferential to the king. Laertes wisely claims that it was the coronation of Claudius, rather than the funeral of King Hamlet, that brought him back to France. He is rewarded with the king's agreement that he may leave the court. This exchange contrasts with the one that follows, in which Claudius encourages Hamlet to remain at court.

Useful quotes

> Therefore, our sometime sister, now our queen,
> The imperial jointress to this warlike state,
> Have we, as 'twere with a defeated joy,
> With an auspicious and a dropping eye,
> With mirth in funeral, and with dirge in marriage,
> In equal scale weighing delight and dole,
> Taken to wife
>
> (Claudius, lines 8–14)

> That it should come to this!
> But two months dead; nay, not so much, not two.
> So excellent a king that was, to this,
> Hyperion to a satyr
>
> (Hamlet, lines 137–40)

> O most wicked speed, to post
> With such dexterity to incestuous sheets!
>
> (Hamlet, lines 156–7)

> Good Hamlet, cast thy nighted colour off,
> And let thine eye look like a friend on Denmark.
>
> (Gertrude, lines 68–9)

> He was a man, take him for all in all,
> I shall not look upon his like again.
>
> (Hamlet, lines 188–9)

> For let the world take note,
> You are the most immediate to our throne;
> And with no less nobility of love
> Than that which dearest father bears his son,
> Do I impart towards you.
>
> (Claudius, lines 108–12)

> My father's spirit in arms? All is not well.
> I doubt some foul play. Would the night were come!
> Till then sit still, my soul. Foul deeds will rise,
> Though all the earth o'erwhelm them, to men's eyes.
>
> (Hamlet, lines 257–60)

? Questions

1 The first section (lines 1–16) of Claudius's opening speech is remarkable for its balancing of opposing ideas, e.g. 'discretion' and 'nature', 'wisest sorrow', 'defeated joy'. What does this suggest to you?

2 Describe the tone of Claudius's first speech.

3 What, do you think, are Claudius's main concerns in this scene?

4 What kind of impression does Claudius make on you (a) as a king; (b) as a person?

5 On the evidence of this scene, describe the relationship between Claudius and Gertrude.

6 Plays always involve some form of conflict. On the evidence of this scene, identify the key conflicts in this play.

7 The contrast between appearance and reality is one of the main themes of the play. How is it developed in this scene?

8 What impression did Hamlet make on you in this scene? Explain your answer.

9 Design a costume for Hamlet based on the information contained within this scene.

10 Comment on Shakespeare's use of the aside and the soliloquy in this scene.

ACT 1 ✟ Scene 3

Laertes is about to leave Elsinore for France. Bidding farewell to his sister, Ophelia, he warns her about Hamlet. He points out that Hamlet, being a prince, cannot simply marry anyone he pleases. He advises Ophelia not to believe Hamlet when he says he loves her. Polonius, their father, then arrives and gives some wise advice to Laertes about his conduct in France. After Laertes departs, Ophelia is again warned about Hamlet, this time by Polonius. When she tells him that Hamlet has made honourable declarations of love to her, he tells her she would be foolish to believe Hamlet, and orders her not to spend any more time with him. She agrees to obey.

Fear it, Ophelia, fear it, my dear sister.
And keep you in the rear of your affection,
Out of the shot and danger of desire.

LAERTES, Act 1, Scene 3, 33–5

Elsinore. A room in the house of Polonius.

Enter LAERTES and OPHELIA.

LAERTES

My necessaries are embarked, farewell,

And sister, as the winds give benefit

And convoy is assistant, do not sleep,

But let me hear from you.

OPHELIA

Do you doubt that?

LAERTES

5   For Hamlet, and the trifling of his favour,

Hold it a fashion and a toy in blood,

A violet in the youth of primy nature,

Forward, not permanent, sweet, not lasting,

The perfume and suppliance of a minute.

No more.

OPHELIA

No more but so?

LAERTES

10   Think it no more;

For nature crescent does not grow alone

In thews and bulk, but, as this temple waxes,

The inward service of the mind and soul

Grows wide withal. Perhaps he loves you now,

15   And now no soil nor cautel doth besmirch

The virtue of his will: but you must fear,

His greatness weighed, his will is not his own;

For he himself is subject to his birth.

He may not, as unvalued persons do,

20   Carve for himself; for on his choice depends

The safety and health of this whole state;

And therefore must his choice be circumscribed

Unto the voice and yielding of that body

Whereof he is the head. Then, if he says he loves you,

25   It fits your wisdom so far to believe it

As he in his particular act and place

May give his saying deed, which is no further

Than the main voice of Denmark goes withal.

Then weigh what loss your honour may sustain

30   If with too credent ear you list his songs,

Notes (left column):

1   *My . . . embarked:* my essential luggage is on board the ship

2–4   *as . . . you:* whenever weather conditions permit a ship to sail from Denmark to France, do not neglect to send me a letter

5–10   *For . . . more:* Hamlet's apparent affection for you ('his favour') is not serious on his part (it is playful, mere 'trifling'). Consider it a passing whim, a diversion for an impulsive young man. It is like a violet, blossoming too early, pleasant during its short existence, but fading quickly

9   *suppliance:* pastime, diversion

10   *No more but so?* Is that all it amounts to?

11   *nature crescent:* the growing and developing human being

12   *thews and bulk:* strength and size
     temple waxes: body grows larger

13–14   *The . . . wide:* continuing the metaphor of the body as a temple, the 'inward service' is the spiritual and mental activity and growth that take place within us as we age

14   *withal:* as well, at the same time

15   *soil:* blot, fault
     cautel: trickery, deceit
     besmirch: stain, contaminate

16   *will:* desire

16–24   *fear . . . head:* be careful to bear in mind that, given Hamlet's high rank ('greatness'), he cannot simply marry whom he chooses, as a person of lesser birth ('unvalued') might be able to do. The welfare of the country may well depend on his choice; in this matter, therefore, he must have the approval of those whom he is to govern eventually as king

20   *Carve for himself:* take what he wants, like a man taking his own meat at the dining table

22   *circumscribed:* limited, confined

23   *yielding:* consent

27   *give . . . deed:* honour his promise

28   *main voice of:* those who have influence in
     withal: along with

30   *credent:* believing, credulous
     list: listen to, pay attention to

Or lose your heart, or your chaste treasure open

To his unmastered importunity.

Fear it, Ophelia, fear it, my dear sister.

And keep you in the rear of your affection,

Out of the shot and danger of desire.   35

The chariest maid is prodigal enough

If she unmask her beauty to the moon.

Virtue itself 'scapes not calumnious strokes.

The canker galls the infants of the spring

Too oft before their buttons be disclosed,   40

And in the morn and liquid dew of youth

Contagious blastments are most imminent.

Be wary then. Best safety lies in fear.

Youth to itself rebels, though none else near.

OPHELIA

I shall the effect of this good lesson keep   45

As watchman to my heart. But, good my brother,

Do not, as some ungracious pastors do,

Show me the steep and thorny way to heaven,

Whiles, like a puffed and reckless libertine,

Himself the primrose path of dalliance treads,   50

And recks not his own rede.

LAERTES

       O fear me not.

I stay too long—

Enter POLONIUS.

      But here my father comes.

A double blessing is a double grace,

Occasion smiles upon a second leave.

POLONIUS

Yet here, Laertes! Aboard, aboard, for shame!   55

The wind sits in the shoulder of your sail,

And you are stayed for. There — my blessing with thee!

And these few precepts in thy memory

Look thou character. Give thy thoughts no tongue,

Nor any unproportioned thought his act.   60

Be thou familiar, but by no means vulgar.

Those friends thou hast, and their adoption tried,

Grapple them unto thy soul with hoops of steel;

But do not dull thy palm with entertainment

---

31 *chaste treasure:* chastity, virginity

32 *unmastered importunity:* uncontrolled persistence

34–5 *keep . . . desire:* this is a metaphor from battle. The battle is between Ophelia and her feelings, and Laertes is telling her to avoid being attacked by these

36–7 *The . . . moon:* the most cautious young maiden is being reckless enough if she lets even the moon see her beauty (the pale moonlight will not show up beauty too dramatically)

38 *Virtue . . . strokes:* even the most virtuous people may not avoid slanderous gossip

39–40 *The . . . disclosed:* the caterpillar ('canker') often damages the young spring blossoms before their buds appear

41–2 *And . . . imminent:* infectious diseases are most threatening in the moist morning air. Laertes is emphasising the vulnerability of the young

44 *Youth . . . near:* even if there is no immediate temptation, youth often rebels against its own best instincts and controls

45 *effect:* purpose, meaning

47 *ungracious pastors:* priests who lack grace or virtue

49 *puffed:* proud, self-conceited
  libertine: rake, free spirit

50 *primrose . . . dalliance:* delightful, easy route of pleasure (leading to hell, in contrast to the thorny way to heaven)

51 *recks . . . rede:* pays no heed to his own advice

51 *fear me not:* do not worry about me

53–4 *A . . . leave:* Laertes has already had a farewell blessing from his father. Now this delay makes it possible for him to take his leave again, and receive a second blessing

55–7 *Yet . . . stayed for:* I am surprised to find you still here! Hurry and board your ship! The wind is favourable and those on board are waiting for you

58–9 *these . . . character:* engrave these few principles on your memory

59–80 *Give . . . any man:* the following is a paraphrase of Polonius's shrewd, cautious lecture, the guiding principle of which is self-interest: Keep your thoughts to yourself, and do not let your actions be out of harmony with the occasion. Be friendly without ever being vulgarly familiar with people. If you find true friends, be resolute in maintaining their friendship, but do not become immediately friendly with . . .

59–80 ... each new untried acquaintance. Do not easily enter a quarrel, but if you do, let your conduct be such that your opponent will not take you for granted. Listen to others a lot, but talk little. Hear and consider each man's opinion, but do not express your own. Dress as expensively as your money will permit, but avoid dressing in a showy, ostentatious way. Your clothes should be rich without being garish. It is safe to take the example of the French upper classes, who are noteworthy for their refined, discriminating taste in dress. Do not borrow or lend; the lender often loses both his money and the friendship of the borrower, and borrowing makes people thriftless. Above all, be true to yourself and to your own highest principles; if you are, you cannot be false to anybody else

81 *season ... thee:* to help this mature in your mind, to make my advice acceptable to you

83 *The ... tend:* it is time for you to leave; go, your servants wait for you

89 *touching:* concerning

90 *Marry:* by (the Virgin) Mary (an oath)
well bethought: I'm glad Laertes thought of raising that subject

92–3 *you yourself ... bounteous:* you have spent a very generous share of your time in listening to what he has to say

65 Of each new-hatched, unfledged comrade. Beware

Of entrance to a quarrel; but, being in,

Bear't that th'opposèd may beware of thee.

Give every man thine ear, but few thy voice.

Take each man's censure, but reserve thy judgement.

70 Costly thy habit as thy purse can buy,

But not expressed in fancy; rich, not gaudy;

For the apparel oft proclaims the man,

And they in France of the best rank and station

Are of a most select and generous chief in that.

75 Neither a borrower nor a lender be,

For loan oft loses both itself and friend,

And borrowing dulls the edge of husbandry.

This above all: to thine own self be true,

And it must follow, as the night the day,

80 Thou canst not then be false to any man.

Farewell: my blessing season this in thee.

LAERTES
Most humbly do I take my leave, my lord.

POLONIUS
The time invites you; go, your servants tend.

LAERTES
Farewell, Ophelia; and remember well

What I have said to you.

OPHELIA
85   'Tis in my memory locked,

And you yourself shall keep the key of it.

LAERTES
Farewell.

Exit.

POLONIUS
What is't, Ophelia, he hath said to you?

OPHELIA
So please you, something touching the Lord Hamlet.

POLONIUS
90 Marry, well bethought:

'Tis told me he hath very oft of late

Given private time to you, and you yourself

Have of your audience been most free and bounteous.

If it be so — as so 'tis put on me,

And that in way of caution — I must tell you,   95

You do not understand yourself so clearly

As it behoves my daughter and your honour.

What is between you? Give me up the truth.

OPHELIA

He hath, my lord, of late made many tenders

Of his affection to me.   100

POLONIUS

Affection? Puh! You speak like a green girl,

Unsifted in such perilous circumstance.

Do you believe his tenders, as you call them?

OPHELIA

I do not know, my lord, what I should think.

POLONIUS

Marry, I'll teach you: think yourself a baby   105

That you have ta'en these tenders for true pay

Which are not sterling. Tender yourself more dearly;

Or — not to crack the wind of the poor phrase,

Running it thus — you'll tender me a fool.

OPHELIA

My lord, he hath importuned me with love   110

In honourable fashion.

POLONIUS

Ay, 'fashion' you may call it; go to, go to.

OPHELIA

And hath given countenance to his speech, my lord,

With almost all the holy vows of heaven.

POLONIUS

Ay, springes to catch woodcocks. I do know,   115

When the blood burns, how prodigal the soul

Lends the tongue vows. These blazes, daughter,

Giving more light than heat, extinct in both,

Even in their promise, as it is a-making,

You must not take for fire. From this time   120

Be something scanter of your maiden presence;

Set your entreatments at a higher rate

Than a command to parley. For Lord Hamlet,

Believe so much in him, that he is young,

---

94   *'tis ... me:* it has been suggested to me

95   *in ... caution:* by way of a warning

96–7 *You ... honour:* your conduct shows that you do not realise what is expected of you as an honourable young woman and as the daughter of me, Polonius

99   *tenders:* offers, expressions

101 *green:* immature

102 *Unsifted ... circumstance:* lacking training and experience in these dangerous matters

105–9 *think ... fool:* Polonius indulges in a complex series of puns on the different meanings of 'tender': Ophelia, in her childlike innocence, has accepted Hamlet's token money ('his tenders') as if it were real money ('sterling'); she must learn to place a higher value on herself ('tender' herself more dearly), because if she does not, she will show herself to him (Polonius) as a fool ('tender me a fool')

108–9 *not ... thus:* Polonius, conscious that he is overstretching his puns, compares the exercise to overworking a horse to the point of breathlessness

110 *importuned ... love:* urgently and persistently declared his love for me

112 *fashion:* Ophelia has just used 'fashion' to mean 'manner'; Polonius picks up the word and distorts its meaning to 'a passing fancy or whim'
    go to: come, come (an expression of disapproval or contempt)

113 *given ... speech:* supported or confirmed his words

115 *springes:* snares, traps
    woodcocks: as the woodcock was considered a stupid bird, Polonius is suggesting that Ophelia is Hamlet's silly, gullible victim

116–17 *When ... vows:* when passion is aroused, rash promises are freely made

117 *blazes:* flames of passion

118–19 *extinct ... a-making:* die away even as the promise is being made

120 *take ... fire:* mistake such passion for the steady flame of real love

121 *something scanter of:* somewhat less available with

122–3 *Set ... parley:* do not enter into negotiations with Hamlet just because he wants a parley or conference. Polonius represents Hamlet's pursuit of Ophelia in military terms: Ophelia must defend the fortress of her honour from Hamlet the besieger

124 *Believe ... young:* his youth makes him unreliable

125–6 *with ... you:* he enjoys greater freedom than you can be permitted

126 *few:* brief, short

127–31 *they ... beguile:* Hamlet's promises of love are like dishonest middlemen whose underhand dealings are hidden behind their convincing outward appearance. They also remind Polonius of hypocrites who frame their immoral proposals in pious language, in order to deceive

128 *investments:* clothes

129 *implorators ... suits:* beggars making improper requests

130 *bawds:* go-betweens, pimps

131 *to beguile:* to cheat and cause you to give way

133 *slander:* abuse, disgrace
moment: moment of, or momentary

135 *Come your ways:* let's go

125 And with a larger tether may he walk

Than may be given you. In few, Ophelia,

Do not believe his vows; for they are brokers,

Not of that dye which their investments show,

But mere implorators of unholy suits,

130 Breathing like sanctified and pious bawds,

The better to beguile. This is for all:

I would not, in plain terms, from this time forth

Have you so slander any moment leisure

As to give words or talk with the Lord Hamlet.

135 Look to't, I charge you. Come your ways.

OPHELIA

I shall obey, my lord.

Exeunt.

Key points

This scene focuses on Polonius and his children, Laertes and Ophelia, whose lives and destinies will determine Hamlet's fate. Similarly, all three doomed members of this family meet their fate as a result of the actions of Hamlet.

- The emphasis in this scene is mainly on Ophelia's relationship with Hamlet. We learn that Hamlet has declared his love for Ophelia. However, neither her brother nor her father believe that Hamlet is sincere. They assume that she has been gullible in taking Hamlet seriously, and that Hamlet intends to take advantage of her.

- Laertes wants to protect his sister from danger. He is concerned for her honour and reputation, which also reflect on the family as a whole. However, his moralising speech, in the form of a sermon, is based on ignorance of the nature of Hamlet's and Ophelia's feelings for each other.

- Ophelia notes that her brother, who has instructed her in virtue, should also follow his own advice.

- The scene suggests that minding other people's business is a family failing; all three members of this family give advice to each other, especially Polonius and Laertes.

- The advice Polonius gives to Laertes is shrewd and practical. However, he seems more concerned with his son's worldly activities than with his moral or spiritual development.

- The scene gives some important glimpses of the kind of man Polonius is, and in particular of the kind of father he is. He certainly likes to talk! Even though he starts out urging Laertes to hurry to his ship, he delays him even longer by preaching to him about his conduct in France.

- Polonius is an authoritarian father. He instructs Ophelia not to spend any more time with Hamlet. Ophelia's response, 'I shall obey, my lord' (line 136), is an undertaking to give up seeing Hamlet. In Shakespeare's day, children (and especially daughters) were expected to obey their parents without question.

- Although Ophelia is present throughout this scene, she does not say much and we learn few details of the Hamlet–Ophelia relationship from her point of view.

Useful quotes

> For Hamlet, and the trifling of his favour,
> Hold it a fashion and a toy in blood,
> A violet in the youth of primy nature,
> Forward, not permanent, sweet, not lasting,
> The perfume and suppliance of a minute.
>
> (Laertes, lines 5–9)

> This above all: to thine own self be true,
> And it must follow, as the night the day,
> Thou canst not then be false to any man.
>
> (Polonius, lines 78–80)

> His greatness weighed, his will is not his own;
> For he himself is subject to his birth.
> He may not, as unvalued persons do,
> Carve for himself
>
> (Laertes, lines 17–20)

> He hath, my lord, of late made many tenders
> Of his affection to me.
>
> (Ophelia, lines 99–100)

> My lord, he hath importuned me with love
> In honourable fashion.
>
> (Ophelia, lines 110–11)

> Do not, as some ungracious pastors do,
> Show me the steep and thorny way to heaven,
> Whiles, like a puffed and reckless libertine,
> Himself the primrose path of dalliance treads,
> And recks not his own rede.
>
> (Ophelia, lines 47–51)

> I would not, in plain terms, from this time forth
> Have you so slander any moment leisure
> As to give words or talk with the Lord Hamlet.
> Look to't, I charge you.
>
> (Polonius, lines 132–5)

Questions ?

1 What, do you think, is Laertes trying to achieve in his lecture to Ophelia?

2 Do Laertes' fears for his sister suggest anything about his own behaviour and character?

3 What view of Hamlet does Polonius try to convey to Ophelia? Does she agree with him?

4 What does this scene tell us about Ophelia's attitude to her brother and her father?

5 From the evidence of this scene, describe Ophelia.

6 Are Laertes and Polonius being fair to Ophelia? Explain.

7 Compare and contrast the advice given to Ophelia by Laertes with that given to her by Polonius.

8 From the evidence of this scene, do you admire Polonius? Give reasons for your answer.

9 Imagine you are one of the characters in this scene. Compose a diary entry giving your thoughts on the relationship between Hamlet and Ophelia, and commenting on the views your family members have on it.

10 Are there any opportunities for comedy in this scene? Explain. It may be helpful to act out some passages in groups of three.

Plot summary

Hamlet, Horatio and Marcellus wait in darkness on the cold battlements for the appearance of the ghost. The sound of trumpets and cannon off stage indicates that Claudius and the members of his court are enjoying their midnight revels. The ghost appears, and beckons to Hamlet to follow it. Horatio and Marcellus try to restrain him, but he obeys the ghost's call.

Thou com'st in such a questionable shape
That I will speak to thee. I'll call thee Hamlet,
King, father, royal Dane. O answer me!

HAMLET, Act 1, Scene 4, 45–7

Elsinore. The guard-platform of the castle.

Enter HAMLET, HORATIO and MARCELLUS.

HAMLET

The air bites shrewdly; it is very cold.

HORATIO

It is a nipping and an eager air.

HAMLET

What hour now?

HORATIO

I think it lacks of twelve.

HAMLET

No, it is struck.   5

HORATIO

Indeed? I heard it not. Then it draws near the season

Wherein the spirit held his wont to walk.

A flourish of trumpets, and cannon shot off.

What does this mean, my lord?

HAMLET

The king doth wake tonight and takes his rouse,

Keeps wassail, and the swaggering upspring reels;   10

And, as he drains his draughts of Rhenish down,

The kettle-drum and trumpet thus bray out

The triumph of his pledge.

HORATIO

Is it a custom?

HAMLET

Ay, marry, is't: 15

But to my mind, though I am native here

And to the manner born, it is a custom

More honoured in the breach than the observance.

This heavy-headed revel east and west

Makes us traduced and taxed of other nations: 20

They clepe us drunkards, and with swinish phrase

Soil our addition; and indeed it takes

From our achievements, though performed at height,

The pith and marrow of our attribute.

So oft it chances in particular men   25

That for some vicious mole of nature in them,

As in their birth — wherein they are not guilty,

---

1 *shrewdly:* sharply, piercingly

2 *eager:* sharp, keen

4 *lacks of:* is a little before

6 *season:* time

7 *held his wont:* was accustomed

  off: sounded off stage

9 *The . . . rouse:* Claudius has stayed up late tonight and is drinking heavily
10 *wassail:* drunken revelry
  upspring: a wild, abandoned dance
11 *Rhenish:* wine from the Rhine valley, Germany
12 *bray out:* make coarse harsh sounds (like a donkey)

13 *pledge:* toast

18 *More . . . observance:* it would be more honourable for Danes to break with this custom than to continue to observe it
19–20 *This . . . nations:* this drunken revelry, which leaves the revellers with heavy heads, gives us a bad name in other countries
20 *traduced and taxed:* slandered and censured
21 *clepe:* call, name
21–2 *with . . . addition:* by dubbing us pigs, sully our good name
23 *performed at height:* (the achievements are) outstanding
24 *pith . . . attribute:* core of our reputation
25–40 *So . . . scandal:* a paraphrase of this key speech is: It often happens that individual men are born with a fault or blemish, for which they cannot be blamed . . .

25–40 *... since they had no say in their parentage. They may suffer because some temperamental feature (e.g. melancholy) is too prominent, and this imbalance can lead even to madness. They may also be cursed with a habit that corrupts their normally acceptable behaviour. Such people, then, have one major defect, whether that be hereditary or the result of chance. They may be gifted with an endless variety of excellent qualities, but, in the opinion of most observers, their single defect will tend to corrupt all their virtues. A small measure ('dram') of evil will often appear to extinguish all the nobility of a man's nature, and bring discredit on him*

41 *Angels ... us!* Hamlet's prayer for protection from evil spirits
ministers: messengers
42 *a ... damned:* a good spirit or a hellish demon
43 *Bring:* whether you bring
44 *Be thy intents:* whether your intentions be

45 *questionable shape:* form that invites questioning or conversation

49 *canonised bones:* his remains were buried according to sacred church rites
hearsèd: placed in a coffin or a hearse
50 *cerements:* burial clothes
sepulchre: tomb, burial place
51 *inurned:* buried, entombed
52–3 *Hath ... again:* has opened its heavy stone jaws to vomit you up again
54 *complete steel:* full armour

56 *fools of nature:* weak, fearful creatures at the mercy of nature
57 *disposition:* self-control, composure
58 *reaches:* understanding, capacity

59 *Wherefore?* Why?

61 *some ... desire:* wanted to communicate something

Since nature cannot choose his origin —

By the o'ergrowth of some complexion,

30 Oft breaking down the pales and forts of reason,

Or by some habit that too much o'erleavens

The form of plausive manners, that these men,

Carrying, I say, the stamp of one defect,

Being nature's livery, or fortune's star,

35 His virtues else be they as pure as grace,

As infinite as man may undergo,

Shall in the general censure take corruption

From that particular fault: the dram of evil

Doth all the noble substance often doubt

To his own scandal.

Enter GHOST.

HORATIO
40   Look, my lord, it comes!
HAMLET
Angels and ministers of grace defend us!

Be thou a spirit of health or goblin damned,

Bring with thee airs from heaven or blasts from hell,

Be thy intents wicked or charitable,

45 Thou com'st in such a questionable shape

That I will speak to thee. I'll call thee Hamlet,

King, father, royal Dane. O answer me!

Let me not burst in ignorance; but tell

Why thy canonised bones, hearsèd in death,

50 Have burst their cerements; why the sepulchre,

Wherein we saw thee quietly inurned,

Hath oped his ponderous and marble jaws

To cast thee up again? What may this mean,

That thou, dead corpse, again in complete steel,

55 Revisits thus the glimpses of the moon,

Making night hideous; and we fools of nature

So horridly to shake our disposition

With thoughts beyond the reaches of our souls?

Say, why is this? Wherefore? What should we do?

GHOST beckons HAMLET.

HORATIO
60 It beckons you to go away with it,

As if it some impartment did desire

To you alone.

MARCELLUS

          Look, with what courteous action

It waves you to a more removèd ground:

But do not go with it.

HORATIO

             No, by no means.

HAMLET

It will not speak; then I will follow it.   65

HORATIO

Do not, my lord.

HAMLET

          Why, what should be the fear?

I do not set my life at a pin's fee;

And for my soul, what can it do to that,

Being a thing immortal as itself?

It waves me forth again. I'll follow it.   70

HORATIO

What if it tempt you towards the flood, my lord,

Or to the dreadful summit of the cliff

That beetles o'er his base into the sea,

And there assume some other horrible form,

Which might deprive your sovereignty of reason   75

And draw you into madness? Think of it:

The very place puts toys of desperation,

Without more motive, into every brain

That looks so many fathoms to the sea

And hears it roar beneath.   80

HAMLET

It waves me still. — Go on; I'll follow thee.

MARCELLUS

You shall not go, my lord.

HAMLET

              Hold off your hands.

HORATIO

Be ruled; you shall not go.

HAMLET

            My fate cries out,

And makes each petty artere in this body

As hardy as the Nemean lion's nerve.   85

Still am I called. Unhand me, gentlemen.

By heaven, I'll make a ghost of him that lets me!

I say, away! — Go on; I'll follow thee.

Exeunt GHOST and HAMLET.

---

63 *removèd ground:* remote spot

67 *fee:* worth

71 *flood:* sea

73 *beetles:* projects, hangs

75 *deprive . . . reason:* take away the control that your reason exerts over your mind

77 *toys of desperation:* desperate fancies or impulses, which might lead to suicide

78 *more motive:* any further cause (the place alone is sufficiently terrible to inspire thoughts of suicide)

79 *fathoms:* a nautical measurement of just over 1.8 metres

84 *petty artere:* small artery

85 *hardy . . . nerve:* strong as the muscle of the fiercest lion (the slaying of the Nemean lion was one of the labours of Hercules)

86 *Unhand me:* let me go

87 *lets:* hinders

89 *waxes:* grows
imagination: fantasies

91 *Have after:* let's go after him
issue: result

92 *state:* government, kingdom

93 *direct it:* control the outcome

93 *Nay:* Marcellus does not agree with Horatio that they should leave matters entirely to God; he wants them to do something to help Hamlet

HORATIO

He waxes desperate with imagination.

MARCELLUS

90 Let's follow; 'tis not fit thus to obey him.

HORATIO

Have after. To what issue will this come?

MARCELLUS

Something is rotten in the state of Denmark.

HORATIO

Heaven will direct it.

MARCELLUS

Nay, let's follow him.

Exeunt.

Key points

This scene gives us a sense of the kind of society Claudius rules over, and of Hamlet's disapproval of the court's drunkenness. It also features Hamlet's first encounter with the ghost of his dead father.

- The most interesting feature of this scene is one that may at first appear an irrelevance. It is Hamlet's commentary on Danish drunkenness and the bad name it gives the Danish people. Hamlet's observations on the drunken revelry of Claudius and his courtiers suggests his own civilised standards. Unlike his uncle, he does not want his reputation associated with so 'swinish' (line 21) a habit as drunkenness.

- Hamlet the intellectual finds a parallel between the predicament of the Denmark he describes, and that of individual human beings. He observes that just as a nation may be damned in the eyes of the world by being associated with a single gross vice such as drunkenness, so, too, a fine individual, whatever his good qualities, may be subject to public criticism for a particular fault.

- Hamlet may be thinking of himself when he deplores the fact that a single defect, whether caused by nature or circumstances, can

undermine the character and reputation of an otherwise good man.

- Hamlet's reflection on how the minutest quantity of evil in a human being can extinguish or conceal the much greater measure of good portrays his intellectual capacity. It is in keeping with his standing in the play as a philosopher and scholar, who is interested in and contemplates many subjects.

- The remark of Marcellus, following the appearance of the ghost, is significant: 'Something is rotten in the state of Denmark' (line 92). This true insight echoes Hamlet's observation at the close of Scene 2: 'All is not well. I doubt some foul play' (lines 257–8).

- Hamlet is excited to see the ghost of his father and eager to find out what he wants. Horatio urges caution; he is fearful for Hamlet's sanity and warns that the ghost may draw him into madness or tempt him to take his own life. Hamlet, however, is determined to speak with the ghost.

Useful quotes

> It beckons you to go away with it,
> As if it some impartment did desire
> To you alone.
>
> (Horatio, lines 60–62)

> This heavy-headed revel east and west
> Makes us traduced and taxed of other nations
>
> (Hamlet, lines 19–20)

> My fate cries out,
> And makes each petty artere in this body
> As hardy as the Nemean lion's nerve.
>
> (Hamlet, lines 83–5)

> Thou com'st in such a questionable shape
> That I will speak to thee. I'll call thee Hamlet,
> King, father, royal Dane. O answer me!
> Let me not burst in ignorance
>
> (Hamlet, lines 45–8)

> Something is rotten in the state of Denmark.
>
> (Marcellus, line 92)

Questions ?

1 What does Horatio think of the ghost and its purposes?

2 Hamlet believes that the ghost wants to be questioned or engaged in conversation. Does the ghost do anything to confirm this?

3 Why does Marcellus come to the conclusion that 'Something is rotten in the state of Denmark' (line 92)? Does any other character think the same?

4 Is Horatio somewhat confused over what is happening? Explain your answer.

5 Imagine you are a journalist who witnesses the events on the castle battlements. Write a short newspaper article on what you saw and heard.

ACT 1 † Scene 5

Plot summary

The ghost has led Hamlet to a remote place on the castle walls, where Hamlet learns that Claudius murdered his father. The ghost expects Hamlet to avenge that crime. Hamlet promises to dedicate himself to this solemn duty.

Hamlet refuses to tell Horatio and Marcellus what transpired during his encounter with the ghost. He forces them to take an oath never to reveal what they have seen, and never to comment, by way of explanation, if they notice anything odd about his behaviour in future. The ghost joins Hamlet in demanding silence from Horatio and Marcellus about what they have seen.

But know, thou noble youth,
The serpent that did sting thy father's life
Now wears his crown.

GHOST, Act 1, Scene 5, 38–40

Elsinore. The battlements of the castle.

Enter GHOST and HAMLET.

HAMLET

Whither wilt thou lead me? Speak. I'll go no further.

GHOST

Mark me.

HAMLET

    I will.

GHOST

        My hour is almost come,

When I to sulphurous and tormenting flames

Must render up myself.

HAMLET

           Alas, poor ghost!

GHOST

Pity me not, but lend thy serious hearing   5

To what I shall unfold.

HAMLET

          Speak. I am bound to hear.

GHOST

So art thou to revenge, when thou shalt hear.

HAMLET

What?

GHOST

I am thy father's spirit,

Doomed for a certain term to walk the night,   10

And for the day confined to fast in fires,

Till the foul crimes done in my days of nature

Are burnt and purged away. But that I am forbid

To tell the secrets of my prison-house,

I could a tale unfold whose lightest word   15

Would harrow up thy soul, freeze thy young blood,

Make thy two eyes, like stars, start from their spheres,

Thy knotted and combinèd locks to part

And each particular hair to stand on end

Like quills upon the fretful porpentine.   20

But this eternal blazon must not be

To ears of flesh and blood. List, list, O list!

If thou didst ever thy dear father love—

---

1 *Whither:* where

2 *Mark me:* listen, pay attention to me

2 *My hour:* daybreak

3–4 *to . . . myself:* must return to the fires of purgatory

6 *bound:* ready, destined

7 *So . . . revenge:* you will also be compelled to seek revenge

11 *fast in fires:* in Shakespeare's time, fasting was regarded as an appropriate purgatorial punishment for earthly gluttony. It may or may not be relevant that King Hamlet was poisoned after a hearty meal (Act 3, Scene 3, line 81)

12 *days of nature:* life on earth

16 *harrow up:* lacerate, tear up

17 *start:* jump
    spheres: sockets, orbits

18 *locks:* hairs

20 *fretful porpentine:* disturbed or irritated porcupine

21–2 *eternal . . . blood:* revelation of the secrets of eternity is too frightful for human ears to endure

22 *List:* listen

HAMLET

O God!

GHOST

25 Revenge his foul and most unnatural murder.

HAMLET

Murder?

GHOST

Murder most foul, as in the best it is,

But this most foul, strange and unnatural.

HAMLET

Haste me to know't, that I, with wings as swift

30 As meditation or the thoughts of love,

May sweep to my revenge.

GHOST

              I find thee apt;

And duller shouldst thou be than the fat weed

That roots itself in ease on Lethe wharf,

Wouldst thou not stir in this. Now, Hamlet, hear:

35 'Tis given out that, sleeping in my orchard,

A serpent stung me; so the whole ear of Denmark

Is by a forgèd process of my death

Rankly abused. But know, thou noble youth,

The serpent that did sting thy father's life

Now wears his crown.

HAMLET

              O my prophetic soul!

40 My uncle?

GHOST

Ay, that incestuous, that adulterate beast,

With witchcraft of his wit, with traitorous gifts —

O wicked wit, and gifts, that have the power

45 So to seduce! — won to his shameful lust

The will of my most seeming-virtuous queen.

O Hamlet, what a falling-off was there!

From me, whose love was of that dignity

That it went hand in hand even with the vow

50 I made to her in marriage; and to decline

Upon a wretch whose natural gifts were poor

To those of mine!

---

27   *Murder . . . is:* even the least revolting murder is still a foul crime

30   *meditation:* the contemplation of God (thoughts of God, and of love, were proverbially carried on wings, and therefore speedy)

31   *apt:* prepared

32–4   *And . . . this:* Lethe was the river in the Greek underworld whose waters caused forgetfulness. The ghost is telling Hamlet that if he does not take revenge he must be a dull, lethargic individual. Like a bloated weed on the banks of the Lethe, he must be in a state of oblivion

35   *'Tis given out:* it is officially stated

36   *the whole ear:* all the people

37   *forgèd process:* false official account

38   *Rankly abused:* grossly deceived

40   *prophetic:* foreknowing. The ghost's revelation has confirmed Hamlet's instincts about the unworthiness of Claudius (Act 1, Scene 2, lines 139–40)

42   *that incestuous . . . beast:* in marrying Gertrude, Claudius can be seen as having committed the crimes of incest and adultery, since marriage to a deceased brother's wife was unlawful. It has been suggested that 'adulterate' indicates that the adultery took place during King Hamlet's lifetime; the rest of this speech adds some weight to such an argument

43   *witchcraft . . . gifts:* he assumes that Claudius used unnatural means to entice Gertrude, i.e. practised black magic, and made use of devilish cunning and presents to win her over

46   *will:* desire

47   *falling-off:* shocking decline in her standards

50–51   *decline upon:* lower herself to accept

52   *To:* compared with

But virtue as it never will be moved,

Though lewdness court it in a shape of heaven,

So lust, though to a radiant angel linked,   55

Will sate itself in a celestial bed

And prey on garbage.

But soft, methinks I scent the morning air;

Brief let me be: sleeping within my orchard,

My custom always of the afternoon,   60

Upon my secure hour thy uncle stole,

With juice of cursèd hebenon in a vial,

And in the porches of my ears did pour

The leperous distilment, whose effect

Holds such an enmity with blood of man   65

That swift as quicksilver it courses through

The natural gates and alleys of the body,

And with a sudden vigour doth posset

And curd, like eager droppings into milk,

The thin and wholesome blood; so did it mine;   70

And a most instant tetter barked about,

Most lazar-like, with vile and loathsome crust,

All my smooth body.

Thus was I, sleeping, by a brother's hand

Of life, of crown, and queen at once dispatched: 75

Cut off even in the blossoms of my sin,

Unhouseled, disappointed, unaneled,

No reckoning made, but sent to my account

With all my imperfections on my head.

O horrible! O horrible! Most horrible!   80

If thou hast nature in thee, bear it not;

Let not the royal bed of Denmark be

A couch for luxury and damned incest.

But howsomever thou pursuest this act,

Taint not thy mind, nor let thy soul contrive   85

Against thy mother aught: leave her to heaven

And to those thorns that in her bosom lodge

To prick and sting her. Fare thee well at once.

The glow-worm shows the matin to be near,

And 'gins to pale his uneffectual fire.   90

Adieu, adieu, adieu, remember me.

Exit.

53–4 *virtue … heaven:* a really virtuous person will not be corrupted, even if the tempter comes in the form of an angel

55–7 *lust … garbage:* a lustful person (i.e. Gertrude), even if married to a wholly virtuous partner (i.e. King Hamlet), will grow tired of a decent relationship and seek satisfaction with someone foul (i.e. Claudius)

57 *garbage:* the offal and entrails of animals. The imagery used by the ghost and Hamlet to characterise Claudius is consistently repulsive

58 *scent:* smell, sniff

61 *secure hour:* unsuspecting, relaxed time

62 *hebenon:* a poison, probably oil of henbane, which, according to ancient tradition, injured the mind when poured into the ear
vial: phial, small bottle

63 *porches:* openings

64 *leperous:* causing scales to form on the body
distilment: concentrated juice, essence

65 *Holds … enmity:* is so deadly, reacts so violently

66 *quicksilver:* liquid mercury
courses: races

67 *gates and alleys:* ducts, veins, arteries

68–70 *sudden … blood:* rapid and violent action curdles the healthy, free-flowing blood, as acid acts on milk

69 *eager droppings:* bitter drops

71–3 *most … All:* immediately a revolting rash of scabs, like leprosy, encrusted

75 *dispatched:* deprived

76 *Cut … sin:* killed when my sins were at their peak

77 *Unhouseled:* deprived of the Eucharist
disappointed: not having made Confession
unaneled: not having received Extreme Unction

78 *No reckoning made:* I had no chance to settle my debts to God
account: judgement

81 *nature:* natural feeling (love of a son for his father)

83 *luxury:* lust

84 *howsomever:* however
act: revenge

85–6 *Taint … aught:* do not allow yourself to become hostile to your mother, or plan any action against her

86 *leave … heaven:* let God judge her

87–8 *those … sting her:* the torments of her own conscience

89 *matin:* morning

90 *'gins … fire:* begins to let its weak light fade

HAMLET

O all you host of heaven! O earth! What else?

And shall I couple hell? O fie! Hold, hold, my heart;

And you, my sinews, grow not instant old,

95   But bear me stiffly up. Remember thee?

Ay, thou poor ghost, while memory holds a seat

In this distracted globe. Remember thee?

Yea, from the table of my memory

I'll wipe away all trivial fond records,

100   All saws of books, all forms, all pressures past,

That youth and observation copied there;

And thy commandment all alone shall live

Within the book and volume of my brain,

Unmixed with baser matter. Yes, by heaven!

105   O most pernicious woman!

O villain, villain, smiling, damnèd villain!

My tables — meet it is I set it down [*writes*]

That one may smile, and smile, and be a villain;

At least I'm sure it may be so in Denmark.

110   So, uncle, there you are. Now to my word;

It is 'Adieu, adieu, remember me'.

I have sworn't.

HORATIO, MARCELLUS [*within*]
           My lord, my lord!

MARCELLUS [*within*]
                    Lord Hamlet!

HORATIO [*within*]
Heaven secure him!

HAMLET
So be it!

MARCELLUS [*within*]
115   Hillo, ho, ho, my lord!

HAMLET
Hillo, ho, ho, boy! Come, bird, come.

Enter HORATIO and MARCELLUS.

MARCELLUS
How is't, my noble lord?

---

92 *host of heaven:* angels

93 *couple:* include. Hamlet considers including hell in case the ghost is really a devil
Hold: carry on, stay strong

94 *sinews:* muscles, physical strength

96–7 *while . . . globe:* as long as my disturbed mind retains any power of memory. A secondary meaning is: as long as this disordered world can keep memories alive. The audience in the Globe theatre would have relished this complex pun

98 *table:* tablet, slate

99 *trivial fond records:* insignificant and foolish recollections

100 *saws of books:* proverbs and other items of wisdom copied from books. The collecting of wise sayings was once a common practice
pressures past: impressions imprinted upon the memory

103 *the . . . brain:* my memory

104 *baser matter:* less significant material

105 *pernicious:* dangerous, destructive. Hamlet's first fierce feeling of anger is inspired by his mother's betrayal of his father

106 *O . . . damnèd villain!* Claudius. His smiling appearance contrasts with the ugly reality beneath

107 *My tables:* Hamlet may produce a notebook at this point
meet . . . down: it is appropriate to make a note of this (observation about smiling villains)

110 *there you are:* I've now recorded my comment on you and your kind
my word: the motto or key phrase for my programme of action from now on

within: from off stage; behind the stage façade

113 *secure him:* make him safe

115–16 *Hillo . . . come:* cries used by falconers to call hawks

HORATIO

What news, my lord?

HAMLET

O wonderful!

HORATIO

Good my lord, tell it.

HAMLET

No, you'll reveal it.

HORATIO

Not I, my lord, by heaven.

MARCELLUS

Nor I, my lord.   120

HAMLET

How say you, then? Would heart of man once think it?

But you'll be secret?

HORATIO, MARCELLUS

Ay, by heaven, my lord.

HAMLET

There's ne'er a villain dwelling in all Denmark

But he's an arrant knave.

HORATIO

There needs no ghost, my lord, come from the grave   125

To tell us this.

HAMLET

Why right, you are in the right;

And so, without more circumstance at all,

I hold it fit that we shake hands and part:

You, as your business and desire shall point you;

For every man hath business and desire,   130

Such as it is; and for mine own poor part,

Look you, I'll go pray.

HORATIO

These are but wild and whirling words, my lord.

HAMLET

I'm sorry they offend you, heartily;

Yes, faith, heartily.

HORATIO

There's no offence, my lord.   135

121 *Would ... it?* Would anybody ever ('once') think such a thing could happen?
122 *be secret:* keep it a secret

123–4 *There's ... knave:* villains in Denmark are all downright bad fellows. Perhaps Hamlet, about to reveal what he has heard, has second thoughts and tries to put his friends off with a meaningless statement

127 *circumstance:* detail, elaboration

133 *wild and whirling:* violently excited, hysterical

HAMLET

Yes, by Saint Patrick, but there is, Horatio,

And much offence too. Touching this vision here,

It is an honest ghost, that let me tell you.

For your desire to know what is between us,

140 O'ermaster't as you may. And now, good friends,

As you are friends, scholars and soldiers,

Give me one poor request.

HORATIO

What is't, my lord? We will.

HAMLET

Never make known what you have seen tonight.

HORATIO, MARCELLUS

My lord, we will not.

HAMLET

     Nay, but swear't.

HORATIO

145   In faith,

My lord, not I.

MARCELLUS

    Nor I, my lord, in faith.

HAMLET

Upon my sword.

MARCELLUS

    We have sworn, my lord, already.

HAMLET

Indeed, upon my sword, indeed.

GHOST cries under the stage.

GHOST [*beneath*]

Swear.

HAMLET

150 Ha, ha, boy! Say'st thou so? Art thou there, truepenny?

Come on, you hear this fellow in the cellarage,

Consent to swear.

HORATIO

    Propose the oath, my lord.

HAMLET

Never to speak of this that you have seen,

Swear by my sword.

GHOST [*beneath*]

Swear.   155

They swear silently.

HAMLET

Hic et ubique? Then we'll shift our ground.

Come hither, gentlemen,

And lay your hands again upon my sword.

Never to speak of this that you have heard,

Swear by my sword.   160

GHOST [*beneath*]

Swear by his sword.

They swear silently.

156 *Hic et ubique?* Here and everywhere? Only God or
the devil could be everywhere at once
157 *hither:* here

Swear by my sword.

HAMLET, Act 1, Scene 5, 154

HAMLET

Well said, old mole! Canst work in th'earth so fast?

A worthy pioneer! Once more remove, good friends.

HORATIO

O day and night, but this is wondrous strange!

HAMLET

165 And therefore as a stranger give it welcome.

There are more things in heaven and earth, Horatio,

Than are dreamt of in your philosophy. But come;

Here as before, never, so help you mercy,

How strange or odd some'er I bear myself

170 (As I perchance hereafter shall think meet

To put an antic disposition on)

That you, at such times seeing me, never shall,

With arms encumbered thus, or this head-shake,

Or by pronouncing of some doubtful phrase,

175 As 'Well, well, we know' or 'We could, an if we would'

Or 'If we list to speak' or 'There be, an if they might'

Or such ambiguous giving out, to note

That you know aught of me — this do swear,

So grace and mercy at your most need help you.

GHOST [*beneath*]

180 Swear.

They swear silently.

HAMLET

Rest, rest, perturbèd spirit! So, gentlemen,

With all my love I do commend me to you,

And what so poor a man as Hamlet is

May do to express his love and friending to you,

185 God willing, shall not lack. Let us go in together;

And still your fingers on your lips, I pray.

The time is out of joint: O cursèd spite,

That ever I was born to set it right!

Nay, come, let's go together.

Exeunt.

162–3 *Well ... pioneer:* Hamlet compares the ghost's mobility to a burrowing mole moving quickly through the ground, and to an excellent digger of mines, as wherever they move, the ghost manages to speak from just below them
163 *remove:* move
164 *wondrous:* extraordinarily

166–7 *There ... philosophy:* not everything in heaven and on earth can be rationally explained. The 'philosophy' (near in meaning to our 'science') is philosophy in general, not just Horatio's
168 *Here as before:* swear here, in the same solemn way as before
169–71 *How ... on:* however strangely I conduct myself (as I may see fit to behave oddly after this)
171 *antic disposition:* grotesque behaviour, suggesting madness

173 *encumbered:* folded
174 *doubtful phrase:* ambiguous remark

176 *list:* wished
'*There ... might*': some of us could explain if we chose to
177 *giving out:* statement
note: indicate
178 *aught:* something (a reason why I should behave oddly)
179 *at ... need:* in your greatest need. This line is similar to the modern 'so help me God'

182 *commend me:* entrust myself

183–5 *And ... lack:* I do not have the means or the power to do much by way of rewarding your love and friendship, but, with God's help, whatever I can do for you, I will

186 *still:* always keep
187 *The ... joint:* the state of Denmark is afflicted with sickness and is disordered
spite: fate, ill fortune
189 *let's go together:* the others have waited to let Hamlet go first; he shows his friendliness and indifference to rank and status by suggesting that they all go together

Key points

This scene provides the first major climax of the play, and marks the end of its first phase, as the crime of Claudius is revealed. This truth sets the main action of the play in motion as it is now Hamlet's task to avenge the murder of his father.

- The ghost tells Hamlet that Claudius poisoned him in his orchard as he slept, thus killing him before he had time to make his peace with God. As a result, he is confined to the fires of purgatory by day and doomed to walk the earth at night until his earthly crimes are purged.

- Hamlet's previous hostility towards his uncle, and his strong resentment of his mother, were based on natural instinct and suspicion. Now he knows the truth, and it is more terrible than anything he might have suspected.

- It is important to note the ghost's revelation that Gertrude was guilty of adultery with Claudius while still married to her late husband. To this crime she has, by marrying Claudius, added the crime of incest. The reference of the ghost to Claudius as 'that incestuous, that adulterate beast' (line 42) provides firm evidence of this.

- The ghost instructs Hamlet not to 'taint' his mind or let his soul 'contrive' in any way against Gertrude, but to leave her to heaven and her own conscience (lines 85–8). It is difficult to comprehend the ghost's demand that Gertrude is not to suffer in any scheme of revenge that Hamlet may undertake; it is scarcely possible to imagine how he can take revenge on Claudius without causing pain to Gertrude.

- Hamlet's first soliloquy showed his struggle to understand his mother's irrational and lustful behaviour (Act 1, Scene 2, lines 138–57). In the present scene, the ghost echoes and elaborates on Hamlet's insights. He suggests that Claudius may have used witchcraft to undermine Gertrude's reason.

- The real significance of the ghost is to be found in the shameful burden of knowledge laid on Hamlet by his revelations, and the task of revenge imposed on him by solemn command and by his sense of duty to his wronged father.

- Hamlet's closing words in this scene show that he recognises his lack of fitness for the task he has been given by the ghost: 'The time is out of joint: O cursèd spite, that ever I was born to set it right!' (lines 187–8). It is clear from these lines that Hamlet regards his task as involving more than personal vengeance on Claudius. He must also restore the health of the whole state ('the time' means 'the state of Denmark') by purging it of the evil with which it has been infected.

- Not surprisingly, given what the ghost has revealed to him and the task that faces him, Hamlet struggles to maintain mental and emotional stability. This struggle is not always successful. His loss of control is conveyed by his deliriously high spirits, his 'wild and whirling words' (line 133) to his companions, and his hysterical remarks about the ghost.

- Hamlet warns his companions that in the future he may think it appropriate to pretend to be mad ('To put an antic disposition on'; line 171) from time to time. What he intends to achieve by behaving as though he is mad is never made fully clear.

Useful quotes

If thou didst ever thy dear father love—
…

Revenge his foul and most unnatural murder.

(Ghost, lines 23, 25)

Haste me to know't, that I, with wings as swift
As meditation or the thoughts of love,
May sweep to my revenge.

(Hamlet, lines 29–31)

The serpent that did sting thy father's life
Now wears his crown.

(Ghost, lines 39–40)

O Hamlet, what a falling-off was there!
From me, whose love was of that dignity
That it went hand in hand even with the vow
I made to her in marriage; and to decline
Upon a wretch whose natural gifts were poor
To those of mine!

(Ghost, lines 47–52)

Thus was I, sleeping, by a brother's hand
Of life, of crown, and queen at once dispatched:
Cut off even in the blossoms of my sin

(Ghost, lines 74–6)

That one may smile, and smile, and be a villain

(Hamlet, line 108)

There are more things in heaven and earth, Horatio,
Than are dreamt of in your philosophy.

(Hamlet, lines 166–7)

As I perchance hereafter shall think meet
To put an antic disposition on

(Hamlet, lines 170–71)

The time is out of joint: O cursèd spite,
That ever I was born to set it right!

(Hamlet, lines 187–8)

? Questions

1 This scene reveals a good deal about the character and personality of the late King Hamlet. Develop this point.

2 Explain, in your own words, the ghost's commands to Hamlet.

3 Contrast the ghost's attitude to Gertrude with his attitude to Claudius.

4 Does Hamlet appear certain that the ghost is his late father's spirit? Explain your answer.

5 How does Hamlet view the task imposed on him by the ghost? Is he looking forward to carrying it out? Give reasons for your answers.

6 Compare Hamlet's attitude to his father with Ophelia's attitude to Polonius in Act 1, Scene 3.

7 Describe Hamlet's conduct after he has spoken with the ghost. Is his behaviour what you would expect in the circumstances?

8 Does Hamlet's attitude to his friends change in the course of this scene? Explain.

9 Comment on Hamlet's 'antic disposition' (line 171). Can you suggest why he has chosen to take it on?

10 Imagine you are Hamlet. Compose a diary entry on your encounter with the ghost.

ACT 1 ⚔ Key moments

Scene 1

- The guards on night watch at the royal castle in Elsinore are uneasy. Some of them have seen the ghost of Hamlet's father. They have invited Horatio, a scholar, to join them and speak to the ghost. Horatio is sceptical.
- The ghost appears and Horatio tries without success to get it to explain its presence.
- The men agree to tell Hamlet what they have seen.

Scene 2

- Claudius explains why he has married Gertrude, his brother's widow, so soon after her husband's death.
- To address the military threat to Denmark posed by young Fortinbras, nephew of the King of Norway, Claudius sends two ambassadors to make peace with the Norwegians.
- Claudius tries to win Hamlet's friendship and approval for his marriage to Gertrude.
- Hamlet remains sullen and hostile. He reveals in a bitter soliloquy that his mother's marriage to Claudius is the cause of his depressed state.
- Horatio and Marcellus tell Hamlet that they have seen his father's ghost; he decides to join them on the guard-platform that night.

Scene 3

- Laertes and Ophelia exchange farewells before Laertes leaves for France. Laertes warns Ophelia not to take Hamlet's declarations of love for her seriously.
- Polonius gives Laertes advice on how he should conduct himself in France.
- Polonius warns Ophelia about Hamlet and orders her not to see him again. She agrees to obey her father's wishes.

Scene 4

- The ghost appears to Hamlet, and indicates that it wants to speak to him alone.
- Horatio and Marcellus try to stop him, but Hamlet follows the ghost.

Scene 5

- The ghost tells Hamlet that Claudius murdered him, and gives Hamlet the task, which he accepts, of taking vengeance on Claudius, without harming Gertrude.
- Hamlet refuses to tell Horatio and Marcellus what happened with the ghost. He swears them to secrecy.
- Hamlet curses the fates for imposing the terrible burden he now has to carry.

ACT 1 ⚔ Speaking and listening

1 Assign the part of the ghost. He will be interviewed by four members of the class, chosen at random. They will question him on how he feels about Hamlet's response to him, why he has given Hamlet such a difficult task to perform, how he ended up where he is, and whether he has any suggestions as to how Hamlet might carry out

2 In groups of three, assign the parts of Polonius, Laertes and Ophelia. Each character should select a short speech or two from Act 1 that gives the audience a sense of his or her nature. As a group, discuss the characteristics revealed in the three speeches, and identify the differences and similarities between these family members.

ACT 2 ✝ Scene 1

Plot summary

Polonius sends his servant Reynaldo to Paris to check on Laertes. He describes in detail how Reynaldo should go about gathering whatever incriminating evidence there is against Laertes. Ophelia, greatly distressed, arrives with disturbing news of an encounter she has just had with a distracted Hamlet. Polonius assumes that Hamlet's madness is a direct result of Ophelia's refusal to see him. He concludes that he has misjudged Hamlet's intentions towards Ophelia, and decides to tell Claudius of Hamlet's feelings for Ophelia in case Hamlet might do something desperate.

You shall do marvellous wisely, good Reynaldo,
Before you visit him, to make inquire
Of his behaviour.

POLONIUS, Act 2, Scene 1, 3–5

Elsinore. A room in the house of Polonius.

Enter POLONIUS and REYNALDO.

POLONIUS

Give him this money and these notes, Reynaldo.

REYNALDO

I will, my lord.

POLONIUS

You shall do marvellous wisely, good Reynaldo,

Before you visit him, to make inquire

Of his behaviour.   5

REYNALDO

My lord, I did intend it.

POLONIUS

Marry, well said; very well said. Look you, sir,

Inquire me first what Danskers are in Paris;

And how, and who, what means, and where they keep,

What company, at what expense; and finding   10

By this encompassment and drift of question

That they do know my son, come you more nearer

Than your particular demands will touch it.

Take you, as 'twere, some distant knowledge of him,

As thus: 'I know his father and his friends,   15

And in part him' — do you mark this, Reynaldo?

REYNALDO

Ay, very well, my lord.

POLONIUS

'And in part him; but,' you may say, 'not well:

But if't be he I mean, he's very wild;

Addicted so and so'. And there put on him   20

What forgeries you please — marry, none so rank

As may dishonour him, take heed of that —

But sir, such wanton, wild and usual slips

As are companions noted and most known

To youth and liberty.

REYNALDO

                              As gaming, my lord.   25

POLONIUS

Ay, or drinking, fencing, swearing, quarrelling,

Drabbing — you may go so far.

---

1 *notes:* letters

4 *inquire:* enquiries

7 *Look you:* make sure you do this

8 *Inquire . . . Danskers:* first find out what Danes

9–10 *And . . . expense:* what they are there for, who they are, what their financial position is, where they are staying, who their friends are, how much they spend

11 *By . . . question:* by this indirect method of enquiry

12–13 *come . . . it:* you will come much closer to finding the truth than you would if you asked straightforward questions

14 *Take . . . him:* pretend you know him slightly

16 *mark:* comprehend, pay attention to

20–21 *And . . . please:* make whatever false accusations you like about him

21 *forgeries:* inventions
rank: gross, foul

23–5 *such . . . liberty:* the undisciplined lapses associated with young men who enjoy freedom

25 *gaming:* gambling

27 *Drabbing:* pursuing prostitutes

29 *as . . . charge:* provided that you make the accusation in a tactful, delicate way

31 *open to incontinency:* guilty of habitual lechery

32 *breathe . . . quaintly:* suggest or hint at his failings so delicately

33 *taints of liberty:* vices one would expect of those who have freedom

34–6 *The . . . assault:* the wild outbursts typical of lively spirits, the uncontrolled impulses to which all men are subject

37 *Wherefore:* why

38 *my drift:* what I'm getting at

39 *fetch of warrant:* trick that can be defended or justified

40 *You . . . son:* for you to attribute these minor vices to my son

41 *As . . . working:* as if he has become a little corrupted through contact with the world

42 *your . . . sound:* the person to whom you are talking with a view to finding out about Laertes

43–5 *Having . . . consequence:* if the person you're sounding out has seen Laertes committing the aforementioned ('prenominate') faults, he is sure to agree with you as follows

46–61 *'Good sir' . . . forth:* Polonius is composing an imaginary speech for the imagined person Reynaldo is to talk to

47 *addition:* title

50 *By the mass:* a mild oath

51 *Where . . . leave?* Where was I? The rambling, garrulous, doting Polonius has lost the thread of his argument

REYNALDO

My lord, that would dishonour him.

POLONIUS

Faith no, as you may season it in the charge.

30 You must not put another scandal on him,

That he is open to incontinency;

That's not my meaning. But breathe his faults so quaintly

That they may seem the taints of liberty,

The flash and outbreak of a fiery mind,

35 A savageness in unreclaimèd blood,

Of general assault.

REYNALDO

                   But, my good lord—

POLONIUS

Wherefore should you do this?

REYNALDO

                     Ay, my lord,

I would know that.

POLONIUS

                   Marry, sir, here's my drift;

And I believe it is a fetch of warrant,

40 You laying these slight sullies on my son,

As 'twere a thing a little soiled in the working,

Mark you, your party in converse, him you would sound,

Having ever seen in the prenominate crimes

The youth you breathe of guilty, be assured

45 He closes with you in this consequence:

'Good sir' or so, or 'friend' or 'gentleman',

According to the phrase or the addition

Of man and country—

REYNALDO

                   Very good, my lord.

POLONIUS

And then, sir, does he this. He does—

50 What was I about to say? By the mass, I was about

To say something! Where did I leave?

REYNALDO

At 'closes in the consequence', at 'friend',

Or 'so' and 'gentleman'—

POLONIUS

At 'closes in the consequence' — ay, marry!

55 He closes thus: 'I know the gentleman;

I saw him yesterday, or t'other day,

Or then or then, with such or such, and, as you say,

There was he gaming; there o'ertook in's rouse;

There falling out at tennis', or perchance,

'I saw him enter such a house of sale',   60

Videlicet, a brothel, or so forth.

See you now?

Your bait of falsehood takes this carp of truth,

And thus do we of wisdom and of reach,

With windlasses and with assays of bias,   65

By indirections find directions out.

So, by my former lecture and advice,

Shall you my son.

You have me, have you not?

REYNALDO

            My lord, I have.

POLONIUS

God buy ye; fare ye well.

REYNALDO

            Good, my lord.   70

POLONIUS

Observe his inclination in yourself.

REYNALDO

I shall, my lord.

POLONIUS

And let him ply his music.

REYNALDO

            Well, my lord.

POLONIUS

Farewell!

Exit REYNALDO.

Enter OPHELIA.

            How now, Ophelia, what's the matter?

OPHELIA

O my lord, my lord, I have been so affrighted!   75

POLONIUS

With what, in the name of God?

OPHELIA

My lord, as I was sewing in my closet,

Lord Hamlet, with his doublet all unbraced,

58 *o'ertook in's rouse:* overcome by drink

59 *falling out:* quarrelling
perchance: perhaps

61 *Videlicet:* namely

63 *Your … truth:* you get the truth by fishing for it with a lie. Polonius is punning: a carp is a fish and also a criticism; in addition, 'carp of truth' can mean 'talk of truth'
64-6 *And … out:* those of us who have wisdom and a far-reaching understanding can acquire information in roundabout, indirect ways
65 *windlasses:* circuitous approaches (a hunting and shooting term)
assays of bias: indirect attempts (a bowling term)
67 *by … advice:* as I have been describing
69 *have me:* have understood me

70 *God buy ye:* good bye to you

71 *Observe … yourself:* take note of his conduct yourself (as well as asking others about it)

73 *ply his music:* practise his music diligently

75 *affrighted:* frightened, alarmed

77 *closet:* private apartment
78 *doublet all unbraced:* jacket unfastened

79 *No hat:* people generally wore hats indoors in Shakespeare's day
fouled: dirty
80 *Ungartered . . . ankle:* without garters, his stockings were hanging like fetters about his ankles
82 *purport:* expression, meaning
83 *loosèd:* released

No hat upon his head, his stockings fouled,

80 Ungartered, and down-gyvèd to his ankle,

Pale as his shirt, his knees knocking each other,

And with a look so piteous in purport,

As if he had been loosèd out of hell

To speak of horrors — he comes before me.

POLONIUS
Mad for thy love?

OPHELIA
85   My lord, I do not know;

But truly, I do fear it.

POLONIUS
                    What said he?

OPHELIA
He took me by the wrist and held me hard.

Then goes he to the length of all his arm

And, with his other hand thus o'er his brow,

88 *Then . . . arm:* he keeps me at arm's length

90 *perusal:* observation, study

91 *As . . . it:* as if he wanted to sketch it

90 He falls to such perusal of my face

As he would draw it. Long stayed he so.

At last, a little shaking of mine arm,

And thrice his head thus waving up and down,

He raised a sigh so piteous and profound

94 *profound:* deep

95 *his bulk:* the upper part of his body

95 As it did seem to shatter all his bulk

And end his being. That done, he lets me go;

And, with his head over his shoulder turned,

He seemed to find his way without his eyes;

For out o'doors he went without their help,

100 *bended their light:* kept his eyes focused

100 And, to the last, bended their light on me.

POLONIUS
Come, go with me. I will go seek the king.

This is the very ecstasy of love,

Whose violent property fordoes itself,

102 *ecstasy:* madness

103 *Whose . . . itself:* the violent nature of love leads to self-destruction

104 *desperate undertakings:* undertake acts of desperation, including suicide

105–6 *As . . . natures:* love is as frequent a cause of reckless human behaviour as is any of the passions that trouble us

And leads the will to desperate undertakings

105 As oft as any passion under heaven

That does afflict our natures. I am sorry.

What, have you given him any hard words of late?

OPHELIA
No, my good lord, but, as you did command,

I did repel his letters, and denied

His access to me.

109 *repel:* reject, send back

POLONIUS

That hath made him mad.   110

I am sorry that with better heed and judgement

I had not quoted him. I feared he did but trifle,

And meant to wreck thee; but, beshrew my jealousy;

By heaven, it is as proper to our age

To cast beyond ourselves in our opinions   115

As it is common for the younger sort

To lack discretion. Come, go we to the king.

This must be known, which, being kept close, might move

More grief to hide, than hate to utter love.

Exeunt.

112 *quoted:* observed
      I . . . trifle: I didn't think he was serious (about Ophelia)
113 *wreck:* ruin
      beshrew my jealousy: a curse on my suspicions
114–17 *proper . . . discretion:* natural for old people like me to be unduly cautious as it is for young people to be reckless

118 *known:* made known, revealed
      close: secret
      move: cause, create
119 *grief:* pain (Hamlet may grow worse)
      utter: reveal, announce

Key points

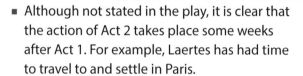

This scene gives us a good insight into Polonius, Claudius's chief counsellor, and the kind of man he is. We also learn, through Ophelia, of Hamlet's strange behaviour.

- Although not stated in the play, it is clear that the action of Act 2 takes place some weeks after Act 1. For example, Laertes has had time to travel to and settle in Paris.

- This scene is dominated by Polonius. He is shown to be a busybody, fond of meddling in everybody's affairs. It does not appear that he has a reason to suspect that Laertes is likely to misbehave in France, yet he asks a servant to spy on him in order to discover whether he is drinking, gambling, swearing, quarrelling or associating with prostitutes. He also wants to know what kind of friends Laertes has. In spying on his son, Polonius is shown to be controlling and dishonest.

- The methods Polonius recommends for gleaning information about the lives of others suggest that he sees himself as a well-practised spymaster. He boasts that men of understanding are in the habit of obtaining information in crooked and roundabout ways: 'By indirections find directions out' (line 66). He also recommends lying as a means of finding out the truth (line 63).

- On the other hand, Polonius's rambling style of speech and his invented conversations could be seen to suggest that he is more of a buffoon than an authoritarian spymaster.

- Ophelia's account of Hamlet's strange appearance and equally strange behaviour has to be understood in the light of recent events. In obedience to her father's command, she has refused to see Hamlet and has rejected his letters. This has isolated Hamlet from sympathetic contact with someone who might have helped him to cope with the immense new weight of suffering and responsibility laid on him by the ghost.

- Ophelia observes, without understanding what the ghost's revelations have done to Hamlet, that he appears to her 'As if he had been loosèd out of hell to speak of horrors' (lines 83–4). This reminds the audience of the ghost and may make us wonder whether the 'madness' Ophelia speaks of has anything to do with Hamlet's intention to adopt an 'antic disposition' (Act 1, Scene 5, line 171). It can be argued that Hamlet knew that his visit to Ophelia would be reported first to Polonius and then to Claudius.

- For reasons of self-interest, Polonius can hardly wait to let Claudius know that he may have the explanation for Hamlet's recent behaviour.

*I did repel his letters, and denied
His access to me.*

OPHELIA, Act 2,
Scene 1, 109–10

Useful quotes

*And thus do we of wisdom and of reach,
With windlasses and with assays of bias,
By indirections find directions out.*

(Polonius, lines 64–6)

*He raised a sigh so piteous and profound
At it did seem to shatter all his bulk
And end his being.*

(Ophelia, lines 94–6)

*I will go seek the king.
This is the very ecstasy of love,
Whose violent property fordoes itself,
And leads the will to desperate undertakings*

(Polonius, lines 101–4)

*I feared he did but trifle,
And meant to wreck thee*

(Polonius, lines 112–13)

? Questions

1 In what ways does this scene expand our understanding of the character of Polonius?

2 Do you agree that Polonius is a considerate father to both his son and his daughter? Give reasons for your answer.

3 'Polonius is a man of high moral standards.' Discuss this statement with reference to the play so far.

4 What conclusions does Polonius draw from Ophelia's account of Hamlet?

5 If you were asked to cast an actor to play the role of Polonius in a film version of *Hamlet*, what characteristics or features would you look for?

6 What important information do Hamlet and the audience have that Polonius and Ophelia do not have? What difference does this make to your interpretation of Ophelia's encounter with Hamlet?

7 Suggest why Shakespeare does not stage Hamlet's visit to Ophelia's closet.

8 Describe and/or make a sketch of Hamlet's appearance and behaviour when he visits Ophelia's closet.

9 Is there any evidence in the scene to suggest that Ophelia is concerned for Hamlet?

10 Is there any evidence in the scene to suggest that Polonius is concerned for Ophelia?

Claudius and Gertrude have invited Hamlet's friends Rosencrantz and Guildenstern to Elsinore in the hope that they will be able to find out what is wrong with Hamlet. The ambassadors return from Norway with the news that Fortinbras is no longer a threat to Denmark. Polonius offers his explanation for Hamlet's behaviour: he has gone mad as a result of Ophelia's refusal to see him. Polonius encounters Hamlet reading a book in the lobby. Hamlet makes fun of Polonius by engaging in an absurd conversation with him. This convinces Polonius that Hamlet is insane. Rosencrantz and Guildenstern attempt to probe Hamlet's mind in the guise of friendship. Their efforts prove futile, because Hamlet soon senses what the real purpose of their visit is.

A new phase opens with the arrival at Elsinore of a touring group of actors. At Hamlet's request, one actor recites a speech. Hamlet arranges for them to perform a play that will contain an extra speech that deals with an event closely resembling the murder of Hamlet's father. He hopes that this speech will force Claudius to reveal the truth about what he has done, and so confirm what the ghost has told him.

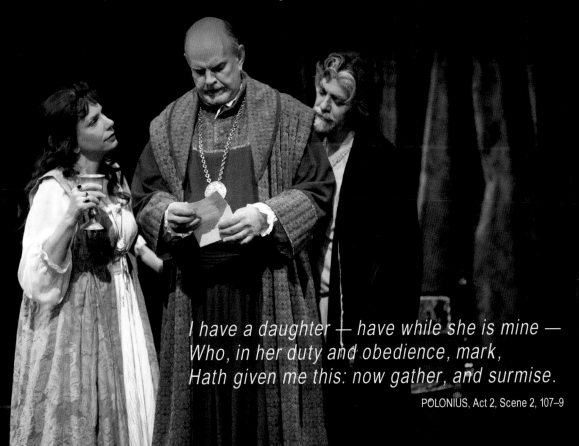

I have a daughter — have while she is mine —
Who, in her duty and obedience, mark,
Hath given me this: now gather, and surmise.

POLONIUS, Act 2, Scene 2, 107–9

Elsinore. A room in the castle.

Enter KING CLAUDIUS, QUEEN GERTRUDE, ROSENCRANTZ, GUILDENSTERN, and ATTENDANTS.

KING CLAUDIUS

Welcome, dear Rosencrantz and Guildenstern!

Moreover that we much did long to see you,

The need we have to use you did provoke

Our hasty sending. Something have you heard

Of Hamlet's transformation; so call it,   5

Sith nor the exterior nor the inward man

Resembles that it was. What it should be,

More than his father's death, that thus hath put him

So much from th'understanding of himself,

I cannot dream of. I entreat you both,   10

That, being of so young days brought up with him,

And sith so neighboured to his youth and haviour,

That you vouchsafe your rest here in our court

Some little time, so by your companies

To draw him on to pleasures, and to gather   15

So much as from occasion you may glean

Whether aught, to us unknown, afflicts him thus,

That, opened, lies within our remedy.

QUEEN GERTRUDE

Good gentlemen, he hath much talked of you;

And sure I am two men there are not living   20

To whom he more adheres. If it will please you

To show us so much gentry and good will

As to expend your time with us a while,

For the supply and profit of our hope,

Your visitation shall receive such thanks   25

As fits a king's remembrance.

ROSENCRANTZ

                      Both your majesties

Might, by the sovereign power you have of us,

Put your dread pleasures more into command

Than to entreaty.

GUILDENSTERN

                    But we both obey,

And here give up ourselves, in the full bent,   30

To lay our service freely at your feet,

To be commanded.

The King is trying to be nice to Hamlet

---

2 *Moreover ... you:* in addition to the fact that I greatly desired to see you. This is a polite fiction on the part of Claudius, who is always anxious to please

4 *sending:* summons to come to court

5 *Hamlet's transformation:* Claudius and Gertrude appear to have observed the 'antic disposition' Hamlet said he might adopt (see Act 1, Scene 5, line 171); Polonius has yet to make his report

6 *Sith nor:* since neither

11 *of ... days:* from so early an age

12 *sith ... haviour:* because since childhood you have had such a close association with his activities

13 *vouchsafe your rest:* agree to stay

15 *draw ... pleasures:* encourage him to take part in pleasurable activities

15–16 *gather ... glean:* find out from whatever opportunities ('occasion') you may have

17 *aught:* anything

18 *opened:* revealed, exposed

21 *more adheres:* is more attached

22 *gentry:* courtesy

23 *expend:* spend

24 *For ... hope:* in order to fulfil our hopes

25–6 *Your ... remembrance:* Gertrude is promising a rich reward

26–9 *Both ... entreaty:* being our monarchs, your majesties could command rather than request ('entreaty') us to perform this task

28 *dread pleasures:* deeply respected wishes

30 *in ... bent:* to the limit, to the best of our ability

KING CLAUDIUS

Thanks, Rosencrantz, and gentle Guildenstern.

QUEEN GERTRUDE

Thanks, Guildenstern, and gentle Rosencrantz.

And I beseech you instantly to visit   35

My too much changèd son. [*to ATTENDANTS*] Go, some of you,

And bring these gentlemen where Hamlet is.

GUILDENSTERN

Heavens make our presence and our practices

Pleasant and helpful to him!

QUEEN GERTRUDE
                               Ay, amen!

*Exeunt ROSENCRANTZ, GUILDENSTERN, and some
ATTENDANTS.*

Enter POLONIUS.

POLONIUS

The ambassadors from Norway, my good lord,   40

Are joyfully returned.

KING CLAUDIUS

Thou still hast been the father of good news.

POLONIUS

Have I, my lord? Assure you, my good liege,

I hold my duty, as I hold my soul,

Both to my God and to my gracious king;   45

And I do think, or else this brain of mine

Hunts not the trail of policy so sure

As it hath used to do, that I have found

The very cause of Hamlet's lunacy.

KING CLAUDIUS

O speak of that; that do I long to hear.   50

POLONIUS

Give first admittance to th'ambassadors;

My news shall be the fruit to that great feast.

KING CLAUDIUS

Thyself do grace to them, and bring them in.

Exit POLONIUS.

He tells me, my dear Gertrude, he hath found

The head and source of all your son's distemper.   55

---

38 *practices:* activities, actions. In Shakespeare's plays, it often carries the suggestion of underhandedness through devious dealings or sinister plots

41 *joyfully:* bearing joyful news

42 *still:* always

43 *liege:* lord to whom allegiance is due

44 *hold:* value

46–8 *or ... do:* unless my ability as an investigator is not what it used to be. Polonius imagines himself as a dog following a scent

47 *policy:* the management of state affairs, which, for Polonius, would include attention to Hamlet's state of mind

52 *My ... feast:* the news I have will be like a dessert after the main course (the report of the ambassadors)

53 *grace:* honour. This is also a pun on the saying of grace before a meal

55 *head ... distemper:* cause and origin of Hamlet's mental derangement

QUEEN GERTRUDE

I doubt it is no other but the main:

His father's death, and our o'erhasty marriage.

KING CLAUDIUS

Well, we shall sift him.

Enter POLONIUS, VOLTEMAND and CORNELIUS.

Welcome, my good friends!

Say, Voltemand, what from our brother Norway?

VOLTEMAND

60   Most fair return of greetings and desires.

Upon our first, he sent out to suppress

His nephew's levies, which to him appeared

To be a preparation 'gainst the Polack;

But, better looked into, he truly found

65   It was against your highness. Whereat, grieved

That so his sickness, age and impotence

Was falsely borne in hand, sends out arrests

On Fortinbras, which he, in brief, obeys,

Receives rebuke from Norway, and in fine

70   Makes vow before his uncle never more

To give th'assay of arms against your majesty.

Whereon old Norway, overcome with joy,

Gives him three thousand crowns in annual fee,

And his commission to employ those soldiers,

75   So levied as before, against the Polack,

With an entreaty, herein further shown

Gives a paper to KING CLAUDIUS.

That it might please you to give quiet pass

Through your dominions for this enterprise,

On such regards of safety and allowance

As therein are set down.

KING CLAUDIUS

80   It likes us well;

And at our more considered time we'll read,

Answer, and think upon this business.

Meantime, we thank you for your well-took labour.

Go to your rest; at night we'll feast together.

85   Most welcome home!

Exeunt VOLTEMAND and CORNELIUS.

56–7 *I ... marriage:* I suspect that the one and only cause is his father's death, followed too closely by our marriage. This suggests that Gertrude is not aware that her first husband was murdered

58 *sift him:* question Polonius carefully

59 *our brother Norway:* my fellow-monarch, the King of Norway

61–2 *Upon ... levies:* as soon as we made our request, he issued orders to suppress the forces commanded by Fortinbras

63 *a ... Polack:* an expedition against Poland

65 *Whereat:* because of this

66 *impotence:* helplessness

67 *borne in hand:* abused, taken advantage of
arrests: orders to halt

69 *Receives ... Norway:* Fortinbras is chastised by the King of Norway, his uncle
fine: conclusion

71 *give ... majesty:* undertake any military action against you

73 *fee:* revenue, income

74 *commission:* royal consent

75 *levied:* assembled, mustered

76 *With ... shown:* about which there is a request set out in this document

77 *quiet pass:* peaceful passage

79–80 *On ... down:* conditions for this passage, covering Denmark's security and permission, are set out in the document

80 *likes:* pleases

81 *at ... time:* when there is more time for consideration of the document

83 *well-took labour:* work well performed

POLONIUS

This business is very well ended.

My liege, and madam, to expostulate

What majesty should be, what duty is,

Why day is day, night night, and time is time,

Were nothing but to waste night, day and time.   90

Therefore, since brevity is the soul of wit,

And tediousness the limbs and outward flourishes,

I will be brief: your noble son is mad;

Mad call I it, for to define true madness,

What is't but to be nothing else but mad?   95

But let that go.

QUEEN GERTRUDE

More matter, with less art.

POLONIUS

Madam, I swear I use no art at all.

That he is mad, 'tis true: 'tis true 'tis pity;

And pity 'tis 'tis true — a foolish figure,

But farewell it, for I will use no art.   100

Mad let us grant him then, and now remains

That we find out the cause of this effect,

Or rather say, the cause of this defect,

For this effect defective comes by cause.

Thus it remains, and the remainder thus.   105

Perpend.

I have a daughter — have while she is mine —

Who, in her duty and obedience, mark,

Hath given me this: now gather, and surmise.

[*reads*] 'To the celestial and my soul's idol, the most   110
beautified Ophelia' — that's an ill phrase, a vile phrase;
'beautified' is a vile phrase. But you shall hear. Thus: [*reads*]
'In her excellent white bosom, these . . .' et cetera.

QUEEN GERTRUDE

Came this from Hamlet to her?

POLONIUS

Good madam, stay a while; I will be faithful.   115

[*reads*] 'Doubt thou the stars are fire;

Doubt that the sun doth move;

Doubt truth to be a liar;

But never doubt I love.

87–96 *My ... go:* displaying his absurd rhetorical powers, Polonius becomes tediously long-winded while, ironically, praising brevity of speech
87 *expostulate:* enquire into, discuss at length
91 *soul of wit:* essence of intelligent discourse
92 *outward flourishes:* external appearance, dress
94–5 *for ... mad:* it would be madness to try to define madness, since we can all recognise it anyway
95 *More ... art:* let us have more meaning and less rhetoric
98 *'tis true 'tis pity:* indeed it is a pity
99 *foolish figure:* nonsensical figure of speech
101 *now remains:* it is now left to us as our duty
104 *For ... cause:* this disorder must have a cause (since every effect has a cause)
105 *Thus ... thus:* that's how things stand, and now I'll proceed to give you my solution to the problem
106 *Perpend:* observe, consider carefully
107 *while ... mine:* until she marries
108 *mark:* look
109 *this:* Polonius displays a letter *gather, and surmise:* draw your own conclusions
111 *beautified:* endowed with beauty. Polonius objects to this phrase because he would have preferred 'beautiful'. Hamlet's word may suggest to him that Ophelia's beauty does not owe everything to nature
115 *stay ... faithful:* wait, I will give you a true report of the contents
116–19 *Doubt ... love:* this may be paraphrased as: There are things that you may question, but you need never question my love for you

120	*ill ... numbers:* not skilled as a writer of verses *art:* skill, craft
121	*reckon my groans:* count up, or recount, my miseries
123–4	*whilst ... him:* while this body is mine, as long as I live
126–8	*more ... ear:* moreover, she has told me all about Hamlet's approaches to her; when, how and where they were made
131	*fain:* greatly desire to
132	*hot ... wing:* passionate love in full flight
133	*I perceived it:* in fact Polonius had to rely on others for information about Hamlet's interest in Ophelia (see Act 1, Scene 3, lines 91–4)
136	*played ... table-book:* been a go-between for them
137	*given ... winking:* turned a blind eye
138	*looked ... sight:* failed to detect the true significance of what I saw
139	*round:* directly, without compromise
140	*my ... bespeak:* I addressed that young madam, my daughter, as follows
141	*out ... star:* beyond your reach
142	*prescripts:* orders
143	*resort:* visits
145	*Which ... advice:* when she had heard my advice, she proceeded to follow it
146	*repelled:* rejected *a ... make:* to make a long story short
148	*watch:* loss of sleep
149	*lightness:* light-headedness, delirium *declension:* decline

120 O dear Ophelia, I am ill at these numbers; I have not art to
reckon my groans: but that I love thee best, O most best,
believe it. Adieu.

> Thine evermore most dear lady, whilst this machine is
> to him, Hamlet.'

125 This, in obedience, hath my daughter shown me,
And more above hath his solicitings,
As they fell out by time, by means and place,
All given to mine ear.

KING CLAUDIUS
> But how hath she
Received his love?

POLONIUS
> What do you think of me?

KING CLAUDIUS
130 As of a man faithful and honourable.

POLONIUS
I would fain prove so. But what might you think
When I had seen this hot love on the wing —
As I perceived it, I must tell you that,
Before my daughter told me — what might you,
135 Or my dear majesty your queen here, think
If I had played the desk or table-book,
Or given my heart a winking, mute and dumb,
Or looked upon this love with idle sight?
What might you think? No, I went round to work,
140 And my young mistress thus I did bespeak:
'Lord Hamlet is a prince, out of thy star.
This must not be.' And then I prescripts gave her:
That she should lock herself from his resort,
Admit no messengers, receive no tokens.
145 Which done, she took the fruits of my advice;
And he, repelled — a short tale to make —
Fell into a sadness, then into a fast,
Thence to a watch, thence into a weakness,
Thence to a lightness, and, by this declension,
150 Into the madness wherein now he raves,
And all we mourn for.

KING CLAUDIUS
> Do you think 'tis this?

QUEEN GERTRUDE

It may be, very like.

POLONIUS

Hath there been such a time, I'd fain know that,

That I have positively said ''Tis so'

When it proved otherwise?

KING CLAUDIUS

        Not that I know.   155

POLONIUS

[points to his head and shoulder] Take this from this, if

    this be otherwise.

If circumstances lead me, I will find

Where truth is hid, though it were hid indeed

Within the centre.

KING CLAUDIUS

        How may we try it further?

POLONIUS

You know sometimes he walks four hours together   160

Here in the lobby.

QUEEN GERTRUDE

        So he does indeed.

POLONIUS

At such a time I'll loose my daughter to him.

Be you and I behind an arras then,

Mark the encounter: if he love her not

And be not from his reason fall'n thereon,   165

Let me be no assistant for a state,

But keep a farm and carters.

KING CLAUDIUS

        We will try it.

Enter HAMLET, reading a book.

QUEEN GERTRUDE

But look, where sadly the poor wretch comes reading.

POLONIUS

Away, I do beseech you both, away.

I'll board him presently. O give me leave.   170

Exeunt KING CLAUDIUS, QUEEN GERTRUDE, and ATTENDANTS.

How does my good Lord Hamlet?

---

152 *like:* likely

156 *Take ... otherwise:* you may have me beheaded if I am wrong. I am prepared to stake my life on my opinion

157–9 *If ... centre:* if I can get some facts or evidence to start with, I will get at the truth, no matter how well it is hidden

159 *How ... further?* How can we test your theory further?

160 *four hours:* this need not be taken literally; it may mean 'many hours' or 'several hours'

162 *I'll ... him:* I'll turn her loose to him. The animal image here indicates the degeneracy of Polonius; he sees no difference between human love and the activity of farmyard animals

163 *an arras:* a tapestry of the kind that covered the walls of expensive houses

164 *Mark:* observe

165 *And ... thereon:* and if that's not why he has lost his wits

166–7 *Let ... carters:* then let me retire from my post as government minister and take up farming

170 *I'll ... presently:* I'll accost him at once
    give me leave: excuse me

172 *God-a-mercy:* thank God

173 *know:* recognise. Hamlet is adopting a distant manner

174 *Excellent . . . fishmonger:* of course I recognise you: you are a fishmonger. It is possible that Hamlet intentionally gives an absurd reply to make Polonius think he is mad. In contemporary slang, a fishmonger could be someone with a weakness for women, or even a pimp, and the daughters of fishmongers were thought to be extremely fertile

176 *honest:* chaste, virtuous. Polonius is even less honest in this sense than a corrupt fishmonger

181–2 *For . . . carrion:* the heat of the sun creates new life from a dead dog as the sun sees its carcass ('carrion') as good for kissing

184 *Let . . . sun:* Ophelia must avoid walking in the sun (in view of what happened to the decaying dog, i.e. a pregnancy may result). The sun is a royal emblem; Hamlet is the son of a king. Hence, Polonius may have to shield her from contact with Hamlet as well
Conception: understanding, and also pregnancy
185 *look to it:* take care of it, take precautions
186 *How . . . that?* What do you make of that?
harping: dwelling

189 *much extremity:* extreme hardship

192 *matter:* subject matter

HAMLET

Well, God-a-mercy.

POLONIUS

Do you know me, my lord?

HAMLET

Excellent well: you are a fishmonger.

POLONIUS

175 Not I, my lord.

HAMLET

Then I would you were so honest a man.

POLONIUS

Honest, my lord?

HAMLET

Ay, sir. To be honest, as this world goes, is to be one man picked out of ten thousand.

POLONIUS

180 That's very true, my lord.

HAMLET

For if the sun breed maggots in a dead dog, being a good kissing carrion — have you a daughter?

POLONIUS

I have, my lord.

HAMLET

Let her not walk in the sun. Conception is a blessing, but
185 as your daughter may conceive, friend, look to it.

POLONIUS

[*aside*] How say you by that? Still harping on my daughter, yet he knew me not at first — he said I was a fishmonger. He is far gone, far gone. And truly in my youth I suffered much extremity for love, very near this. I'll speak to him
190 again. [*to HAMLET*] What do you read, my lord?

HAMLET

Words, words, words.

POLONIUS

What is the matter, my lord?

HAMLET

Between who?

POLONIUS

I mean the matter that you read, my lord.

HAMLET

Slanders, sir; for the satirical rogue says here that old men have grey beards, that their faces are wrinkled, their eyes purging thick amber and plum-tree gum, and that they have a plentiful lack of wit, together with most weak hams. All which, sir, though I most powerfully and potently believe, yet I hold it not honesty to have it thus set down; for yourself, sir, shall grow old as I am, if like a crab you could go backward.

POLONIUS

[*aside*] Though this be madness, yet there is method in't.

[*to HAMLET*] Will you walk out of the air, my lord?

HAMLET

Into my grave?

195
200
205

195 *satirical rogue:* author of the satirical book Hamlet is carrying

197 *purging . . . gum:* discharging thick yellowish resin (like sap from trees)
198 *wit:* intelligence
199 *hams:* thighs
201 *set down:* printed
201–2 *shall . . . backward:* if you could crawl back through your life again, you would be as young as I am now. Hamlet is arguing that it is unfair to poke fun at old age (although he is doing so himself) because the old would prefer to be young
203 *method:* logic
204 *out . . . air:* Polonius is asking Hamlet if he would like to leave the fresh air and go indoors. Fresh air was thought to be bad for sick people; confinement to a dark room was a treatment for madness
205 *Into my grave:* Hamlet takes the previous question literally. If he goes away from the air, there will be nowhere else to go but to his death

Though this be madness, yet there is method in't.
POLONIUS, Act 2, Scene 2, 203

206 *pregnant:* full of meaning

207–9 *A . . . of:* mad people can often express themselves with more point and meaning than sane, reasonable people can

209 *suddenly:* immediately

213–14 *You . . . withal:* I am extremely glad to be rid of you

224 *As . . . earth:* we are getting along like ordinary, average people, neither enjoying great prosperity nor enduring great adversity

226 *On . . . button:* we are not at the highest point of fortune

227 *Nor . . . shoe:* nor are you despised or trodden underfoot by fortune

POLONIUS

[*aside*] Indeed, that is out of the air. How pregnant sometimes his replies are! A happiness that often madness hits on, which reason and sanity could not so prosperously be delivered of. I will leave him, and suddenly contrive the

210 means of meeting between him and my daughter. [*to HAMLET*] My honourable lord, I will most humbly take my leave of you.

HAMLET

You cannot, sir, take from me anything that I will more willingly part withal — except my life, except my life,

215 except my life.

POLONIUS

Fare you well, my lord.

HAMLET

These tedious old fools!

Enter ROSENCRANTZ and GUILDENSTERN.

POLONIUS

You go to seek the Lord Hamlet; there he is.

ROSENCRANTZ

[*to POLONIUS*] God save you, sir!

Exit POLONIUS.

GUILDENSTERN

220 My honoured lord!

ROSENCRANTZ

My most dear lord!

HAMLET

My excellent good friends! How dost thou, Guildenstern?

Ah, Rosencrantz! Good lads, how do ye both?

ROSENCRANTZ

As the indifferent children of the earth.

GUILDENSTERN

225 Happy, in that we are not over-happy;

On Fortune's cap we are not the very button.

HAMLET

Nor the soles of her shoe?

ROSENCRANTZ

Neither, my lord.

HAMLET

Then you live about her waist, or in the middle of her favours?

GUILDENSTERN

Faith, her privates we.   230

HAMLET

In the secret parts of Fortune? O most true; she is a strumpet. What news?

ROSENCRANTZ

None, my lord, but that the world's grown honest.

HAMLET

Then is doomsday near. But your news is not true. Let me question more in particular: what have you, my good   235 friends, deserved at the hands of Fortune that she sends you to prison hither?

GUILDENSTERN

Prison, my lord?

HAMLET

Denmark's a prison.

ROSENCRANTZ

Then is the world one.

HAMLET

A goodly one; in which there are many confines, wards,   240 and dungeons; Denmark being one of the worst.

ROSENCRANTZ

We think not so, my lord.

HAMLET

Why, then, 'tis none to you; for there is nothing either good or bad, but thinking makes it so; to me it is a prison.

ROSENCRANTZ

Why then your ambition makes it one; 'tis too narrow for   245 your mind.

HAMLET

O God, I could be bounded in a nutshell and count myself a king of infinite space, were it not that I have bad dreams.

230 *privates:* a pun referring to both ordinary individuals of lowly rank, and the sexual parts of the body

232 *strumpet:* prostitute

234 *Then … near:* according to the Book of Revelations, those who live to see doomsday, or the Day of Judgement, will be marked as honest

237 *hither:* here

240 *goodly:* splendid
confines: cells

243 *'tis none:* it is not one (a prison)
243–4 *there … so:* what makes one person happy makes another sad. Denmark may appear a prison to Hamlet and a happy land to Rosencrantz and Guildenstern

245 *ambition:* desire to be king
'tis: Denmark is

247 *bounded in:* confined to. Hamlet rejects the idea that he wants the throne
248 *bad dreams:* these were considered a major symptom of melancholy

249–50 *Which ... dream:* the dreams you have mentioned are signs of ambition. The actual achievements of the ambitious man are only a poor shadow or reflection of what he hoped for

251 *shadow:* delusion

252–3 *Truly ... shadow:* ambitious dreams are even less substantial than any other kind

254–5 *Then ... shadows:* Hamlet's logical faculty is at work and he seems to be arguing that since ambition is the mere shadow of a shadow, the only solid beings ('bodies') capable of casting a shadow must be those without ambition ('beggars'), leaving ambitious monarchs and heroes in the shadows of beggars

256 *fay:* faith
reason: carry on this argument

257 *wait upon you:* be your escorts or attendants

258–60 *No ... attended:* I will not have you attending on me. I will not class you with my servants; indeed, to be honest, I am very poorly served

260–61 *But ... Elsinore?* But, may I ask you, as true and tested friends, what you are doing here?

262 *occasion:* purpose, motive

263–4 *Beggar ... halfpenny:* Hamlet returns to the beggar/king-shadow images above. He is a beggar at the moment, a man who can only dream of being a king, and is therefore 'poor' in his ability to reward them, but nevertheless, his poor thanks are worth a halfpenny more than his two friends deserve (he realises that they have not come to visit him of their own free will, but because Claudius sent for them)

269 *anything ... purpose:* say anything you like, provided you do not give me a straight answer (he is being sarcastic)

271 *modesties ... colour:* sense of decency or shame makes it impossible for you to disguise

---

GUILDENSTERN

Which dreams indeed are ambition, for the very substance

250 of the ambitious is merely the shadow of a dream.

HAMLET

A dream itself is but a shadow.

ROSENCRANTZ

Truly, and I hold ambition of so airy and light a quality that it is but a shadow's shadow.

HAMLET

Then are our beggars bodies, and our monarchs and

255 outstretched heroes the beggars' shadows. Shall we to the court? For, by my fay, I cannot reason.

ROSENCRANTZ, GUILDENSTERN

We'll wait upon you.

HAMLET

No such matter. I will not sort you with the rest of my servants; for, to speak to you like an honest man, I am most

260 dreadfully attended. But, in the beaten way of friendship, what make you at Elsinore?

ROSENCRANTZ

To visit you, my lord; no other occasion.

HAMLET

Beggar that I am, I am even poor in thanks, but I thank you, and sure, dear friends, my thanks are too dear a halfpenny.

265 Were you not sent for? Is it your own inclining? Is it a free visitation? Come, come, deal justly with me; come, come; nay, speak.

GUILDENSTERN

What should we say, my lord?

HAMLET

Why, anything but to the purpose. You were sent for, and

270 there is a kind of confession in your looks, which your modesties have not craft enough to colour. I know the good king and queen have sent for you.

ROSENCRANTZ

To what end, my lord?

HAMLET

That, you must teach me. But let me conjure you, by the rights of our fellowship, by the consonancy of our youth, by the obligation of our ever-preserved love, and by what more dear a better proposer can charge you withal, be even and direct with me, whether you were sent for, or no?

275

ROSENCRANTZ [aside to GUILDENSTERN]

What say you?

HAMLET

Nay, then, I have an eye of you. If you love me, hold not off.

280

GUILDENSTERN

My lord, we were sent for.

HAMLET

Hamlet is depressed

I will tell you why; so shall my anticipation prevent your discovery, and your secrecy to the king and queen moult no feather. I have of late, but wherefore I know not, lost all my mirth, forgone all custom of exercise. And indeed it goes so heavily with my disposition that this goodly frame, the earth, seems to me a sterile promontory; this most excellent canopy, the air, look you, this brave o'erhanging firmament, this majestical roof fretted with golden fire, why, it appears no other thing to me but a foul and pestilent congregation of vapours. What a piece of work is a man! How noble in reason, how infinite in faculties, in form and moving how express and admirable, in action how like an angel, in apprehension how like a god: the beauty of the world, the paragon of animals. And yet, to me, what is this quintessence of dust? Man delights not me: no, nor woman neither, though by your smiling you seem to say so.

285

290

295

ROSENCRANTZ

My lord, there was no such stuff in my thoughts.

HAMLET

Why did ye laugh then when I said 'man delights not me'?

300

ROSENCRANTZ

To think, my lord, if you delight not in man, what lenten entertainment the players shall receive from you. We coted them on the way, and hither are they coming to offer you service.

---

274 *conjure you:* ask you in such a way that you will have to answer

274–8 *by ... with me:* I'm appealing to our friendship for each other, to the harmonious companionship of our youthful days, to the fondness that has always existed between us, and whatever arguments a more skilled persuader might propose, to tell me straight

280 *have ... you:* see what you are at
hold not off: do not reject my appeal

282 *anticipation:* telling you before you tell me

283–4 *your ... feather:* the secret you share with Claudius and Gertrude will remain intact as you have not betrayed their confidence

284 *of late:* recently

285 *forgone ... of:* abandoned my habit of

286 *it ... disposition:* I am so depressed

287 *sterile promontory:* barren headland. Shakespeare's stage was shaped like a promontory, surrounded by the audience

288–90 *most ... fire:* this is best understood if the structure of Shakespeare's stage is kept in mind. The roof of the inner stage had an elaborate inlaid ceiling ('canopy') representing the sky ('firmament'), painted with stars ('golden fire') and known as the 'heavens'. Hamlet's 'look you' shows that he is explaining his feelings in terms of what the audience could see

291 *foul ... vapours:* nasty mass of clouds

291–2 *piece of work:* masterpiece, work of art

292–3 *infinite in faculties:* possessing unlimited abilities

293 *express:* fitted to its purpose

294 *apprehension:* understanding

295 *paragon:* most complete, most perfect

296 *quintessence:* pure essence

301–2 *lenten entertainment:* miserable reception

302 *players:* actors

303 *coted:* overtook

HAMLET

305 He that plays the king shall be welcome, his majesty shall have tribute of me; the adventurous knight shall use his foil and target; the lover shall not sigh *gratis*; the humorous man shall end his part in peace; the clown shall make those laugh whose lungs are tickled o' th' sere; and

310 the lady shall say her mind freely, or the blank verse shall halt for't. What players are they?

ROSENCRANTZ

Even those you were wont to take delight in, the tragedians of the city.

HAMLET

How chances it they travel? Their residence, both in

315 reputation and profit, was better both ways.

ROSENCRANTZ

I think their inhibition comes by the means of the late innovation.

HAMLET

Do they hold the same estimation they did when I was in the city? Are they so followed?

ROSENCRANTZ

320 No, indeed, are they not.

HAMLET

How comes it? Do they grow rusty?

ROSENCRANTZ

Nay, their endeavour keeps in the wonted pace; but there is, sir, an aery of children, little eyases, that cry out on the top of question, and are most tyrannically clapped for it:

325 these are now the fashion, and so berattle the common stages (so they call them) that many wearing rapiers are afraid of goose-quills and dare scarce come thither.

HAMLET

What, are they children? Who maintains 'em? How are they escoted? Will they pursue the quality no longer than they

330 can sing? Will they not say afterwards, if they should grow themselves to common players (as it is like most will, if their means are not better), their writers do them wrong, to make them exclaim against their own succession?

---

307 *foil and target:* sword and shield
gratis: in vain, for nothing
308 *in peace:* without interruption
309 *whose . . . sere:* who laugh at the smallest provocation
310–11 *mind . . . for't:* piece in full, or else the rhythm of the verse will suffer because of the gaps

312 *were wont:* used

313 *tragedians:* actors

314 *How . . . travel?* Why are they touring?
314–15 *Their . . . ways:* had they maintained a fixed abode, they would be better off financially and in terms of their reputation

316–17 *their . . . innovation:* they have limited their stay in the city because of changing fashions there. It has been suggested that 'innovation' refers to a government decree limiting theatrical performances in London in Shakespeare's time

318 *Do . . . did:* are they as popular as they were

322 *their . . . pace:* they still perform to a high standard
323–4 *an aery . . . it:* a group of child actors, with squeaky voices, who are attracting loud applause
323 *aery:* nest
eyases: unfledged hawks

326 *rapiers:* swords (worn by men of fashion)

327 *goose-quills:* pens (used by playwrights)
dare . . . thither: are afraid to attend the theatre for fear of being ridiculed

329 *escoted:* paid

329–30 *Will . . . sing?* Will they continue to act when their voices break?
330–31 *grow . . . players:* eventually become professional actors
333 *exclaim . . . succession:* satirise their future profession

ROSENCRANTZ

Faith, there has been much to-do on both sides; and the
nation holds it no sin to tarre them to controversy. There   335
was, for a while, no money bid for argument unless the
poet and the player went to cuffs in the question.

HAMLET

Is't possible?

GUILDENSTERN

O, there has been much throwing about of brains.

HAMLET

Do the boys carry it away?   340

ROSENCRANTZ

Ay, that they do, my lord; Hercules and his load too.

HAMLET

It is not very strange; for my uncle is king of Denmark,
and those that would make mows at him while my father
lived, give twenty, forty, fifty, an hundred ducats a-piece
for his picture in little. 'Sblood, there is something in this   345
more than natural, if philosophy could find it out.

Flourish of trumpets within.

GUILDENSTERN

There are the players.

HAMLET

Gentlemen, you are welcome to Elsinore. Your hands?
Come then, the appurtenance of welcome is fashion and
ceremony: let me comply with you in this garb, lest my   350
extent to the players, which I tell you must show fairly
outward, should more appear like entertainment than
yours. You are welcome, but my uncle-father and aunt-
mother are deceived.

GUILDENSTERN

In what, my dear lord?   355

HAMLET

I am but mad north-north-west: when the wind is
southerly, I know a hawk from a handsaw.

Enter POLONIUS.

334–5 *Faith … controversy:* indeed, adults and children have satirised each other; and the people see no harm in inciting them to keep arguing with each other
336–7 *no … question:* no theatre that would pay a writer for a play unless its plot featured fights between the children's writers and the adult players
339 *much .... brains:* a great battle of wits
340 *carry it away:* win the day
341 *Hercules … load:* Hercules bearing the world on his shoulders (this was the sign of the Globe theatre, where Shakespeare's company performed). Rosencrantz is saying that the boy actors are stealing the popularity of even well-established companies
343 *make mows at:* show contempt for, pull faces at. Hamlet finds nothing strange in the fact that popular opinion is so fickle
345 *picture in little:* miniature portrait / *'Sblood:* by God's blood (an oath)
346 *more than natural:* abnormal / *philosophy:* science
348 *Your hands?* Give me your hands (to shake)
349–50 *appurtenance … ceremony:* welcome should be accompanied by some formal ceremony
350 *comply … garb:* greet you in this manner (i.e. a handshake)
351 *extent:* behaviour
351–2 *show fairly outward:* have an impressive, pleasant appearance
352–3 *more … yours:* seem like a warmer reception than I have given to you
356–7 *but … handsaw:* only occasionally mad (at just one, i.e. 'north-north-west', of the sixteen main points of the compass): during my longer spells of normality ('when the wind is southerly'), I am in full control of my faculties and can distinguish a hawk from a heron ('handsaw')

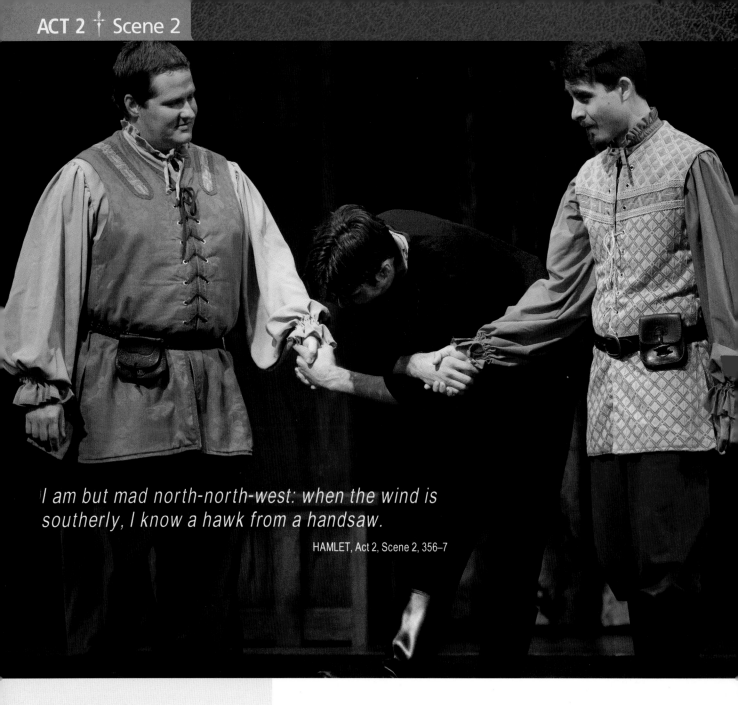

I am but mad north-north-west: when the wind is southerly, I know a hawk from a handsaw.

HAMLET, Act 2, Scene 2, 356–7

359–60 *at ... hearer:* Hamlet wants Rosencrantz and Guildenstern to arrange themselves one on either side of him, so that he may exchange offensive comments with them about Polonius

361 *swaddling clouts:* baby clothes

362 *Happily:* perhaps

363 *twice a child:* in his second childhood

365–6 *You ... indeed:* Hamlet pretends to be deep in conversation with Rosencrantz and Guildenstern

POLONIUS

Well be with you, gentlemen!

HAMLET

[*lowers his voice*] Hark you, Guildenstern, and you too, at
360 each ear a hearer: that great baby you see there is not yet
out of his swaddling clouts.

ROSENCRANTZ

Happily he is the second time come to them. For they say
an old man is twice a child.

HAMLET

I will prophesy he comes to tell me of the players; mark
365 it. [*raises his voice*] You say right, sir, a Monday morning,
'twas then, indeed.

POLONIUS

My lord, I have news to tell you.

HAMLET

My lord, I have news to tell you. When Roscius was an actor in Rome—

POLONIUS

The actors are come hither, my lord.   370

HAMLET

Buzz, buzz!

POLONIUS

Upon mine honour—

HAMLET

Then came each actor on his ass—

POLONIUS

The best actors in the world, either for tragedy, comedy, history, pastoral, pastoral-comical, historical-pastoral,   375
tragical-historical, tragical-comical-historical-pastoral, scene individable, or poem unlimited. Seneca cannot be too heavy, nor Plautus too light. For the law of writ and the liberty, these are the only men.

HAMLET

O Jephthah, judge of Israel, what a treasure hadst thou!   380

POLONIUS

What a treasure had he, my lord?

HAMLET

Why,

    'One fair daughter and no more,

    The which he lovèd passing well.'

POLONIUS [*aside*]

Still on my daughter.   385

HAMLET

Am I not in the right, old Jephthah?

POLONIUS

If you call me Jephthah, my lord, I have a daughter that I love passing well.

368 *Roscius:* the most famous actor in ancient Rome

371 *Buzz:* an expression of contempt

373 *Then . . . ass:* Hamlet seems to be quoting from a ballad

376–7 *scene . . . unlimited:* plays having only one long single scene, or plays with many scenes
377–8 *Seneca . . . light:* Seneca wrote tragedies; Plautus wrote comedies
378–9 *For . . . men:* these are the only actors capable of doing justice to plays, whether they are composed strictly according to classical rules or written freely without regard to those rules

380 *Jephthah:* an Old Testament leader who sought to please God by sacrificing his daughter

384 *passing:* extremely

385 *Still . . . daughter:* always talking about Ophelia. Polonius is certain that Hamlet's love for her is the cause of his madness

389 *that follows not:* it does not follow that because you have a daughter you love her

392, 394 *'As ... was':* Hamlet continues reciting the ballad

395 *row ... chanson:* stanza of that religious ballad

396 *abridgement:* interruption (the players have arrived)

399 *valanced:* fringed with a beard

400 *beard:* outwit, outface
lady: Hamlet addresses the boy-actor who plays the female roles
401 *By'r lady:* by Our Lady (an oath)
nearer to heaven: taller
402 *chopine:* high-heeled shoe
403 *uncurrent gold:* a gold coin that is no longer legal tender
403–4 *cracked ... ring:* broken; there is a pun on 'ring', meaning pure sound and cracked coin
404–5 *e'en ... see:* go about our business with enthusiasm and confidence. French falconers were noted for these traits
406 *straight:* immediately
quality: skill, ability
407 *passionate speech:* speech full of powerful feeling

411 *pleased ... general:* lacked wide general appeal; like caviar, it was not appreciated by those unused to such exotic fare
413 *cried ... of:* are superior to
414 *digested:* shaped, ordered
modesty: restraint
415 *cunning:* art, skill
415–16 *no ... savoury:* it was not flavoured with spicy touches (possibly coarse jokes and allusions)
417 *indict:* convict
418 *an ... sweet:* a decent, straightforward style, good as well as delightful
419 *more ... fine:* more dignified rather than showy
420 *Aeneas' ... Dido:* Aeneas, the Trojan who escaped from Troy when it was burned by the Greeks, told the story of its fall to Dido, Queen of Carthage
420–21 *thereabout of it:* around the part
421 *Priam's slaughter:* Priam, King of Troy, was killed by Pyrrhus

HAMLET
Nay, that follows not.

POLONIUS
390 What follows then, my lord?

HAMLET
Why,
　'As by lot, God wot,'
and then, you know,
　'It came to pass, as most like it was.'

395 The first row of the pious chanson will show you more, for look where my abridgement comes.
Enter four or five PLAYERS.

You are welcome, masters; welcome, all. I am glad to see thee well. Welcome, good friends. O, my old friend, why thy face is valanced since I saw thee last: comest thou to 400 beard me in Denmark? What, my young lady and mistress! By'r lady, your ladyship is nearer to heaven than when I saw you last, by the altitude of a chopine. Pray God, your voice, like a piece of uncurrent gold, be not cracked within the ring. Masters, you are all welcome. We'll e'en 405 to't like French falconers, fly at anything we see: we'll have a speech straight. Come, give us a taste of your quality. Come, a passionate speech.

FIRST PLAYER
What speech, my good lord?

HAMLET
I heard thee speak me a speech once, but it was never 410 acted, or if it was, not above once. For the play, I remember, pleased not the million, 'twas caviare to the general, but it was (as I received it, and others, whose judgements in such matters cried in the top of mine) an excellent play, well digested in the scenes, set down with as much modesty 415 as cunning. I remember one said there were no sallets in the lines to make the matter savoury, nor no matter in the phrase that might indict the author of affectation, but called it an honest method, as wholesome as sweet, and by very much more handsome than fine. One speech in it 420 I chiefly loved: 'twas Aeneas' tale to Dido. And thereabout of it especially, when he speaks of Priam's slaughter. If it

live in your memory, begin at this line — let me see, let
me see:

> 'The rugged Pyrrhus, like th'Hyrcanian beast,'

'Tis not so. It begins with Pyrrhus: 425

> 'The rugged Pyrrhus, he whose sable arms,
> Black as his purpose, did the night resemble
> When he lay couchèd in th'ominous horse,
> Hath now this dread and black complexion smeared
> With heraldry more dismal. Head to foot   430
> Now is he total gules; horridly tricked
> With blood of fathers, mothers, daughters, sons,
> Baked and impasted with the parching streets
> That lend a tyrannous and damnèd light
> To their lord's murder. Roasted in wrath and fire,   435
> And thus o'ersizèd with coagulate gore,
> With eyes like carbuncles, the hellish Pyrrhus
> Old grandsire Priam seeks.'

So, proceed you.

POLONIUS

'Fore God, my lord, well spoken, with good accent and   440
good discretion.

FIRST PLAYER

> 'Anon he finds him
> Striking too short at Greeks; his antique sword,
> Rebellious to his arm, lies where it falls,
> Repugnant to command. Unequal matched,   445
> Pyrrhus at Priam drives, in rage strikes wide,
> But with the whiff and wind of his fell sword
> Th'unnervèd father falls. Then senseless Ilium,
> Seeming to feel this blow, with flaming top
> Stoops to his base, and with a hideous crash   450
> Takes prisoner Pyrrhus' ear. For lo, his sword,
> Which was declining on the milky head
> Of reverend Priam, seemed i' th'air to stick:
> So, as a painted tyrant, Pyrrhus stood,
> And like a neutral to his will and matter,   455
> Did nothing.
> But, as we often see, against some storm,
> A silence in the heavens, the rack stand still,
> The bold winds speechless, and the orb below

Glossary

424 *th'Hyrcanian beast:* a tiger

426–38 *'The ... seeks':* this stirring speech has been written in a bombastic style, rather than the restrained manner preferred by Hamlet
426 *sable arms:* black armour
428 *couchèd ... horse:* hidden in the ill-omened horse (the wooden horse used by the Greeks to deceive the Trojans)
430 *heraldry more dismal:* the more deadly red of blood (that now marks his armour)
431 *total gules:* completely red
    tricked: painted

433 *Baked ... streets:* the blood has dried and baked into a crust in the heat of the burning city

436 *o'ersizèd ... gore:* smeared all over with clotted blood
437 *carbuncles:* fiery red gems
438 *grandsire:* grandfather

441 *discretion:* understanding

442 *Anon:* soon

443 *Striking too short:* Priam's tired blows fall short of their mark
444 *Rebellious to:* not obeying
445 *Repugnant to command:* he is not able to lift it again

447–8 *with ... falls:* with the breeze created by his enemy's cruel sword, the feeble old man falls
448–51 *senseless ... ear:* the unfeeling stronghold of Troy, seeming to feel the blow to Priam, crashes to the ground in flames, and the terrible din attracts the attention of Pyrrhus

452 *declining ... head:* falling on the white head

454 *as ... tyrant:* as motionless as a tyrant in a painting
455 *like ... matter:* passively (his ability to perform his task suspended)

457 *against:* before

458 *the rack:* clouds

459 *orb:* earth

460 *hush:* silent

461 *rend the region:* split the air

462 *Arousèd . . . a-work:* his newly aroused desire for revenge inspires him to further action

463 *Cyclops:* giants employed by Vulcan, the Roman god of metalworkers

464 *Mars:* Roman god of war
forged . . . eterne: made to survive forever

465 *remorse:* pity

468 *synod:* assembly

469 *fellies:* rim

470–71 *bowl . . . fiends:* roll the hub (which is all that remains of Fortune's wheel) down to the devils in hell

473 *a jig . . . bawdry:* comic dances and bawdy stories. Hamlet, annoyed at Polonius for interrupting, mocks his poor taste

475 *the moblèd queen:* Hecuba (Priam's widow)

478–9 *threat'ning . . . rheum:* appearing likely to quench the flames of Troy with her blinding tears

479 *clout:* cloth, rag

480 *diadem:* crown

481 *lank:* shrunken
o'erteemèd loins: Hecuba was exhausted from childbearing (Priam fathered fifty sons, many of them, presumably, Hecuba's)

483–4 *Who . . . pronounced:* anyone who had witnessed this sight would have bitterly denounced the treachery of fate (for allowing Hecuba to suffer thus)

488–91 *The . . . gods:* the immediate and overwhelming emotion she created would have drawn tears from the flaming stars, and aroused sorrow in the gods, if the gods have any feeling for the affairs of human beings

---

460 As hush as death, anon the dreadful thunder
Doth rend the region; so, after Pyrrhus' pause,
Arousèd vengeance sets him new a-work;
And never did the Cyclops' hammers fall
On Mars's armour, forged for proof eterne,
465 With less remorse than Pyrrhus' bleeding sword
Now falls on Priam.
Out, out, thou strumpet Fortune! All you gods,
In general synod, take away her power,
Break all the spokes and fellies from her wheel,
470 And bowl the round nave down the hill of heaven,
As low as to the fiends.'

POLONIUS
                    This is too long.

HAMLET
It shall to the barber's, with your beard! [*to FIRST PLAYER*] Prithee, say on — he's for a jig or a tale of bawdry, or he sleeps. Say on, come to Hecuba.

FIRST PLAYER
475 'But who, ah woe, had seen the moblèd queen—'

HAMLET
'The moblèd queen'?

POLONIUS
That's good; 'moblèd queen' is good.

FIRST PLAYER
'Run barefoot up and down, threat'ning the flames
With bisson rheum; a clout upon that head
480 Where late the diadem stood, and for a robe,
About her lank and all o'erteemèd loins,
A blanket in the alarm of fear caught up;
Who this had seen, with tongue in venom steeped
'Gainst Fortune's state would treason have pronounced.
485 But if the gods themselves did see her then,
When she saw Pyrrhus make malicious sport
In mincing with his sword her husband's limbs,
The instant burst of clamour that she made,
Unless things mortal move them not at all,
490 Would have made milch the burning eyes of heaven
And passion in the gods.'

POLONIUS

Look, whether he has not turned his colour, and has tears in's eyes. Prithee, no more.

HAMLET

'Tis well. I'll have thee speak out the rest soon. [*to POLONIUS*] Good my lord, will you see the players well 495 bestowed? Do you hear? Let them be well used; for they are the abstract and brief chronicles of the time. After your death you were better have a bad epitaph than their ill report while you live.

POLONIUS

My lord, I will use them according to their desert. 500

HAMLET

God's bodkin, man, much better! Use every man after his desert, and who shall 'scape whipping? Use them after your own honour and dignity: the less they deserve, the more merit is in your bounty. Take them in.

POLONIUS

Come, sirs. 505

HAMLET

Follow him, friends; we'll hear a play tomorrow.

Exeunt POLONIUS and the PLAYERS except the FIRST.

Dost thou hear me, old friend, can you play *The Murder of Gonzago*?

FIRST PLAYER

Ay, my lord.

HAMLET

We'll ha't tomorrow night. You could, for a need, study a 510 speech of some dozen or sixteen lines, which I would set down and insert in't, could you not?

FIRST PLAYER

Ay, my lord.

HAMLET

Very well. Follow that lord, and look you mock him not.

Exit FIRST PLAYER.

492 *he:* the player
turned his colour: gone pale

496 *bestowed:* lodged
used: looked after
497 *abstract . . . time:* people who provide a record and summary of events as they happen

500 *use . . . desert:* treat them as they deserve

501 *God's bodkin:* by the sacred host, the body of Christ (an oath)
502 *'scape:* escape, avoid. Players without a licence were regarded as vagabonds and whipped as a punishment in Shakespeare's time
502–4 *Use . . . bounty:* treat them as if they were people of your importance and status; your generosity will have all the greater merit if you treat people better than they deserve

510 *ha't:* have it performed
for a need: if necessary

512 *insert in't:* include them in the performance

515 My good friends, I'll leave you till night. You are welcome
to Elsinore.

ROSENCRANTZ

Good my lord.

HAMLET

Ay, so, God buy ye!

Exeunt ROSENCRANTZ and GUILDENSTERN.

Now I am alone.

O what a rogue and peasant slave am I!

520 Is it not monstrous that this player here,
But in a fiction, in a dream of passion,
Could force his soul so to his own conceit
That from her working all his visage wanned,
Tears in his eyes, distraction in's aspect,

525 A broken voice, and his whole function suiting
With forms to his conceit; and all for nothing!
For Hecuba!
What's Hecuba to him, or he to Hecuba,
That he should weep for her? What would he do,

530 Had he the motive and the cue for passion
That I have? He would drown the stage with tears
And cleave the general ear with horrid speech,
Make mad the guilty and appal the free,
Confound the ignorant, and amaze indeed

535 The very faculties of eyes and ears. Yet I,
A dull and muddy-mettled rascal, peak,
Like John-a-dreams, unpregnant of my cause,
And can say nothing; no, not for a king,
Upon whose property and most dear life

540 A damned defeat was made. Am I a coward?
Who calls me villain, breaks my pate across,
Plucks off my beard and blows it in my face,
Tweaks me by the nose, gives me the lie in the throat,
As deep as to the lungs? Who does me this?

545 Ha! 'Swounds, I should take it: for it cannot be
But I am pigeon-livered and lack gall
To make oppression bitter, or ere this
I should have fatted all the region kites
With this slave's offal. Bloody, bawdy villain!

---

519 *peasant:* this was a term of abuse for a base, low individual

521 *But:* simply, merely

522 *Could ... conceit:* could make himself believe in something he (the player) only imagined

523 *her working:* this activity of his soul
visage wanned: face turned pale

524 *in's aspect:* in his expression

525–6 *his whole ... conceit:* everything in his outward behaviour matched his imaginary experience ('conceit')

526 *nothing:* something unreal

530 *cue for passion:* cause for feeling

532 *cleave ... speech:* deafen the audience with horrifying words

533 *appal the free:* shock even those who are innocent

534 *Confound the ignorant:* confuse those who know nothing about the crime that has been committed

534–5 *amaze ... ears:* astonish the senses of sight and hearing

536 *muddy-mettled:* dull-spirited

536–7 *peak ... cause:* mope around like a dreamy idler, not prepared to do my duty

541 *pate:* head

543–4 *gives ... lungs:* accuses me of being a liar

545 *Ha ... take it:* indeed, by God's wounds, I would put up with such insults without reply

546 *pigeon-livered:* as meek and patient as a dove

546–7 *gall ... bitter:* the strength of spirit necessary to make me resent the injury and insult I now suffer

547 *ere:* before

548–9 *fatted ... offal:* fattened all the birds of prey in the air with the guts of Claudius

Remorseless, treacherous, lecherous, kindless villain! 550

O vengeance!

Why, what an ass am I. This is most brave,

That I, the son of a dear father murdered,

Prompted to my revenge by heaven and hell,

Must, like a whore, unpack my heart with words, 555

And fall a-cursing, like a very drab,

A scullion! Fie upon't! Foh!

About, my brains. Hum, I have heard

That guilty creatures sitting at a play

Have by the very cunning of the scene 560

Been struck so to the soul that presently

They have proclaimed their malefactions;

For murder, though it have no tongue, will speak

With most miraculous organ. I'll have these players

Play something like the murder of my father 565

Before mine uncle. I'll observe his looks.

I'll tent him to the quick: if he do blench,

I know my course. The spirit that I have seen

May be a devil, and the devil hath power

T'assume a pleasing shape; yea, and perhaps 570

Out of my weakness and my melancholy,

As he is very potent with such spirits,

Abuses me to damn me. I'll have grounds

More relative than this: the play's the thing

Wherein I'll catch the conscience of the king. 575

Exit.

552 *most brave:* really admirable (Hamlet is being sarcastic at his own expense)

555 *unpack . . . words:* relieve my feelings with talk (instead of action)
556 *drab:* prostitute
557 *scullion:* foul-mouthed servant

558 *About:* get working

560 *cunning . . . scene:* skill and artfulness involved in the performance
561–2 *struck . . . malefactions:* so moved by what they have seen that they instantly confess their crimes aloud

564 *With . . . organ:* in strange, even miraculous, ways

567 *tent . . . quick:* probe him where he will feel pain *blench:* flinch

571–3 *Out . . . damn me:* by taking advantage of my present wayward mental state and my depression ('melancholy'), the ghost may be trying to delude ('abuses') me into damning my soul by killing an innocent man
573–4 *grounds . . . this:* more convincing reasons for proceeding against Claudius than a ghost's word
575 *conscience:* knowledge

the play's the thing
Wherein I'll catch the conscience of the king.
HAMLET, Act 2, Scene 2, 574–5

Key points

Hamlet's strange behaviour has become a matter for comment at court and much of this scene is devoted to attempts to find an explanation for it, without success.

- Early on we learn that the diplomatic mission to Norway has been a success and Denmark is no longer under threat from Fortinbras. This outcome suggests that Claudius is an effective leader.

- The main focus of the scene is on a fascinating battle of wits between Hamlet and a variety of people he despises and cannot trust, including Claudius, Polonius, Rosencrantz and Guildenstern. He outwits all of them, duping and ridiculing Polonius, and forcing a confession from Rosencrantz and Guildenstern.

- Claudius has sent for Rosencrantz and Guildenstern because he 'cannot dream of' (line 10) what is bothering Hamlet. He hopes that Hamlet will confide in his old friends. Although he pretends to be concerned about Hamlet, the audience can see that he is a liar and a hypocrite who is only concerned about himself.

- Polonius is almost gloating as he tells Claudius and Gertrude that the cause of Hamlet's madness must be unrequited love. He is delighted to bring them the information that he has obtained from Ophelia. He claims that he 'will find where truth is hid, though it were hid indeed within the centre' (lines 157–9).

- Polonius enjoys being the centre of attention. His speeches are full of rhetorical flourishes and elaborate puns. Such word play was valued in Shakespeare's day, but it often sacrificed meaning in favour of surface ornamentation. Gertrude has to ask Polonius to provide 'more matter with less art' (line 96). Polonius replies that he uses 'no art at all' (line 97), but then continues to embellish his words.

- Polonius volunteers to use his daughter as a trap for Hamlet. He appears to have no qualms about this. He will arrange for Ophelia and Hamlet to meet 'accidentally', and Claudius and Polonius will spy on the encounter. The aim of this plot is to prove that Hamlet has lost his mind as a result of Ophelia's rejection of his love. Polonius is convinced that this is the case.

- Although the scene is the longest in the play, it does little to advance the outward action. This, however, is its whole point, since it serves to suggest Hamlet's inactivity. Several weeks have passed since he met the ghost, but he does not appear to have framed a plan of vengeance against Claudius. But for the accidental arrival of the players, it might not have occurred to Hamlet to use a play as a means to confirm the ghost's narrative.

- Instead, he participates in casual banter with Polonius and in theatrical gossip with Rosencrantz and Guildenstern, and enjoys an engaging speech by one of the players about an episode in the Trojan Wars. These events, dramatising Hamlet's loss of interest in his task of vengeance, are a natural preparation for his outburst of self-criticism at the end: 'O what a rogue and peasant slave am I' (line 519). He feels ashamed that he has not fulfilled his duty to avenge his father's murder.

- Hamlet expresses doubts about the nature of the ghost he has seen and conversed with in Act 1, Scene 5. Now he wonders whether this spirit was really his father's ghost, or was it a devil trying to take advantage of his low spirits by tempting him to commit murder. This speculation is not unreasonable. Hamlet has nothing but the word of a ghost that Claudius murdered his father. If he were to make a public accusation against his uncle based on a statement made to him in private by a ghost, he could hardly expect to be taken seriously. He wants firmer evidence of his uncle's guilt.

- By the close of the scene Hamlet has devised a clever plan to test Claudius. He is hoping that a dramatic version of the ghost's story of his father's murder, to be enacted in the presence of Claudius, will uncover the latter's guilt. If Claudius is guilty, the play will catch his conscience as if in a trap and force him into some show of guilt. If Claudius is innocent, he is unlikely to recoil in horror.

KING CLAUDIUS

With all my heart; and it doth much content me

To hear him so inclined.   25

Good gentlemen, give him a further edge

And drive his purpose on to these delights.

ROSENCRANTZ

We shall, my lord.

Exeunt ROSENCRANTZ and GUILDENSTERN.

KING CLAUDIUS

         Sweet Gertrude, leave us too;

For we have closely sent for Hamlet hither,

That he, as 'twere by accident, may here   30

Affront Ophelia.

Her father and myself — lawful espials —

Will so bestow ourselves that, seeing unseen,

We may of their encounter frankly judge,

And gather by him, as he is behaved,   35

If't be th'affliction of his love or no

That thus he suffers for.

QUEEN GERTRUDE

         I shall obey you.

And for your part, Ophelia, I do wish

That your good beauties be the happy cause

Of Hamlet's wildness. So shall I hope your virtues   40

Will bring him to his wonted way again,

To both your honours.

OPHELIA

         Madam, I wish it may.

Exit QUEEN GERTRUDE.

POLONIUS

Ophelia, walk you here. [*to KING CLAUDIUS*] Gracious, so please you,

We will bestow ourselves. [*to OPHELIA*] Read on this book,

That show of such an exercise may colour   45

Your loneliness. We are oft to blame in this —

'Tis too much proved — that with devotion's visage

And pious action we do sugar o'er

The devil himself.

---

24 *much content me:* there is irony here as it would certainly not make Claudius happy if he knew what use Hamlet proposes to make of the play

26 *give ... edge:* encourage him further

29 *closely:* secretly, privately
hither: to come here

31 *Affront:* meet face to face with

32 *lawful espials:* spies who have a right to be there

33 *bestow:* place, position
seeing unseen: we will see, but remain unseen

35–7 *gather ... for:* we will be able to judge from his behaviour whether or not his problems are due to unhappiness in love

39 *good beauties:* virtuous charms

40 *wildness:* a polite word for madness

40–42 *virtues ... honours:* influence will restore him to normality, to the credit of both of you. Gertrude appears to have a marriage between Hamlet and Ophelia in mind, when Hamlet regains his mental balance

43 *Gracious:* your grace

44 *bestow:* hide

45–6 *That .... loneliness:* if you appear to be engaged in a religious exercise (the book is a religious one) it may help to account for your being alone

46 *oft to blame:* often guilty of hypocrisy

47–9 *with ... himself:* a seemingly holy appearance and the performance of religious acts can hide, or gloss over, extreme wickedness

50–54 *How … burden:* the audience now has a firm indication of Claudius's guilt

50 *conscience:* sense of right and wrong, moral sense

51–3 *The … word:* just as the prostitute's cheek is ugly under the pleasant make-up that conceals it, my own ugly guilt is disguised by my plausible language

54 *burden:* burden of guilt and unhappiness. This is one of the human touches that Shakespeare uses to make Claudius a convincing character

56–69 *To … life:* this passage may be paraphrased as: Whether human existence is worthwhile or not, whether death is preferable to life, is a question I must try to answer. Until I do, I cannot decide whether it is better and nobler for a rational being to suffer the random blows of fate patiently, or to struggle against them, dying in the struggle. Death is no more than a sleep. If to die were to sleep forever, and forever to be unaware of the miseries of human nature, then such a death and such a sleep would be devoutly welcomed. But if in the sleep of death we were to retain our human consciousness, the notion of this would make us pause and consider what troublesome dreams might come to us. It is the consideration of what may happen in death that makes people who are troubled by misfortune put up with their suffering for so long

70 *whips … time:* humiliations and sufferings inflicted on people during their earthly lives

71 *contumely:* insulting behaviour

72 *disprized:* unvalued

73 *insolence of office:* arrogance of those in authority

73–4 *spurns … takes:* rebukes and insults that decent, long-suffering people patiently accept from those less noble than themselves

75 *his quietus make:* settle his account, gain release from the troubles of life

76 *bare bodkin:* mere dagger
fardels: burdens

79–80 *undiscovered … returns:* world beyond the grave, whose boundaries nobody crosses twice. Hamlet seems to have forgotten his earlier encounter with a ghost; however, he is engaged in a general reflection on life and death and a particular reference would be out of place

81 *ills:* sufferings and trials

KING CLAUDIUS

O 'tis too true!

50 [*aside*] How smart a lash that speech doth give my
        conscience!

The harlot's cheek, beautied with plastering art,

Is not more ugly to the thing that helps it

Than is my deed to my most painted word.

O heavy burden!

POLONIUS

55 I hear him coming; let's withdraw, my lord.

Exeunt KING CLAUDIUS and POLONIUS.

Enter HAMLET.

HAMLET

To be, or not to be — that is the question;

Whether 'tis nobler in the mind to suffer

The slings and arrows of outrageous fortune,

Or to take arms against a sea of troubles,

60 And, by opposing, end them. To die, to sleep —

No more, and by a sleep to say we end

The heartache and the thousand natural shocks

That flesh is heir to — 'tis a consummation

Devoutly to be wished. To die, to sleep;

65 To sleep, perchance to dream. Ay, there's the rub.

For in that sleep of death what dreams may come

When we have shuffled off this mortal coil

Must give us pause; there's the respect

That makes calamity of so long life.

70 For who would bear the whips and scorns of time,

Th'oppressor's wrong, the proud man's contumely,

The pangs of disprized love, the law's delay,

The insolence of office, and the spurns

That patient merit of th'unworthy takes,

75 When he himself might his quietus make

With a bare bodkin? Who would fardels bear,

To grunt and sweat under a weary life,

But that the dread of something after death,

The undiscovered country from whose bourn

80 No traveller returns, puzzles the will

And makes us rather bear those ills we have

Than fly to others that we know not of?

Thus, conscience does make cowards of us all;

And thus, the native hue of resolution

Is sicklied o'er with the pale cast of thought,   85

And enterprises of great pith and moment

With this regard their currents turn awry,

And lose the name of action. — Soft you now,

The fair Ophelia? —

                            Nymph, in thy orisons

Be all my sins remembered.

OPHELIA

                      Good my lord,   90

How does your honour for this many a day?

HAMLET

I humbly thank you; well, well, well.

OPHELIA

My lord, I have remembrances of yours

That I have longed long to re-deliver;

I pray you now receive them.

HAMLET

                  No, not I;   95

I never gave you aught.

OPHELIA

My honoured lord, you know right well you did;

And, with them, words of so sweet breath composed

As made the things more rich. Their perfume lost,

Take these again; for to the noble mind   100

Rich gifts wax poor when givers prove unkind.

There, my lord.

HAMLET

Ha, ha! Are you honest?

OPHELIA

My lord?

HAMLET

Are you fair?   105

OPHELIA

What means your lordship?

---

83 *conscience ... all:* either: once we reflect on the implications of some action, and become conscious of where it may lead us, we tend to become afraid of performing it; or: our inner voice that tells us right from wrong makes us fear doing what we know is morally evil or dubious

84–5 *the ... thought:* when we have time to think, our normal desire for action ('resolution') is impaired, like a healthy person whose ruddy complexion ('native hue') is given a pale tinge

86–8 *enterprises ... action:* ambitious, important undertakings turn from their proper course because too great a time is spent thinking about them, and they are not proceeded with

89 *Nymph:* beautiful girl

89–90 *in ... remembered:* remember me in your prayers (Ophelia is reading a religious book)

92 *I ... well:* this is a formal, distant reply

93 *remembrances:* souvenirs, keepsakes

94 *re-deliver:* give back

96 *I ... aught:* Hamlet's denial may be because Ophelia has changed and is no longer the woman he loved; or his view of all women may have changed for the worse as a result of Gertrude's conduct; or he may be aware that he is being spied upon

98 *words ... composed:* sweet-sounding words

99 *Their perfume lost:* now that your words have lost their sweetness

101 *Rich ... poor:* in the eyes of their recipients, expensive gifts lose their value

103 *honest:* meaning both truthful and chaste

107–8 *That ... beauty:* if Ophelia is both chaste and beautiful, her chastity should permit nobody to have easy access to her beauty, to take advantage of it. Hamlet is implying that the beauty of women makes them vulnerable

109 *commerce:* dealings

111–13 *for ... likeness:* it is much easier for beauty to corrupt chastity than it is for chastity to purify beauty

112 *bawd:* procurer, pimp

113 *sometime:* once

114 *paradox:* here, an idea that most people would not accept
gives it proof: proves it is true (Hamlet is thinking of his mother)

116–17 *for ... it:* Hamlet is picturing a gardener grafting ('inoculating') a slip from a cultivated tree (representing virtue) onto a wild stock (representing original sin). Whatever is done, some of the flavour ('relish') of vice will remain

120–21 *Get ... sinners:* enter a convent, where you will remain chaste and not produce sinners

121 *indifferent honest:* reasonably well behaved

124–5 *more ... act them in:* the capacity to commit more offences than I can imagine, plan or carry out in the time available to me

127 *arrant knaves:* absolute, downright bad fellows

128 *father:* this sudden mention of Polonius has led to speculation that Hamlet has seen the eavesdropping Polonius, and perhaps Claudius as well

HAMLET

That if you be honest and fair, your honesty should admit no discourse to your beauty.

OPHELIA

Could beauty, my lord, have better commerce

110 Than with honesty?

HAMLET

Ay, truly; for the power of beauty will sooner transform honesty from what it is to a bawd, than the force of honesty can translate beauty into his likeness. This was sometime a paradox, but now the time gives it proof. I did love you once.

OPHELIA

115 Indeed, my lord, you made me believe so.

HAMLET

You should not have believed me; for virtue cannot so inoculate our old stock but we shall relish of it. I loved you not.

OPHELIA

I was the more deceived.

HAMLET

120 Get thee to a nunnery. Why wouldst thou be a breeder of sinners? I am myself indifferent honest; but yet I could accuse me of such things that it were better my mother had not borne me: I am very proud, revengeful, ambitious, with more offences at my beck than I have thoughts to put them

125 in, imagination to give them shape, or time to act them in. What should such fellows as I do crawling between earth and heaven? We are arrant knaves all; believe none of us. Go thy ways to a nunnery. Where's your father?

OPHELIA

At home, my lord.

HAMLET

130 Let the doors be shut upon him, that he may play the fool nowhere but in his own house. Farewell.

OPHELIA

O help him, you sweet heavens!

HAMLET

If thou dost marry, I'll give thee this plague for thy dowry: be thou as chaste as ice, as pure as snow, thou shalt not escape calumny. Get thee to a nunnery. Go, farewell. 135 Or, if thou wilt needs marry, marry a fool; for wise men know well enough what monsters you make of them. To a nunnery, go, and quickly too, farewell.

OPHELIA

O heavenly powers, restore him!

HAMLET

I have heard of your paintings too, well enough. God hath 140 given you one face and you make yourselves another, you jig, you amble, and you lisp, and nickname God's creatures, and make your wantonness your ignorance. Go to, I'll no more on't, it hath made me mad. I say we will have no more marriages: those that are married already, 145 all but one, shall live; the rest shall keep as they are. To a nunnery, go.

Exit.

OPHELIA

O what a noble mind is here o'erthrown!
The courtier's, soldier's, scholar's eye, tongue, sword;
Th'expectancy and rose of the fair state, 150
The glass of fashion and the mould of form,
The observed of all observers, quite, quite down!
And I, of ladies most deject and wretched,
That sucked the honey of his music vows,
Now see that noble and most sovereign reason, 155
Like sweet bells jangled, out of tune and harsh;
That unmatched form and feature of blown youth
Blasted with ecstasy. O, woe is me,
T'have seen what I have seen, see what I see!

Enter KING CLAUDIUS and POLONIUS.

---

132 *him:* Hamlet (Ophelia believes that he is mad)

133 *plague:* curse

135 *calumny:* slander

137 *what . . . them:* how wives betray their husbands by being unfaithful to them

139 *restore:* cure

140 *paintings:* cosmetics, make-up

142 *jig . . . lisp:* walk and talk in silly, affected ways
nickname: find new, absurd names for
143 *make your wantonness:* blame your deliberately offensive and silly behaviour on
143–4 *Go . . . on't:* off with you; I don't want anything more to do with women and their ways
146 *all but one:* except Claudius
rest: unmarried

149 *The . . . sword:* Hamlet is seen as having had the qualities of an ideal man
150 *Th'expectancy . . . state:* the heir to the throne, on whom all hopes were built, and the finest flower of Danish manhood
151 *The . . . form:* the model for both fashion and behaviour ('form')
152 *The . . . observers:* honoured and respected by all who knew him
quite down: reduced to a pitiful state of dejection
153 *deject:* dejected, downcast
154 *music vows:* pleasant, harmonious declarations of love
157–8 *That . . . ecstasy:* the incomparable beauty of his youth blighted ('blasted') by madness

160	*affections:* feelings, passions
161–2	*Nor . . . madness:* his words, although a little disordered, were not those of a madman
163	*sits on brood:* dwells on (like a bird about to hatch eggs)
164–5	*doubt . . . danger:* fear that whatever plans Hamlet is hatching will prove dangerous when revealed
167–8	*he . . . tribute:* he will be sent on a diplomatic mission to England to collect revenue owed to Denmark
169	*Haply:* perhaps
170	*variable objects:* various noteworthy sights
171	*This . . . heart:* whatever unidentified grief is troubling him
172	*Whereon . . . beating:* which is constantly disturbing his mind, like a noise that won't stop
173	*From . . . himself:* off his normal behaviour
174	*It . . . well:* that is a good idea
176	*neglected:* unrequited, unreturned
179	*hold it fit:* think it appropriate
180–81	*entreat . . . grief:* plead with him to reveal the cause of his sorrow
181	*be . . . him:* treat him firmly
182–3	*in . . . conference:* within earshot of their conversation
183	*find him not:* does not discover the truth about him

KING CLAUDIUS

160 Love? His affections do not that way tend;
Nor what he spake, though it lacked form a little,
Was not like madness. There's something in his soul
O'er which his melancholy sits on brood.
And I do doubt the hatch and the disclose
165 Will be some danger; which to prevent,
I have in quick determination
Thus set it down: he shall with speed to England,
For the demand of our neglected tribute.
Haply the seas and countries different,
170 With variable objects, shall expel
This something-settled matter in his heart,
Whereon his brains still beating puts him thus
From fashion of himself. What think you on't?

POLONIUS

It shall do well. But yet do I believe
175 The origin and commencement of his grief
Sprung from neglected love. — How now, Ophelia?
You need not tell us what Lord Hamlet said;
We heard it all. — My lord, do as you please;
But if you hold it fit, after the play
180 Let his queen mother all alone entreat him
To show his grief. Let her be round with him;
And I'll be placed, so please you, in the ear
Of all their conference. If she find him not,
To England send him, or confine him where
Your wisdom best shall think.

KING CLAUDIUS

185   It shall be so.
Madness in great ones must not unwatched go.
Exeunt.

[handwritten note] claudius acts immediately
– Hamlet doesn't

Key points

By the end of this scene, Claudius's strategies to discover what is wrong with Hamlet leave him convinced that Hamlet is neither lovesick nor mad, but that he is a threat that must be dealt with.

- This scene contains the most celebrated speech in the play: Hamlet's 'To be or not to be' soliloquy (lines 56–88). Although Hamlet is not alone on stage, this speech is considered a soliloquy because Hamlet is talking to himself and does not realise that anyone else can hear him. It is also important to note that Hamlet is not discussing his own particular circumstances or problems, but reflecting in a general way on matters affecting all human beings. Nowhere in the thirty-three lines does Hamlet make any direct reference to himself.

- Shakespeare's main purpose in writing this speech may have been to show Hamlet as a Renaissance thinker, fond of discussing philosophical problems. Read in this way, the speech becomes a conventional meditation or intellectual exercise. The word 'question' in the first line of the soliloquy has a specialised meaning. It refers to the subject for discussion in a debate between philosophers. Hamlet is an intellectual, capable of handling an abstract argument with skill and subtlety. The first line might then be interpreted: 'To exist or not to exist – here is an interesting subject with which I may divert myself.'

- The soliloquy is not a meditation on suicide, although the possibility of ending one's life by suicide is raised, only to be dismissed as too risky (lines 76–82). Contrary to common opinion, there is nothing in Hamlet's reflections here to suggest that he is contemplating his own suicide.

- Claudius and Polonius had earlier agreed to arrange an 'accidental' meeting between Hamlet and Ophelia to test the theory advanced by Polonius that Hamlet's unrequited love for Ophelia has led to his supposed madness. In this scene, the planned meeting takes place, with Claudius and Polonius concealed behind a tapestry.

- A key issue is how to account for Hamlet's ferocious and cruel verbal assault on Ophelia (lines 95–147). One explanation is that he may be overcome by anger that she has refused to see him, has returned his letters, has shown no sympathy for his pitiful condition on his last visit to her, and now delivers a final blow to his self-esteem by returning his gifts. However, that resentment is not obvious in his initial response to seeing 'the fair Ophelia' (line 89).

- Another explanation is that Hamlet knows, or suspects, that Ophelia is being used as a decoy to test his state of mind, and also, perhaps, that Claudius and Polonius are listening. This would provoke a strong sense of betrayal, and would certainly make sense of the threatening and abusive remarks Hamlet makes about Claudius (lines 145–6) and Polonius (lines 130–31).

- One of the main themes of Hamlet's outburst is female chastity. A related theme is his horrified sense of the consequences of marriage. He rejects Ophelia out of a sense of disgust with the processes of love and marriage. This disgust is inspired by his mother's example. While he is insulting Ophelia, he is thinking of his mother. He can see no reason why Ophelia should not prove equally false.

- Hamlet's treatment of Ophelia indicates his contempt for all women, and shows the extent to which he has lost a sense of balance or proportion. He fails to realise that one woman's behaviour does not give him cause to brand all women as sinners.

- The audience is given a strong indication in this scene of Claudius's guilt (lines 50–54). We also see that Claudius is a shrewd character, who recognises that Hamlet may prove a threat to him, and is taking steps to avoid the danger.

Useful quotes

Nor do we find him forward to be sounded,
But, with a crafty madness, keeps aloof
When we would bring him on to some confession
Of his true state.

(Guildenstern, lines 7–10)

'Tis too much proved — that with devotion's visage
And pious action we do sugar o'er
The devil himself.

(Polonius, lines 47–9)

How smart a lash that speech doth give my conscience!
The harlot's cheek, beautied with plastering art,
Is not more ugly to the thing that helps it
Than is my deed to my most painted word.
O heavy burden!

(Claudius, lines 50–54)

Or, if thou wilt needs marry, marry a fool; for wise men
know well enough what monsters you make of them.

(Hamlet, lines 136–7)

O what a noble mind is here o'erthrown!
The courtier's, soldier's, scholar's eye, tongue, sword;
Th'expectancy and rose of the fair state,
The glass of fashion and the mould of form,
The observed of all observers, quite, quite down!

(Ophelia, lines 148–52)

Love? His affections do not that way tend;
Nor what he spake, though it lacked form a little,
Was not like madness. There's something in his soul
O'er which his melancholy sits on brood.

(Claudius, lines 160–63)

Madness in great ones must not unwatched go.

(Claudius, line 186)

? Questions

1 Do Rosencrantz and Guildenstern provide the king and queen with an accurate report of their meeting with Hamlet? Explain.

2 In what way does Gertrude's attitude to Ophelia differ from that of Polonius and Laertes?

3 There is one detail in this scene that shows that, for all his villainy, Claudius has a conscience. Elaborate on this.

4 In a Hindi version of *Hamlet*, the first line of the soliloquy, 'To be, or not to be …', was subtitled as follows: 'Shall I live, or do myself in? I do not know.' Is this a reasonably accurate version of what Hamlet has in mind here?

5 It has been suggested that in his soliloquy (lines 56–88) Hamlet has forgotten all about the ghost. What evidence is there for this?

6 Describe Hamlet's views on love and marriage, as stated to Ophelia, and try to account for these.

7 Compare and contrast the Hamlet we see on stage during the soliloquy (lines 56–88) with the Hamlet who advises Ophelia to enter a convent (lines 120–28). Which of the two Hamlets do you prefer? Give your reasons.

8 Imagine you are Ophelia. Compose a diary entry in which you discuss the events of this scene.

9 Two schemes emerge at the end of the scene for dealing with Hamlet. What are they and do they make sense?

10 Draw up a list detailing the props needed for a stage version of this scene.

ACT 3 † Scene 2

Hamlet gives the First Player some advice on speaking the lines he has written for him. He then pays tribute to the stoical Horatio for his freedom from the whims of passion. He asks Horatio to study Claudius during the play. Following some banter between Hamlet on the one hand, and Claudius, Polonius and Ophelia on the other, the performance begins with a mime or dumb show. It features the pouring of poison into the ears of a sleeping king, and the poisoner's successful wooing of the king's widow. The spoken version follows. The poisoner is Lucianus, the nephew of the king. When Lucianus pours his poison into the king's ear, Claudius rises in outrage, and Polonius calls a halt to the performance. Hamlet now feels he has adequate confirmation of the ghost's word. Rosencrantz and Guildenstern confront Hamlet with news of Claudius's displeasure, and of Gertrude's desire to see her son. Polonius arrives to repeat Gertrude's invitation to an immediate interview. Hamlet, in soliloquy, gives way to murderous thoughts, but resolves to avoid harming his mother.

> *What should a man do but be merry?*
> *For look you how cheerfully my mother looks,*
> *and my father died within these two hours.*

HAMLET, Act 3, Scene 2, 114–16 .

Elsinore. A hall in the castle.

Enter HAMLET and three PLAYERS.

HAMLET *This shows hamlets [?]*

Speak the speech, I pray you, as I pronounced it to you, trippingly on the tongue; but if you mouth it, as many of your players do, I had as lief the town-crier spoke my lines. Nor do not saw the air too much with your hand, thus,

5 but use all gently, for in the very torrent, tempest, and (as I may say) whirlwind of your passion, you must acquire and beget a temperance that may give it smoothness. O, it offends me to the soul to hear a robustious periwig-pated fellow tear a passion to tatters, to very rags, to split

10 the ears of the groundlings, who for the most part are capable of nothing but inexplicable dumb shows and noise. I would have such a fellow whipped for o'erdoing Termagant. It out-Herods Herod. Pray you avoid it.

FIRST PLAYER

I warrant your honour.

HAMLET

15 Be not too tame neither, but let your own discretion be your tutor. Suit the action to the word, the word to the action; with this special observance, that you o'erstep not the modesty of nature: for anything so overdone is from the purpose of playing, whose end, both at the first, and

20 now, was and is, to hold, as 'twere, the mirror up to nature, to show virtue her own feature, scorn her own image, and the very age and body of the time his form and pressure. Now this overdone, or come tardy off, though it make the unskilful laugh, cannot but make the judicious grieve;

25 the censure of the which one must in your allowance o'erweigh a whole theatre of others. O, there be players that I have seen play, and heard others praise, and that highly (not to speak it profanely) that, neither having the accent of Christians nor the gait of Christian, pagan nor

30 man, have so strutted and bellowed that I have thought some of nature's journeymen had made men and not made them well, they imitated humanity so abominably.

---

1 *pronounced:* recited

2 *trippingly:* smoothly
mouth: over-emphasise

3 *had as lief:* would be as well pleased if

5 *use all gently:* do everything with grace and ease

5–7 *for ... smoothness:* even the most powerful emotions must be conveyed with restraint

8 *robustious:* turbulent, furious

8–9 *periwig-pated fellow:* actor wearing a wig

9–10 *tear ... groundlings:* ruin the emotional effect by deafening the humble spectators who stand in the yard around the stage

11 *capable of:* responsive to

11–12 *inexplicable ... noise:* meaningless spectacles and noisy speeches (rather than dignified, well-acted plays)

13 *Termagant ... Herod:* stock characters from the older drama, both noisy and violent
out-Herods Herod: rants and shouts even louder than Herod

14 *warrant:* can guarantee, can assure

15 *tame:* reserved
discretion: good sense

17–18 *with ... nature:* take particular care not to go beyond what is natural

18–19 *from ... playing:* contrary to, or remote from, the aim of drama

19–22 *whose ... pressure:* the purpose ('end') of drama is, and always was, to provide an image of actual life ('the mirror'), to reveal the shape and appearance of virtue and folly ('scorn') and to show the world its likeness

23 *come tardy off:* if it fails to achieve its aim

24 *unskilful:* people without taste or discrimination
judicious: people with good judgement

25–6 *censure ... others:* hostile verdict of one good judge must count for more with you than the praise of a theatre full of tasteless people

28 *profanely:* offensively

29–30 *accent ... man:* speech of Christians (i.e. civilised) nor the walk of any human being at all

30 *strutted and bellowed:* swaggered and roared

31 *journeymen:* unskilled common workmen

FIRST PLAYER

I hope we have reformed that indifferently with us, sir.

HAMLET

O, reform it altogether. And let those that play your
clowns speak no more than is set down for them; for there   35
be of them that will themselves laugh, to set on some
quantity of barren spectators to laugh too, though in the
meantime some necessary question of the play be then to
be considered. That's villainous, and shows a most pitiful
ambition in the fool that uses it. Go, make you ready.   40

Exeunt PLAYERS.

Enter POLONIUS, ROSENCRANTZ and GUILDENSTERN.

How now, my lord? Will the king hear this piece of work?

POLONIUS

And the queen too, and that presently.

HAMLET

Bid the players make haste.

Exit POLONIUS.

Will you two help to hasten them?

ROSENCRANTZ, GUILDENSTERN

We will, my lord.   45

Exeunt ROSENCRANTZ and GUILDENSTERN.

HAMLET

What, ho, Horatio!

Enter HORATIO.

HORATIO

Here, sweet lord, at your service.

HAMLET

Horatio, thou art e'en as just a man
As e'er my conversation coped withal.

HORATIO

O my dear lord—

HAMLET

                Nay, do not think I flatter;   50
For what advancement may I hope from thee
That no revenue hast but thy good spirits

---

33 *reformed . . . us:* corrected that kind of fault
reasonably well

36 *be of them:* are some among them

37 *barren:* foolish, stupid

42 *presently:* at once

48 *e'en:* even
just: well balanced
49 *e'er . . . withal:* I have ever met with in my dealings
with people

51 *advancement:* promotion, gain, advantage

To feed and clothe thee? Why should the poor be flattered?

No, let the candied tongue lick absurd pomp,

55 And crook the pregnant hinges of the knee

Where thrift may follow fawning. Dost thou hear?

Since my dear soul was mistress of her choice

And could of men distinguish, her election

Hath sealed thee for herself; for thou hast been

60 As one, in suffering all, that suffers nothing,

A man that Fortune's buffets and rewards

Hast ta'en with equal thanks. And blest are those

Whose blood and judgement are so well commeddled,

That they are not a pipe for Fortune's finger

65 To sound what stop she please. Give me that man

That is not passion's slave, and I will wear him

In my heart's core, ay, in my heart of heart,

As I do thee. Something too much of this.

There is a play tonight before the king.

70 One scene of it comes near the circumstance

Which I have told thee of my father's death.

I prithee, when thou seest that act afoot,

Even with the very comment of thy soul

Observe mine uncle. If his occulted guilt

75 Do not itself unkennel in one speech,

It is a damnèd ghost that we have seen,

And my imaginations are as foul

As Vulcan's stithy. Give him heedful note,

For I mine eyes will rivet to his face:

80 And after we will both our judgements join

In censure of his seeming.

HORATIO
                              Well, my lord.

If he steal aught the whilst this play is playing,

And 'scape detecting, I will pay the theft.

Flourish of trumpets and kettle-drums.

HAMLET

They are coming to the play; I must be idle. Get you a place.

Danish march. Enter KING CLAUDIUS, QUEEN GERTRUDE,
POLONIUS, OPHELIA, ROSENCRANTZ, GUILDENSTERN,
LORDS, and ATTENDANTS carrying torches.

54–6 *let . . . fawning:* flatterers are best advised to direct their flattery to those who will respond by giving them something in return

54 *candied tongue:* sweet tongue of the flatterer, who has the gift of sweet talk, and licks, like a dog, those ridiculous people who are impressed by flattery

56 *thrift:* profit

57 *mistress . . . choice:* free to choose (a friend)

59 *sealed:* marked out

60 *As . . . nothing:* two meanings of 'suffer' are involved here. Horatio is a man who endures everything, but is harmed by nothing

61–2 *that . . . thanks:* reacts with evenness of temper to whatever good or ill fate may bring (Horatio is a stoic)

63 *blood:* passions
commeddled: blended, in harmony

64–5 *a pipe . . . please:* at the mercy of fate or circumstances

66 *passion's slave:* at the mercy of his emotions

66–7 *wear . . . of heart:* treasure him

68 *Something . . . this:* enough of this

70 *comes near:* recalls

71 *Which . . . death:* Hamlet has apparently confided in Horatio since the events of Act 1, Scene 5

72 *act afoot:* episode in performance

73–4 *Even . . . uncle:* give Claudius's behaviour your fullest attention and consideration

74–5 *occulted . . . speech:* hidden guilt does not show itself (like a dog breaking out from a kennel) when he hears the speech I have composed

76 *It . . . seen:* then the ghost we have seen is an evil spirit

77–8 *imaginations . . . stithy:* mind is filled with hellish ('foul') and false suspicions concerning Claudius

78 *Vulcan's stithy:* the forge of Vulcan, the Roman god of blacksmiths, a place as black as hell
Give . . . note: observe him carefully

79 *rivet:* fix firmly

80–81 *after . . . seeming:* we will later compare our opinions of his looks and behaviour

82–3 *steal . . . theft:* gets away with concealing anything, I am prepared to answer for it

84 *idle:* unoccupied (i.e. appear to have nothing particular in mind)

KING CLAUDIUS

How fares our cousin Hamlet?   85

HAMLET

Excellent, in faith; of the chameleon's dish: I eat the air, promise-crammed: you cannot feed capons so.

KING CLAUDIUS

I have nothing with this answer, Hamlet.
These words are not mine.

HAMLET

No, nor mine now. [*to POLONIUS*] My lord, you played   90
once in the university, you say?

POLONIUS

That did I, my lord; and was accounted a good actor.

HAMLET

What did you enact?

POLONIUS

I did enact Julius Caesar. I was killed in the Capitol. Brutus killed me.   95

HAMLET

It was a brute part of him to kill so capital a calf there. Be the players ready?

ROSENCRANTZ

Ay, my lord; they stay upon your patience.

QUEEN GERTRUDE

Come hither, my dear Hamlet, sit by me.

HAMLET

No, good mother, here's metal more attractive.   100

Turns to OPHELIA.

POLONIUS

[*to KING CLAUDIUS*] O, ho! Do you mark that?

HAMLET

Lady, shall I lie in your lap?

Sits at OPHELIA's feet.

86–7 *Excellent ... so:* Hamlet deliberately misinterprets a question about how he fares (does), by talking about how he fares (eats). He says that like the chameleon, he is living on air (with a pun on 'heir'), since he is fed with mere promises, the main one being that he will one day succeed Claudius. The reference to capons (cocks fattened before being killed) may be a hint that he suspects Claudius of murderous intent towards him

88–9 *I ... mine:* I can make no sense of your answer; it has no relevance to my question

90 *played:* acted, performed

94–5 *I ... me:* Shakespeare's play *Julius Caesar* was first performed in 1599, a year or so before *Hamlet*. It is an interesting speculation that in the earlier play, the actor now playing Polonius played Caesar, while the Hamlet actor played Brutus

96 *It ... there:* a series of puns on Brutus-brute and Capitol-capital
calf: fool

98 *patience:* convenience

100 *metal more attractive:* more magnetic metal (i.e. Ophelia). This is a snub to Gertrude, but also, Hamlet could not watch the king's face properly if he sat beside the royal couple

OPHELIA

No, my lord.

HAMLET

I mean, my head upon your lap?

OPHELIA

105   Ay, my lord.

HAMLET

Do you think I meant country matters?

OPHELIA

I think nothing, my lord.

HAMLET

That's a fair thought to lie between maids' legs.

OPHELIA

What is, my lord?

HAMLET

110   Nothing.

OPHELIA

You are merry, my lord.

HAMLET

Who, I?

OPHELIA

Ay, my lord.

HAMLET

O God, your only jig-maker. What should a man do but be
115   merry? For look you how cheerfully my mother looks, and
my father died within these two hours.

OPHELIA

Nay, 'tis twice two months, my lord.

HAMLET

So long? Nay then, let the devil wear black, for I'll have a
suit of sables. O heavens, die two months ago, and not
120   forgotten yet? Then there's hope a great man's memory
may outlive his life half a year, but, by'r lady, he must build
churches then or else shall he suffer not thinking on,
with the hobby-horse, whose epitaph is 'For O, for O, the
hobby-horse is forgot!'

106   *country matters:* lovemaking

108   *fair:* pleasant, pure

114   *your only jig-maker:* I'm the best merrymaker anywhere

114–16   *What ... hours:* why shouldn't we all be merry; look how merry my mother is, she who lost her husband only within the last two hours. This is typical of Hamlet's irreverence and bitter sarcasm

118–19   *So ... sables:* to mourn the dead for four months is going rather far. To the devil with mourning, I'm going to wear something luxurious and fashionable

122   *shall ... on:* he will be forgotten

123   *hobby-horse:* in Shakespeare's time, this was a byword for anything that was forgotten

Trumpets sound. A dumb show follows:

Enter a King and a Queen very lovingly; the Queen embracing him, and he her. She kneels, and makes show of protestation unto him. He takes her up, and declines his head upon her neck. He lies down upon a bank of flowers. She, seeing him asleep, leaves him. Anon comes in another man; takes off his crown, kisses it, and pours poison in the sleeper's ears, and leaves him. The Queen returns, finds the King dead, and makes passionate action. The poisoner, with some two or three mutes, comes in again, seeming to condole with her. The dead body is carried away. The poisoner woos the Queen with gifts. She seems harsh a while, but in the end accepts his love.

Exeunt PLAYERS.

dumb show: a mime to introduce the insert-play (lines 141–248), in this case it sets forth the whole action in detail

Anon: soon after

passionate action: gestures that indicate her shock and grief

condole: lament, express sorrow

126 *miching mallecho:* lurking wickedness (i.e. the dumb show is all about a wicked deed stealthily, or sneakily, undertaken)

127 *Belike ... play:* probably this dumb show sets forth the plot ('argument') of the play

128 *fellow:* the player who will deliver the prologue

131–3 *Ay ... means:* Hamlet, addicted to punning, which was an admired accomplishment in Shakespeare's time, makes an indecent one here

134 *naught:* offensive

136 *stooping ... clemency:* placing ourselves at your mercy

138 *posy ... ring:* a saying short enough to engrave on the inside of a ring. Hamlet expected a more elaborate speech

140 *As woman's love:* Hamlet has Gertrude, whom he is watching, in mind, not Ophelia

141–6 *Full ... bands:* the insert-play, composed of rhyming couplets, is artificial, repetitive and verbose in style. Here, the Player King takes six lines to say: 'We are thirty years married.' He says it three times
141 *Phoebus' cart:* the chariot of the sun god
142 *Neptune's ... ground:* sea and land. Neptune was the god of the sea, and Tellus the god of the earth
143 *borrowed sheen:* brightness given by the sun
145 *Hymen:* the goddess of marriage
146 *commutual:* answering to each other
bands: bonds of marriage

OPHELIA

125 What means this, my lord?

HAMLET

Marry, this is miching mallecho; it means mischief.

OPHELIA

Belike this show imports the argument of the play.

Enter PLAYER as Prologue.

HAMLET

We shall know by this fellow. The players cannot keep counsel; they'll tell all.

OPHELIA

130 Will he tell us what this show meant?

HAMLET

Ay, or any show that you will show him: be not you ashamed to show, he'll not shame to tell you what it means.

OPHELIA

You are naught, you are naught. I'll mark the play.

PROLOGUE

135   For us, and for our tragedy,

    Here stooping to your clemency,

    We beg your hearing patiently.

Exit.

HAMLET

Is this a prologue, or the posy of a ring?

OPHELIA

'Tis brief, my lord.

HAMLET

140 As woman's love.

Enter two PLAYERS as King and Queen.

PLAYER KING

Full thirty times hath Phoebus' cart gone round

Neptune's salt wash and Tellus' orbèd ground,

And thirty dozen moons with borrowed sheen

About the world have times twelve thirties been,

145 Since love our hearts, and Hymen did our hands,

Unite commutual in most sacred bands.

PLAYER QUEEN

So many journeys may the sun and moon

Make us again count o'er ere love be done!

But woe is me, you are so sick of late,

So far from cheer and from your former state,   150

That I distrust you. Yet, though I distrust,

Discomfort you, my lord, it nothing must.

For women fear too much, even as they love,

And women's fear and love hold quantity,

In neither aught, or in extremity.   155

Now, what my love is, proof hath made you know;

And as my love is sized, my fear is so:

Where love is great, the littlest doubts are fear;

Where little fears grow great, great love grows there.

PLAYER KING

Faith, I must leave thee, love, and shortly too.   160

My operant powers their functions leave to do,

And thou shalt live in this fair world behind,

Honoured, beloved, and haply one as kind

For husband shalt thou—

PLAYER QUEEN

               O confound the rest!

Such love must needs be treason in my breast.   165

In second husband let me be accurst!

None wed the second but who killed the first.

HAMLET [*aside*]

That's wormwood.

PLAYER QUEEN

The instances that second marriage move

Are base respects of thrift, but none of love.   170

A second time I kill my husband dead,

When second husband kisses me in bed.

PLAYER KING

I do believe you think what now you speak,

But what we do determine oft we break.

Purpose is but the slave to memory,   175

Of violent birth, but poor validity,

Which now, like fruit unripe, sticks on the tree,

But fall, unshaken, when they mellow be.

147–8 *So . . . done:* may we be together for thirty years more

151 *distrust:* feel anxious (about)

152 *Discomfort . . . must:* it must not worry you

154 *hold quantity:* are in proportion

155 *In . . . extremity:* either fear and love are totally absent, or they are present to an extreme degree

157 *And . . . so:* my fear is as great as my love

161 *My . . . do:* my vital faculties are ceasing to perform

162–4 *And . . . shalt thou:* after I have died, you will enjoy honour and love from another husband who may prove as kind as I have been

164 *confound the rest:* a curse on what you're about to say

166 *acurst:* cursed

167 *None . . . first:* the only women who remarry are those who have murdered their first husbands. This does not necessarily mean that Hamlet, by means of his insert-play, is accusing Gertrude of murder, although it is commonly taken to imply that Hamlet considers her an accomplice in King Hamlet's death, because she marries his murderer

168 *wormwood:* a bitter plant, used as a medicine. Hamlet seems to be suggesting that the previous line will prove a bitter medicine for the king, and more particularly the queen, to swallow

169–70 *instances . . . love:* second marriages are motivated by profit and material advantage; love has nothing to do with them

171–2 *A . . . bed:* every expression of love for a second husband is equivalent to murdering the first

175–8 *Purpose . . . be:* the strongest, most violent resolutions depend on our remembering to keep them. The trouble with resolutions is that the strong feelings that prompted them soon cool, and are forgotten

179–80 *Most ... debt:* it is inevitable that resolutions, which are debts owing only to ourselves, should remain unhonoured and forgotten

183–4 *The ... destroy:* the very strength of such passions as grief and joy makes their translation into action very difficult

186 *Grief ... accident:* grief turns to joy, and joy to grief, for trivial reasons
187 *for aye:* forever

189–90 *For ... fortune love:* a problem that still remains to be solved is whether love follows fortune, or fortune follows love

191 *down ... flies:* fallen from favour, watch how his followers abandon him
192 *poor advanced:* person who has been down, but is now in authority
193 *hitherto ... tend:* up to this point in my argument it appears that love follows fortune
194 *who ... friend:* those who are prosperous will always have friends
195–6 *who ... enemy:* those in need find that their friends blossom into enemies
197–200 *orderly ... own:* to return to the beginning of my argument, what we would like to see happen and what fate has in store for us tend to be incompatible, so that our plans are always doomed to frustration. We are free to think, but not to decide what will happen as a result of our thoughts

202 *die thy thoughts:* your resolution will be forgotten

204 *Sport ... night:* may I have no pastimes by day, or rest by night

206 *An anchor's cheer:* the lifestyle of a hermit

207–8 *Each ... destroy:* may whatever influence changes happiness to misery cause my dearest hopes to be blighted
209 *Both ... strife:* may endless discord follow me both in this life and the next

211 *it:* her oath

213–14 *fain ... sleep:* I would like to while away the tiresome day by sleeping

---

Most necessary 'tis that we forget
180   To pay ourselves what to ourselves is debt.
What to ourselves in passion we propose,
The passion ending, doth the purpose lose.
The violence of either grief or joy
Their own enactures with themselves destroy.
185   Where joy most revels, grief doth most lament.
Grief joys, joy grieves, on slender accident.
This world is not for aye, nor 'tis not strange
That even our loves should with our fortunes change.
For 'tis a question left us yet to prove,
190   Whether love lead fortune, or else fortune love.
The great man down, you mark his favourite flies.
The poor advanced makes friends of enemies.
And hitherto doth love on fortune tend;
For who not needs shall never lack a friend,
195   And who in want a hollow friend doth try,
Directly seasons him his enemy.
But, orderly to end where I begun,
Our wills and fates do so contrary run
That our devices still are overthrown;
200   Our thoughts are ours, their ends none of our own.
So think thou wilt no second husband wed,
But die thy thoughts when thy first lord is dead.

PLAYER QUEEN
Nor earth to me give food, nor heaven light,
Sport and repose lock from me day and night,
205   To desperation turn my trust and hope,
An anchor's cheer in prison be my scope,
Each opposite that blanks the face of joy
Meet what I would have well, and it destroy.
Both here and hence pursue me lasting strife,
210   If, once a widow, ever I be wife!

HAMLET
If she should break it now!

PLAYER KING
'Tis deeply sworn. Sweet, leave me here a while;
My spirits grow dull, and fain I would beguile
The tedious day with sleep.

Sleeps.

PLAYER QUEEN

Sleep rock thy brain,

And never come mischance between us twain! 215

Exit.

HAMLET

Madam, how like you this play?

QUEEN GERTRUDE

The lady protests too much, methinks.

HAMLET

O but she'll keep her word.

KING CLAUDIUS

Have you heard the argument? Is there no offence in't?

HAMLET

No, no, they do but jest, poison in jest; no offence in the 220
world.

KING CLAUDIUS

What do you call the play?

HAMLET

The Mousetrap. Marry, how? Tropically. This play is the
image of a murder done in Vienna. Gonzago is the duke's
name; his wife, Baptista. You shall see anon. 'Tis a knavish 225
piece of work, but what of that? Your majesty, and we
that have free souls, it touches us not. Let the galled jade
wince, our withers are unwrung.

Enter a PLAYER as Lucianus.

This is one Lucianus, nephew to the king.

OPHELIA

You are as good as a chorus, my lord. 230

HAMLET

I could interpret between you and your love, if I could see
the puppet's dallying.

OPHELIA

You are keen, my lord, you are keen.

HAMLET

It would cost you a groaning to take off mine edge.

OPHELIA

Still better and worse. 235

215 *mischance:* bad fortune
twain: two

217 *The ... methinks:* it seems to me that the lady's
declarations of love are rather overdone

219 *Have ... in't?* Are you familiar with the plot? I hope
there is nothing in it to cause insult or annoyance.
The king may be addressing Polonius, although
Hamlet replies

220–21 *they ... world:* there is no crime involved here;
after all, this is only a play, depicting a make-
believe poisoning

223 *The Mousetrap:* this is Hamlet's own name for the
play, based on his earlier determination to 'catch
the conscience of the king' (Act 2, Scene 2, line 575)
how? How do you think it got that name?
Tropically: metaphorically

224 *image:* accurate representation

227 *that ... souls:* who are free from guilt
touches us not: does not affect us

227–8 *Let ... unwrung:* a horse in poor condition ('galled
jade') may wince, but our bones are not chafed.
In other words: Let those who are guilty feel hurt
by what they see and hear; those of us who are
innocent can remain unaffected

229 *nephew:* making the murderer the king's nephew
allows the scene to be interpreted as a threat on
Hamlet's part to the life of Claudius

230 *chorus:* the function of the chorus in a play was to
interpret the events of the play for the audience

231–2 *I ... dallying:* if I saw a puppet show with you and
your lover as the characters, I would be able to
provide dialogue for it

233 *keen:* witty

234 *It ... edge:* Hamlet, deliberately misinterpreting
Ophelia's use of 'keen', takes her to mean 'full of
desire', and suggests that his desire can be abated
only by lovemaking

235 *better and worse:* cleverer on the one hand, and
more offensive on the other

236 *mistake:* take other men for. Hamlet is punning on Ophelia's 'better and worse', which reminds him of the marriage vows and his mother's infidelity
murderer: addressed to the actor playing Lucianus

236–7 *Pox! ... begin!* A curse on you! Stop making these ridiculous faces and begin the action!

237–8 *Come ... revenge:* Hamlet is misquoting from an old play, the anonymous *True Tragedy of Richard III*. In the original it was herds of beasts that bellowed

239 *drugs fit:* appropriate poison
time agreeing: a suitable time

240 *Confederate ... seeing:* the ideal opportunity with nobody else looking on

241 *rank:* vile, foul

242 *With ... blasted:* carrying the triple curse of the goddess of witchcraft

243 *dire property:* fatal qualities

244 *On ... immediately:* instantly take away healthy life

245–8 *He ... wife:* Hamlet provokes Claudius by giving a summary of the main elements of the insert-play, which are also the main features of the crime Claudius has committed, its motives and consequences: the poisoning, the desire to be king and the marriage to the widow

246 *extant:* in existence, in written form

250 *frighted ... fire:* Hamlet is feigning surprise that the king should take fright at the sight of a fictitious crime

252 *Give o'er:* stop, abandon

255–8 *Why ... away:* Hamlet recites an old ballad, the theme of which is appropriate to the present situation. The wounded ('stricken') deer, Claudius, must now be on his guard, while the unscathed one, Hamlet ('The hart ungallèd'), can enjoy his leisure and his sleep

HAMLET

So you mistake your husbands. — Begin, murderer. Pox! Leave thy damnable faces, and begin! Come, the croaking raven doth bellow for revenge.

LUCIANUS

Thoughts black, hands apt, drugs fit, and time agreeing

240 Confederate season, else no creature seeing,

Thou mixture rank, of midnight weeds collected,

With Hecate's ban thrice blasted, thrice infected,

Thy natural magic and dire property,

On wholesome life usurp immediately.

Pours the poison into the sleeping king's ears.

HAMLET

245 He poisons him in the garden for his estate. His name's Gonzago. The story is extant, and writ in choice Italian. You shall see anon how the murderer gets the love of Gonzago's wife.

KING CLAUDIUS stands.

OPHELIA

The king rises.

HAMLET

250 What, frighted with false fire!

QUEEN GERTRUDE

How fares my lord?

POLONIUS

Give o'er the play.

KING CLAUDIUS

Give me some light — away!

POLONIUS

Lights, lights, lights!

Exeunt all but HAMLET and HORATIO.

HAMLET

255   Why, let the stricken deer go weep,

The hart ungallèd play;

For some must watch, while some must sleep,

So runs the world away.

Would not this, sir, and a forest of feathers, if the rest of my
fortunes turn Turk with me, with two Provincial roses on   260
my razed shoes, get me a fellowship in a cry of players, sir?

HORATIO
Half a share.

HAMLET
A whole one, I.
    For thou dost know, O Damon dear,
    This realm dismantled was   265
    Of Jove himself, and now reigns here
    A very, very — pajock.

HORATIO
You might have rhymed.

HAMLET
O good Horatio, I'll take the ghost's word for a thousand
pound. Didst perceive?   270

HORATIO
Very well, my lord.

HAMLET
Upon the talk of the poisoning?

HORATIO
I did very well note him.

Enter ROSENCRANTZ and GUILDENSTERN.

HAMLET
Ah ha! Come, some music! Come, the recorders!
    For if the king like not the comedy,   275
    Why then, belike, he likes it not, perdy.
Come, some music!

GUILDENSTERN
Good my lord, vouchsafe me a word with you.

HAMLET
Sir, a whole history.

GUILDENSTERN
The king, sir—   280

HAMLET
Ay, sir, what of him?

259–61 *Would … players:* my skills as producer and part-writer of so successful a play as we have just seen would entitle me to a partnership in a company ('cry') of actors (actors wore feathers in their hats and rosettes on their shoes). If my fortunes worsen ('turn Turk'), I can fall back on this occupation

262 *Half a share:* Horatio is less enthusiastic. After all, he implies, the achievement was only partly Hamlet's, since he had to rely on the players

263 *A … I:* I still insist that I deserve a full share or partnership

264–7 *For … pajock:* Hamlet recites another verse. He calls Horatio 'Damon', a virtuous shepherd and good friend. 'Jove' represents Hamlet's father, whose kingdom ('realm') was usurped ('dismantled') by Claudius

267 *pajock:* a disreputable, uncouth individual

270 *Didst perceive?* Did you see (how Claudius reacted)?

275 *the comedy:* a general word for a play, but Hamlet may be using it ironically
276 *perdy:* by God (from the French *par Dieu*)

278 *vouchsafe:* grant

280 *sir:* a more appropriate form of address would have been 'my lord'. Hamlet's repetition of 'sir' in the next line may indicate disapproval

282 *Is ... distempered:* since he withdrew from the play to his private apartments, he has been terribly out of sorts, distracted in mind

284 *choler:* anger

285–7 *Your ... choler:* you would be wise to report this to his doctor because if I tried to eliminate his angry humour by purging it, my treatment would only make his condition worse. Choler, or anger, was thought to be caused by bile, which had to be purged to be cured. The cure could involve bleeding the patient, an idea maliciously present to Hamlet's mind here

288–9 *put ... affair:* speak to me in an orderly fashion and don't wander so much from the subject I have raised

290 *I am tame:* I have ceased to be wild; I am rational
Pronounce: speak

291 *in ... spirit:* who is greatly distressed

294 *Nay ... breed:* your answer does not show proper manners or breeding
295 *wholesome:* rational, sane
296 *pardon:* permission to go

300 *wit's diseased:* mind is not functioning properly

301 *command:* have for the asking

303 *matter:* object of your visit

GUILDENSTERN

Is in his retirement marvellous distempered.

HAMLET

With drink, sir?

GUILDENSTERN

No, my lord, rather with choler.

HAMLET

285   Your wisdom should show itself more richer to signify this to the doctor; for, for me to put him to his purgation would perhaps plunge him into more choler.

GUILDENSTERN

Good my lord, put your discourse into some frame and start not so wildly from my affair.

HAMLET

290   I am tame, sir. Pronounce.

GUILDENSTERN

The queen, your mother, in most great affliction of spirit, hath sent me to you.

HAMLET

You are welcome.

GUILDENSTERN

Nay, good my lord, this courtesy is not of the right breed.
295   If it shall please you to make me a wholesome answer, I will do your mother's commandment: if not, your pardon and my return shall be the end of my business.

HAMLET

Sir, I cannot.

GUILDENSTERN

What, my lord?

HAMLET

300   Make you a wholesome answer. My wit's diseased. But, sir, such answer as I can make, you shall command, or rather as you say, my mother. Therefore no more, but to the matter. My mother, you say—

ROSENCRANTZ

Then thus she says: your behaviour hath struck her into amazement and admiration.   305

HAMLET

O wonderful son, that can so astonish a mother! But is there no sequel at the heels of this mother's admiration? Impart.

ROSENCRANTZ

She desires to speak with you in her closet ere you go to bed.   310

HAMLET

We shall obey, were she ten times our mother. Have you any further trade with us?

ROSENCRANTZ

My lord, you once did love me.

HAMLET

And do still, by these pickers and stealers.

ROSENCRANTZ

Good my lord, what is your cause of distemper? You do   315
surely bar the door upon your own liberty if you deny your griefs to your friend.

HAMLET

Sir, I lack advancement.

ROSENCRANTZ

How can that be, when you have the voice of the king himself for your succession in Denmark?   320

HAMLET

Ay, sir, but 'while the grass grows' — the proverb is something musty.

Enter a PLAYER with recorders.

O, the recorders! Let me see one — to withdraw with you, why do you go about to recover the wind of me, as if you would drive me into a toil?   325

GUILDENSTERN

O, my lord, if my duty be too bold, my love is too unmannerly.

---

305   *admiration:* astonishment, bewilderment

306–8   *But … Impart:* something must follow on my mother's astonishment; tell me

309   *closet:* private apartment
ere: before

312   *trade with us:* business with me. Hamlet uses the royal plural here, thus distancing himself from his former friends. The abruptness of his question, and his use of the word 'trade', makes it clear that he no longer regards them as friends

314   *pickers and stealers:* hands

315   *your … distemper:* the reason you are disturbed. Rosencrantz thinks Hamlet will find relief for his supposed mental distress if he confides in a 'friend'

318   *advancement:* promotion

319–20   *you … Denmark:* the king has publicly announced that you will succeed him as King of Denmark (see Act 1, Scene 2, line 109)

321–2   *but … musty:* to quote a well-worn proverb, 'while the grass grows the horse starves'. Hamlet is hinting that a promise of kingship in an indefinite future does not satisfy him

323   *withdraw:* speak in private

324–5   *why … toil:* the image is of a hunter who allows the hunted animal to get his scent; the animal then flees from the hunter, but runs into a prepared trap or net ('toil'). Hamlet is accusing Guildenstern of plotting to trap him

326–7   *if … unmannerly:* if I have appeared forward and insolent, it is my love for you that has caused me to go beyond the bounds of proper behaviour

328 *that:* how love can take improper forms

334 *know ... of:* have no skill at

335 *govern these ventages:* control the finger-holes

337 *discourse:* utter

338 *stops:* holes to cover

341–9 *Why ... me:* Hamlet lectures Guildenstern on his presumption. The man who cannot play a recorder thinks he can sound out the depths of Hamlet's soul and mind. If the secrets of a musical instrument will not yield themselves up to Guildenstern's efforts, how can he expect to probe the dark mysteries of Hamlet's being?
345 *compass:* register
346 *organ:* recorder

348 *fret:* irritate (to fret an instrument is to provide markers on it to guide the fingers while playing)

351 *would:* wishes to
presently: immediately

HAMLET

I do not well understand that. Will you play upon this pipe?

GUILDENSTERN

330 My lord, I cannot.

HAMLET

I pray you.

GUILDENSTERN

Believe me, I cannot.

HAMLET

I do beseech you.

GUILDENSTERN

I know no touch of it, my lord.

HAMLET

335 It is as easy as lying: govern these ventages with your fingers and thumb, give it breath with your mouth, and it will discourse most eloquent music. Look you, these are the stops.

GUILDENSTERN

But these cannot I command to any utterance of harmony;
340 I have not the skill.

HAMLET

Why, look you now, how unworthy a thing you make of me! You would play upon me; you would seem to know my stops; you would pluck out the heart of my mystery; you would sound me from my lowest note to the top of
345 my compass: and there is much music, excellent voice, in this little organ; yet cannot you make it speak. 'Sblood, do you think I am easier to be played on than a pipe? Call me what instrument you will, though you can fret me, yet you cannot play upon me.

Enter POLONIUS.

350 God bless you, sir!

POLONIUS

My lord, the queen would speak with you, and presently.

HAMLET

Do you see yonder cloud that's almost in shape of a camel?

POLONIUS

By th' mass and 'tis like a camel indeed.

HAMLET

Methinks it is like a weasel.

POLONIUS

It is backed like a weasel.   355

HAMLET

Or like a whale?

POLONIUS

Very like a whale.

HAMLET

Then I will come to my mother by and by — [*aside*] they
fool me to the top of my bent — I will come by and by.

POLONIUS

I will say so.   360

Exit.

HAMLET

'By and by' is easily said. Leave me, friends.

Exeunt all but HAMLET.

'Tis now the very witching time of night,

When churchyards yawn, and hell itself breathes out

Contagion to this world: now could I drink hot blood,

And do such bitter business as the day   365

Would quake to look on. Soft, now to my mother.

O heart, lose not thy nature; let not ever

The soul of Nero enter this firm bosom;

Let me be cruel, not unnatural.

I will speak daggers to her, but use none;   370

My tongue and soul in this be hypocrites;

How in my words somever she be shent,

To give them seals never, my soul, consent!

Exit.

352–7 *Do ... whale:* there is fine irony here. Hamlet, who is posing as a madman, gets the sane Polonius to agree to a set of contradictory statements

358 *by and by:* immediately

359 *top ... bent:* limit of my endurance

362 *witching time:* time when witches are active

364 *Contagion:* infectious evil

365–6 *do ... on:* perform deeds too horrible to be contemplated in daylight

367 *nature:* natural love for a mother

368 *Nero:* Roman emperor who put his mother to death after she had poisoned her husband

371 *My ... hypocrites:* my tongue will speak the daggers that my soul will not let me use. He can see himself as a hypocrite because he will not put his feelings into action

372–3 *How ... consent!* However bitterly she is rebuked by me ('shent'), may I never translate my words into acts ('give them seals')!

[Handwritten annotations:] Hamlets purpose has been renewed

[Handwritten annotations:] The only person Hamlet can trust is Horatio. He really wants to hurt Gertrude

Key points

In this scene, by means of the play within the play (or insert-play), Hamlet highlights his uncle's guilty secret and provokes a strong response, which he takes as confirmation of Claudius's guilt.

- The scene opens with Hamlet telling the actors how to act. He has clearly given some thought to the principles of good acting.

- Hamlet pays tribute to Horatio. He admires Horatio's balance of 'blood and judgement' (line 63; passion and reason). He trusts him enough to ask for his help in observing Claudius's response to the play.

- The heart of this scene, and the second great climax of the play (the first being the ghost's revelation), is the performance of the dumb show or mime and the play it introduces: *The Murder of Gonzago*.

- In setting out the plot of the insert-play, the dumb show allows the audience to pay less attention to the players and concentrate on what is really interesting: the reactions of Claudius, Gertrude and the others to what they see enacted before them.

- The dumb show reveals the plot of the insert-play in advance and in detail. *The Murder of Gonzago*, or *The Mousetrap* as Hamlet calls it, adds nothing new to the action of the dumb show. The only difference between the dumb show and the insert-play is that in the former we do not know the relationship between the poisoner and his victim. So why does Claudius, who loses his nerve as he watches the play, remain unmoved during the dumb show?

- We know that Claudius is not easily given to panic. We should remember that a very short time after killing his brother, he calmly talked to his assembled courtiers about his grief at his 'dear brother's death' (Act 1, Scene 2, lines 1–4). Such a man should have no great difficulty suppressing his reaction to a theatrical enactment of his crime. Thus, his iron self-control should keep his feelings in check.

- *The Murder of Gonzago* begins at a leisurely pace without implications for either Gertrude or Claudius. However, the lines begin to hit home: 'In second husband let me be accurst! None wed the second but who killed the first' (lines 166–7), and Claudius becomes worried: 'Have you heard the argument? Is there no offence in't?' (line 219).

- The fact that the insert-play's murderer (Lucianus) is the king's nephew rather than his brother adds a new dimension of interest. The Danish courtiers who are watching do not know that Claudius killed his brother; they will therefore interpret this episode as a threat on Hamlet's part to the life of Claudius. From Hamlet's point of view, Lucianus is a representation of himself in the role of avenger, and of Claudius in the role of poisoner. Claudius must see the episode as a threat, as an attempt to make him betray his guilt and as evidence that Hamlet knows his secret.

- Claudius is pushed to breaking-point when Hamlet applies his most potent piece of psychological torture: 'He poisons him in the garden for his estate … You shall see anon how the murderer gets the love of Gonzago's wife' (lines 245, 247–8). For Hamlet, this is an unbloody act of vengeance against Claudius, since it destroys his sense of security.

- Hamlet is delighted at the outcome. However, as Horatio's more measured response suggests, Hamlet's triumph is not complete. He may now have satisfied himself that Claudius has murdered his father, but in doing so he has revealed his knowledge of this to the king, who will promptly take measures to counteract the threat posed by Hamlet to his security. It is soon reported that the king is 'marvellous distempered' (line 282) and the queen is 'in most great affliction of spirit' (line 291).

Useful quotes

> Give me that man
> That is not passion's slave, and I will wear him
> In my heart's core, ay, in my heart of heart,
> As I do thee.
>
> (Hamlet, lines 65–8)

> What should a man do but be
> merry? For look you how cheerfully my mother looks, and
> my father died within these two hours.
>
> (Hamlet, lines 114–16)

> Give me some light — away!
>
> (Claudius, line 253)

> O good Horatio, I'll take the ghost's word for a thousand
> pound.
>
> (Hamlet, lines 269–70)

> Soft, now to my mother.
> O heart, lose not thy nature; let not ever
> The soul of Nero enter this firm bosom;
> Let me be cruel, not unnatural.
> I will speak daggers to her, but use none
>
> (Hamlet, lines 366–70)

Questions ?

1 Why, do you think, has Hamlet chosen Horatio as the one person in whom he confides?

2 The play within the play is a vital part of the plot of *Hamlet*. Why is this so?

3 Describe Ophelia's role in this scene.

4 'The lady protests too much, methinks' (line 217). Explain Gertrude's comment.

5 After this scene the relationship between Claudius and Hamlet cannot be the same as it was before. Explain.

6 Consider the significance of Lucianus as representing (a) Hamlet; (b) Claudius.

7 Claudius and Gertrude react differently to the poisoning episode. Suggest reasons for this.

8 Hamlet tells Rosencrantz, 'I lack advancement' (line 318). What is he implying?

9 Hamlet suggests that the purpose of a play is to provide a mirror image of actual life so as to reveal the shape and appearance of virtue and folly in the world (lines 19–22). Say why you agree or disagree with this view.

10 Imagine you are a theatre critic. Write a review of the production of *The Murder of Gonzago* as performed before the king at Elsinore Castle.

Plot summary

Claudius decides to send Hamlet to England immediately. He will be escorted there by Rosencrantz and Guildenstern. Alone, Claudius reflects on what he has done, and tries to pray. He realises that he cannot win forgiveness for his crime unless he gives up the crown and Gertrude. He feels unable to do this, and therefore is unable to pray. Hamlet comes upon the kneeling Claudius and is tempted to kill him there and then. He fears this will send Claudius to heaven and decides to postpone the act of vengeance to a time when he can catch his uncle committing some evil act that will bring about his damnation.

I like him not, nor stands it safe with us
To let his madness range.

CLAUDIUS, Act 3, Scene 3, 1–2

Elsinore. A room in the castle.

Enter KING CLAUDIUS, ROSENCRANTZ and GUILDENSTERN.

KING CLAUDIUS

I like him not, nor stands it safe with us

To let his madness range. Therefore prepare you.

I your commission will forthwith dispatch,

And he to England shall along with you.

The terms of our estate may not endure   5

Hazard so near us as doth hourly grow

Out of his brows.

GUILDENSTERN

                    We will ourselves provide.

They completely agree with the king

Most holy and religious fear it is

To keep those many many bodies safe

That live and feed upon your majesty.   10

ROSENCRANTZ

The single and peculiar life is bound

With all the strength and armour of the mind

To keep itself from noyance; but much more

That spirit upon whose weal depends and rests

The lives of many. The cess of majesty   15

Dies not alone; but, like a gulf, doth draw

What's near it with it. It is a massy wheel,

Fixed on the summit of the highest mount,

To whose huge spokes ten thousand lesser things

Are mortised and adjoined; which, when it falls,   20

Each small annexment, petty consequence,

Attends the boisterous ruin. Never alone

Did the king sigh, but with a general groan.

KING CLAUDIUS

Arm you, I pray you, to this speedy voyage;

For we will fetters put upon this fear,   25

Which now goes too free-footed.

ROSENCRANTZ, GUILDENSTERN

We will haste us.

Exeunt ROSENCRANTZ and GUILDENSTERN.

Enter POLONIUS.

Not Hamlets true friends

POLONIUS

My lord, he's going to his mother's closet.

Behind the arras I'll convey myself

1–2 *I . . . range:* I don't like his conduct, nor is my life safe as long as I allow this madman free scope

3 *I . . . dispatch:* I shall have your official orders prepared on the spot

5–7 *The . . . brows:* my position as king will not survive the plots he is contriving, plots that originate in his head and that by the hour pose a greater threat to me

7 *ourselves provide:* get ourselves ready

8 *Most . . . is:* it is a sacred obligation

10 *upon:* at the expense of

11 *peculiar:* individual

13 *noyance:* harm
much more: it is even more important for
14 *weal:* welfare

15–16 *cess . . . alone:* death, or deposition, of a king is not a single death
16 *gulf:* whirlpool

17–20 *It . . . adjoined:* the king is like the Wheel of Fortune. Just as the wheel has subsidiary parts fixed ('mortised') to its spokes, so, too, the king and his subjects are intimately bound together

21–2 *small . . . ruin:* insignificant follower is part of the massive process of destruction

23 *general:* common, public

24 *Arm you:* get yourselves ready

25 *fetters . . . fear:* seek to control this dangerous threat

28 *closet:* private rooms
29 *Behind . . . myself:* I'll position myself stealthily behind the wall tapestry

30	*process:* proceedings
	I'll ... home: I'm certain she'll speak to him most severely
32	*meet:* appropriate
33	*nature ... partial:* mothers are naturally prejudiced in favour of their sons
34	*of vantage:* for benefit or profit; also from a good vantage point

30   To hear the process — I'll warrant she'll tax him home,

And as you said, and wisely was it said,

'Tis meet that some more audience than a mother,

Since nature makes them partial, should o'erhear

The speech of vantage. Fare you well, my liege.

35   I'll call upon you ere you go to bed,

And tell you what I know.

KING CLAUDIUS

Thanks, dear my lord.

Exit POLONIUS.

Kings soliloquy

O my offence is rank, it smells to heaven.

37	*rank:* foul

It hath the primal eldest curse upon't:

38	*primal eldest:* earliest, oldest. The first murder to be cursed by God was Cain's murder of his brother, Abel

A brother's murder! Pray can I not,

39	*brother's murder:* the audience now has absolute confirmation of Claudius's guilt
39–41	*Pray ... intent:* my desire to pray is as strong as my will to pray, and yet I cannot do so because my guilty feelings overpower my efforts
42–4	*to ... neglect:* with two duties to perform, I debate which one I should begin with, and end up performing neither

40   Though inclination be as sharp as will:

why doesnt he kill Hamlet – guilt

My stronger guilt defeats my strong intent;

And, like a man to double business bound,

I stand in pause where I shall first begin,

cant get forgiveness because he cant pray for it

And both neglect. What if this cursèd hand

45   Were thicker than itself with brother's blood,

Is there not rain enough in the sweet heavens

47–8	*Whereto ... offence?* What is the use of mercy unless it can come face to face with sin ('offence') and overcome it?

To wash it white as snow? Whereto serves mercy

insight into Claudius' mind

But to confront the visage of offence?

49–51	*this ... down:* the two main reasons for praying are to seek help in avoiding evil and to seek forgiveness if we have done evil, as in the Lord's Prayer: 'Lead us not into temptation, but deliver us from evil'
51	*up:* to heaven (for pardon)

And what's in prayer but this twofold force,

50   To be forestallèd ere we come to fall,

Or pardoned being down? Then I'll look up.

My fault is past. But O, what form of prayer

Guilt but not remorse

53	*serve my turn:* suit my circumstances

Can serve my turn? 'Forgive me my foul murder'?

That cannot be, since I am still possessed

– must feel up to what he has done

55	*effects:* gains

55   Of those effects for which I did the murder,

My crown, mine own ambition, and my queen.

May one be pardoned and retain th'offence?

57	*May ... th'offence?* May one expect forgiveness for a sin while still retaining the benefits and advantages gained by the sin?
58–61	*In ... law:* such is the corruption found in human affairs that a criminal can use the very proceeds ('prize') of his crime to bribe those in authority, and so escape justice
61	*above:* in heaven
62	*shuffling:* evasion, deceit
62–3	*the ... nature:* our deeds are exposed for what they are
63–5	*we ... evidence:* we must give evidence about our worst sins as we are confronted with them
65	*rests:* remains, is left for me to do
66	*Try ... not:* let me try what I can achieve by repenting, which ought to ensure forgiveness for any sin
67	*it:* repentance achieve

In the corrupted currents of this world

Offence's gilded hand may shove by justice,

60   And oft 'tis seen the wicked prize itself

Buys out the law. But 'tis not so above;

There, is no shuffling; there, the action lies

In his true nature; and we ourselves compelled,

Even to the teeth and forehead of our faults,

65   To give in evidence. What then? What rests?

Try what repentance can, what can it not?

Yet what can it, when one cannot repent?

O wretched state! O bosom black as death!

O limèd soul that, struggling to be free,

Art more engaged. Help, angels! Make assay!   70

Bow, stubborn knees; and, heart with strings of steel,

Be soft as sinews of the newborn babe!

All may be well.

Retires and kneels.

Enter HAMLET.

HAMLET [*aside*]

Now might I do it pat, now he is praying;

And now I'll do't, and so he goes to heaven,   75

And so am I revenged. That would be scanned:

A villain kills my father, and for that,

I, his sole son, do this same villain send

To heaven.

Why, this is hire and salary, not revenge.   80

He took my father grossly, full of bread,

With all his crimes broad blown, as flush as May,

And how his audit stands, who knows, save heaven?

But in our circumstance and course of thought,

'Tis heavy with him: and am I then revenged   85

To take him in the purging of his soul,

When he is fit and seasoned for his passage?

No.

Up, sword; and know thou a more horrid hent,

When he is drunk asleep, or in his rage,   90

Or in the incestuous pleasure of his bed,

At game, a-swearing, or about some act

That has no relish of salvation in't;

Then trip him, that his heels may kick at heaven,

And that his soul may be as damned and black   95

As hell, whereto it goes. My mother stays,

This physic but prolongs thy sickly days.

Exit.

KING CLAUDIUS

[*rising*] My words fly up, my thoughts remain below.

Words without thoughts never to heaven go.

Exit.

Handwritten annotations:

PRAYER SCENE

Dark imagery

Begging angels to help him pray

If you die while praying you go to heaven

Hamlet making sure he'll go to hell

Shows us the kind of King Claudius is

Is his excuse for not killing Claudius true?

Claudius' guilt & Hamlets hesitation

Appearance vs Reality

Marginal glosses:

69 *limèd:* caught in a trap with bird-lime

70 *engaged:* stuck
assay: a determined attempt

71 *with ... steel:* hardened by crime

74 *pat:* immediately

75 *I'll do't:* Hamlet draws his sword at this point

76 *scanned:* closely examined, interpreted

80 *hire and salary:* the action of a hired, paid assassin

81 *grossly ... bread:* shamefully unprepared for death (because he had been indulging his appetites)

82 *broad blown:* in full bloom

83 *audit:* final account with God

84–5 *But ... him:* from what it seems, his state is perilous

86–7 *take ... passage:* kill him when he is making his peace with God, and would die in a state of grace

89 *know ... hent:* wait for a more terrible occasion to be grasped again
hent: grip

92 *At game:* gambling

93 *relish:* taste

96 *stays:* is waiting

97 *physic:* medicine (Claudius's prayer, which has saved him from instant death, but cannot preserve his life much longer)

98–9 *My words ... go:* Claudius has failed in his attempt to make his peace with God

Key points

Hamlet's play has struck fear into Claudius. What was a family matter has become an affair that concerns the country and Hamlet is to be sent to England. Also in this scene, Hamlet has an opportunity to kill Claudius, but decides not to take it.

- Claudius makes immediate arrangements to have the official orders (the commission) prepared for Rosencrantz and Guildenstern to take Hamlet to England. Although it has been argued to the contrary, there is no evidence at this stage that these orders will contain a provision for Hamlet's execution by the English authorities as soon as he arrives. The king's anxiety is to get Hamlet out of Denmark. A plan to have him killed is not mentioned until later in the play.

- Through a soliloquy, this scene gives us a glimpse of the inner Claudius, the private man (lines 37–73). His struggles with his conscience, his guilt and his sense that he is trapped in a situation from which he cannot break free, all combine to make this his best moment in the play. It is probably the only occasion on which it is possible to feel pity for him.

- Just as this is the best moment for Claudius, it is Hamlet's worst. It is difficult to defend Hamlet's hope of finding a more damning occasion on which he will kill Claudius.

- Some commentators, who cannot imagine Hamlet meaning what he says here about Claudius, suggest that we are not to take his words seriously. They argue that Hamlet is not prepared to kill Claudius under any circumstances, whether he is praying or not, and is simply looking for a reason not to kill him. His claim that he will have to wait until Claudius is totally unprepared for death is thus to be seen as an excuse.

- Another reason given for Hamlet's failure to kill Claudius when he has him at his mercy is that his instincts revolt against stabbing a defenceless enemy in the back.

- However, historians of Elizabethan drama remind us that *Hamlet* is a revenge tragedy. In Shakespeare's time, revengers were expected to promote the damnation as well as the death of their victims, and to rejoice in this. We see this later when Laertes hopes fervently that the devil will take Hamlet's soul (Act 5, Scene 1, line 244).

- Like other tragedies, revenge tragedies have five Acts, and the deed of vengeance is reserved for the final Act. Shakespeare could not have allowed Hamlet to kill Claudius halfway through the play. Had he done so, the remaining scenes would have little point, and the play as a whole would lack the dramatic power of the *Hamlet* we have.

- Hamlet's decision not to kill Claudius in this scene is one of the profoundest ironies of the play. Hamlet spares him because he believes Claudius is in a state of grace; however, the truth is that Claudius is unable to pray. Hamlet is behaving as he does because he is a Christian; otherwise, he could take his vengeance without further thought, or without being able to offer the excuse he does here for postponing it.

And now I'll do't, and so he goes to heaven, And so am I revenged.

HAMLET, Act 3, Scene 3, 75–6

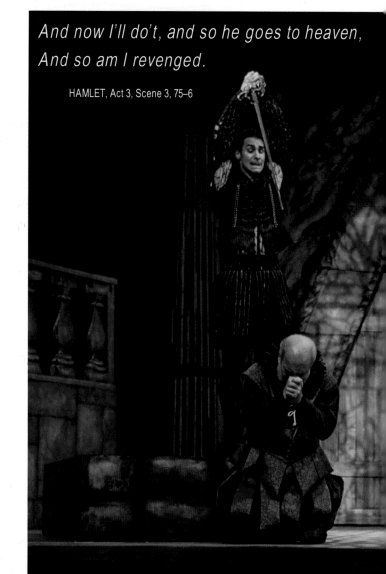

Useful quotes

> I like him not, nor stands it safe with us
> To let his madness range.
>
> (Claudius, lines 1–2)

> Pray can I not,
> Though inclination be as sharp as will:
> My stronger guilt defeats my strong intent
>
> (Claudius, lines 39–41)

> My lord, he's going to his mother's closet.
> Behind the arras I'll convey myself
> To hear the process …
> 'Tis meet that some more audience than a mother,
> Since nature makes them partial, should o'erhear
> The speech of vantage.
>
> (Polonius, lines 28–30, 32–4)

> Up, sword; and know thou a more horrid hent,
> When he is drunk asleep, or in his rage,
> Or in the incestuous pleasure of his bed …
> Then trip him, that his heels may kick at heaven,
> And that his soul may be as damned and black
> As hell, whereto it goes.
>
> (Hamlet, lines 89–91, 94–6)

> O my offence is rank, it smells to heaven.
> It hath the primal eldest curse upon't:
> A brother's murder!
>
> (Claudius, lines 37–9)

> My words fly up, my thoughts remain below.
> Words without thoughts never to heaven go.
>
> (Claudius, lines 98–9)

Questions ?

1 Rosencrantz and Guildenstern talk to Claudius about the sacredness, dignity and social importance of kingship. What, do you think, are their motives in talking to the king like this? Can you find any irony in their pronouncements?

2 Can you detect whether Claudius is pleased or not with the speeches of Rosencrantz and Guildenstern? Explain.

3 The play within the play enacted in the previous scene is already having two kinds of effect on Claudius. Comment on these.

4 In his prayer soliloquy (lines 37–73), Claudius is a very troubled man. What troubles him most?

5 Do you think Claudius is sincere in what he is saying? Explain.

6 Why does Claudius find it impossible to repent?

7 In what ways does the prayer scene provide us with a new and unexpected view of Claudius? Do his words make you feel any sympathy, pity or admiration for him?

8 What reason does Hamlet give for sparing Claudius? Explain why you do or do not think that this reason is genuine.

9 In what ways is the theme of the contrast between appearance and reality developed in this scene?

10 If you were asked to cast an actor to play the role of Claudius in a film version of Hamlet, what characteristics or features would you look for?

ACT 3 † Scene 4

Plot summary

Gertrude intends to chastise Hamlet. Polonius conceals himself behind an arras, or tapestry, in Gertrude's apartment, so that he can eavesdrop on the interview between Hamlet and Gertrude. Hamlet is determined to show his mother the error of her ways. Gertrude thinks her life may be in danger and calls for help. Polonius echoes her call from behind the arras and is stabbed to death by Hamlet, who does not know whom he has killed until he lifts up the arras.

The ghost appears, unseen throughout by Gertrude, accusing Hamlet of forgetting the duty of vengeance and pleading with him to help Gertrude in her inner struggle. Hamlet urges his mother to end her relationship with Claudius. Gertrude asks Hamlet for advice, and promises not to breathe a word of what he has said to her. He tells her that he does not trust Rosencrantz and Guildenstern, sensing that they have been appointed by Claudius to lead him into danger. He contemptuously drags the body of Polonius out of the apartment.

O Hamlet, speak no more.
Thou turn'st mine eyes into my very soul,
And there I see such black and grainèd spots
As will not leave their tinct.

GERTRUDE, Act 3, Scene 4, 88–91

Elsinore. The queen's apartment.

Enter QUEEN GERTRUDE and POLONIUS.

POLONIUS
He will come straight. Look you lay home to him,
Tell him his pranks have been too broad to bear with,
And that your grace hath screened and stood between
Much heat and him. I'll silence me even here.
Pray you be round with him.   5

HAMLET [*within*]
Mother, mother, mother!

QUEEN GERTRUDE
                      I'll warrant you,
Fear me not. Withdraw, I hear him coming.

POLONIUS hides behind the arras.

Enter HAMLET.

HAMLET
Now, mother, what's the matter?

QUEEN GERTRUDE
Hamlet, thou hast thy father much offended.

HAMLET
Mother, you have my father much offended.   10

QUEEN GERTRUDE
Come, come, you answer with an idle tongue.

HAMLET
Go, go, you question with a wicked tongue.

QUEEN GERTRUDE
Why, how now, Hamlet?

HAMLET
                        What's the matter now?

QUEEN GERTRUDE
Have you forgot me?

HAMLET
                      No, by the rood, not so!
You are the queen, your husband's brother's wife,   15
And, would it were not so, you are my mother.

QUEEN GERTRUDE
Nay, then, I'll set those to you that can speak.

1 *He . . . him:* he will come immediately; deal severely with him
2 *broad:* uncontrolled, unrestrained

4 *Much heat:* the anger of Claudius
   even: just
5 *round:* frank, plain-spoken

6 *warrant:* guarantee

9 *thy father:* Claudius

10 *my father:* King Hamlet

11 *idle:* foolish

14 *forgot me:* forgotten that you are speaking to your mother

14 *by the rood:* by Christ's cross (an oath)

16 *would:* I wish

17 *I'll . . . speak:* if you won't listen to what I have to say to you, I'll send for people who will be able to deal with you

19–20 *You... of you:* you will not move until I have held up a mirror ('glass') and shown you the depths of your soul. Hamlet may well be manhandling or restraining Gertrude as he speaks

21–2 *What ... ho!* Gertrude appears to have misunderstood what Hamlet proposes to do, and may be interpreting 'inmost part' quite literally

24 *rat:* treacherous individual
Dead ... ducat: I bet I've killed him (a ducat was a gold coin)
pass: thrust with his sword

30 *As ... king?* Gertrude's astonished question may be taken as proof that she was not involved in the murder of King Hamlet

30 *'twas my word:* that's what I said

32 *took ... better:* thought you were your master (i.e. Claudius)
33 *Thou ... danger:* you now know the risks involved in being a busybody
34 *Leave:* stop

36 *penetrable:* receptive, capable of being affected
37 *If ... so:* if wicked habits have not made it as hard as brass
38 *That ... sense:* to such an extent that it is now fortified against feeling

HAMLET

Come, come, and sit you down; you shall not budge;

You go not till I set you up a glass

20 Where you may see the inmost part of you.

QUEEN GERTRUDE

What wilt thou do? Thou wilt not murder me?

Help, help, ho!

POLONIUS [*behind the arras*]

What, ho! help, help, help!

HAMLET

[*draws his sword*] How now! A rat? Dead for a ducat, dead!

Makes a pass through the arras.

POLONIUS [*behind*]

O, I am slain!

Falls and dies.

QUEEN GERTRUDE

25   O me, what hast thou done?

HAMLET

Nay, I know not. Is it the king?

QUEEN GERTRUDE

O what a rash and bloody deed is this!

HAMLET

A bloody deed! Almost as bad, good mother,

As kill a king, and marry with his brother.

QUEEN GERTRUDE

As kill a king?

HAMLET

30   Ay, lady, 'twas my word.

Lifts up the arras and sees POLONIUS.

Thou wretched, rash, intruding fool, farewell!

I took thee for thy better. Take thy fortune;

Thou findest to be too busy is some danger.

[*to QUEEN GERTRUDE*] Leave wringing of your hands. Peace, sit you down,

35 And let me wring your heart, for so I shall,

If it be made of penetrable stuff,

If damnèd custom have not brazed it so

That it is proof and bulwark against sense.

QUEEN GERTRUDE

What have I done, that thou dar'st wag thy tongue

In noise so rude against me?

HAMLET

                Such an act   40

That blurs the grace and blush of modesty,

Calls virtue hypocrite, takes off the rose

From the fair forehead of an innocent love

And sets a blister there, makes marriage vows

As false as dicers' oaths. O such a deed   45

As from the body of contraction plucks

The very soul, and sweet religion makes

A rhapsody of words. Heaven's face does glow,

Yea, this solidity and compound mass,

With heated visage, as against the doom,   50

Is thought-sick at the act.

QUEEN GERTRUDE

                Ay me, what act,

That roars so loud, and thunders in the index?

HAMLET

Look here upon this picture, and on this,

The counterfeit presentment of two brothers.

See what a grace was seated on this brow: 55

Hyperion's curls, the front of Jove himself,

An eye like Mars to threaten and command,

A station like the herald Mercury

New-lighted on a heaven-kissing hill,

A combination and a form indeed,   60

Where every god did seem to set his seal

To give the world assurance of a man.

This was your husband. Look you now, what follows:

Here is your husband, like a mildewed ear,

Blasting his wholesome brother. Have you eyes?   65

Could you on this fair mountain leave to feed,

And batten on this moor? Ha! Have you eyes?

You cannot call it love; for at your age

The heyday in the blood is tame, it's humble,

And waits upon the judgement, and what judgement   70

Would step from this to this? Sense sure you have,

Else could you not have motion; but sure that sense

39–40 *thou … me:* you dare to scold me so unkindly

40–51 *Such… the act:* this may be paraphrased as: An act that stains your modesty, makes a mockery of your claims to virtue, spoils the original beauty of your love for your first husband, brands you as a harlot, and makes your marriage vows a sham like the oaths taken by gamblers. What you have done has deprived the marriage ceremony of its meaning, and turned its solemn religious language into a senseless jumble of words. The sky blushes above the earth, as though in anticipation of the Day of Judgement ('the doom'). It is sick with horror as it contemplates your crime

51–2 *what … index?* What kind of a deed can you be about to describe that can justify such a terrifying list of features?

53 *Look … on this:* Hamlet shows her two pictures; they may be hanging on the wall, or, more likely, Hamlet may be wearing a miniature portrait of his father and Gertrude one of Claudius

54 *counterfeit presentment:* representation in portrait form

55–62 *See … man:* Hamlet pictures his father as a man possessing the distinctive qualities of the major gods: the beauty of Hyperion (god of light), the forehead of Jove (king of the gods), the warlike capacity of Mars, and the graceful movement of Mercury (god of communication and travel). A human image so invested with godlike qualities as to constitute the ideal man

64–5 *mildewed … brother:* rotten ear of corn infecting or blighting ('Blasting') the healthy ears around it. There is a reminder here of the poisoning through the ear that ended King Hamlet's life

66 *leave:* cease

67 *batten:* fatten

69–70 *heyday … the judgement:* wild passions of youth have subsided and are submissive, obeying reason

71 *Sense:* the five senses

72 *motion:* the power of movement

73 *apoplexèd:* paralysed

73–6 *for ... difference:* even if you were mad, your senses would not have been so overpowered ('thralled') that you would fail to retain some ability to discriminate between two radically different men

77 *cozened ... hoodman-blind:* cheated you into picking the first man that came to hand, as if you were playing blind man's buff

79 *sans all:* without all the other senses

81 *so mope:* act so mistakenly (even if she was defective in all but part of one of her five senses)

82–5 *Rebellious ... fire:* if a middle-aged woman can surrender, as you have, to the flames of passion, young hot-blooded people may as well give up the idea of preserving their virtue

85–8 *Proclaim ... will:* there is no point in condemning the young if the force of their passions attack them, when we find their elders ('frost') giving way to similar passions, and allowing their reason to put itself at the service of self-indulgence

90 *black ... spots:* dark and ingrained sins (presumably including the adultery Hamlet has accused her of)

91 *will ... tinct:* cannot have their stains removed

92 *enseamèd:* greasy

93 *Stewed:* bathed, steeped

94 *sty:* Hamlet is picturing Gertrude and Claudius as pigs

97 *the tithe:* of the tenth part

98 *precedent lord:* first husband
vice of kings: king who is both a villain and a clown. Vice was a character in morality plays, and was the clownish ally of the devil

99–101 *A ... pocket:* like a petty criminal, he stole the kingdom, the royal authority and the crown ('diadem') furtively (as 'from a shelf'), not having the courage to take it by force

99 *cutpurse:* thief who steals purses by cutting them away from the belt to which they are attached

Is apoplexed; for madness would not err,

Nor sense to ecstasy was ne'er so thralled

75 But it reserved some quantity of choice

To serve in such a difference. What devil was't

That thus hath cozened you at hoodman-blind?

Eyes without feeling, feeling without sight,

Ears without hands or eyes, smelling sans all,

80 Or but a sickly part of one true sense

Could not so mope.

O shame, where is thy blush? Rebellious hell,

If thou canst mutine in a matron's bones,

To flaming youth let virtue be as wax

85 And melt in her own fire. Proclaim no shame

When the compulsive ardour gives the charge,

Since frost itself as actively doth burn,

And reason panders will.

QUEEN GERTRUDE
　　　　　　O Hamlet, speak no more.

Thou turn'st mine eyes into my very soul,

90 And there I see such black and grainèd spots

As will not leave their tinct.

HAMLET
　　　　　　　　Nay, but to live

In the rank sweat of an enseamèd bed,

Stewed in corruption, honeying and making love

Over the nasty sty—

QUEEN GERTRUDE
　　　　　O speak to me no more.

95 These words, like daggers, enter in mine ears.

No more, sweet Hamlet.

HAMLET
　　　　　　A murderer and a villain,

A slave that is not twentieth part the tithe

Of your precedent lord, a vice of kings,

A cutpurse of the empire and the rule,

100 That from a shelf the precious diadem stole,

And put it in his pocket—

QUEEN GERTRUDE
　　　　　　No more!

[handwritten margin notes:] Gertrude very easy to manipulate

Hamlet said "I will speak daggers"

comparing physical relationship to pigs in a stir

HAMLET

A king of shreds and patches— *[handwritten: cruel side of Hamlet]*

Enter GHOST.

Save me, and hover o'er me with your wings,

You heavenly guards! What would your gracious figure?

QUEEN GERTRUDE

Alas, he's mad!   105

HAMLET

Do you not come your tardy son to chide,

That, lapsed in time and passion, lets go by

The important acting of your dread command?

O say!

GHOST

Do not forget. This visitation   110

Is but to whet thy almost blunted purpose.

But look, amazement on thy mother sits,

O step between her and her fighting soul,

Conceit in weakest bodies strongest works,

Speak to her, Hamlet.   115

HAMLET

How is it with you, lady?

QUEEN GERTRUDE

Alas, how is't with you, *[handwritten: Gertrude cannot see the ghost]*

That you do bend your eye on vacancy

And with the incorporal air do hold discourse?

Forth at your eyes your spirits wildly peep,   120

And, as the sleeping soldiers in th'alarm,

Your bedded hair, like life in excrements,

Start up and stand on end. O gentle son,

Upon the heat and flame of thy distemper

Sprinkle cool patience. Whereon do you look?   125

HAMLET

On him, on him! Look you, how pale he glares!

His form and cause conjoined, preaching to stones

Would make them capable. Do not look upon me;

Lest with this piteous action you convert

My stern effects. Then what I have to do   130

Will want true colour, tears perchance for blood.

---

102 *shreds and patches:* poor and ill-matching qualities, or dressed like a fool (i.e. a clown)

103–4 *Save ... figure:* Hamlet is addressing the ghost

104 *would:* is your wish

105 *Alas, he's mad!* Gertrude does not see the ghost

106 *tardy:* slow, lazy, procrastinating
chide: rebuke, scold

107 *lapsed ... passion:* having allowed time to pass and passion to cool

107–8 *lets ... command:* defers the urgent performance of your solemn order

111 *whet:* sharpen, encourage

112 *amazement:* bewilderment

114 *Conceit:* imagination

118 *bend ... vacancy:* turn your attention to empty space

119 *with ... discourse:* converse with the bodiless air

120 *Forth ... peep:* you look astonished
Forth at: out of

121–3 *And ... end:* your hair is standing on end, like sleeping soldiers who were suddenly aroused from their beds by the call to arms and who now stand to attention

122 *like ... excrements:* as if these outgrowths of hair had a life of their own

124 *distemper:* illness; here, raging madness

127–8 *His ... capable:* his outward appearance ('form') and the reason for his visit ('cause') would together make even stones respond with feeling to his words

129–30 *this ... effects:* these pitiful gestures you turn aside the grim deeds I intend to perform

131 *want ... blood:* lack its properly bloody character, by causing him to shed his own tears instead of the blood of Claudius

134 *all that is:* everything that is here

138 *in . . . lived:* wearing the clothes he did when he was alive
139 *portal:* door

140–42 *the . . . in:* mere invention on your part; madness ('ecstasy') is very accomplished at this kind of hallucination

143 *temperately:* steadily, calmly

145–7 *bring . . . from:* try me out, and I will repeat what I have said, something a madman would shy away ('gambol') from

148–9 *Lay . . . speaks:* do not try to ease your conscience or soothe your soul by telling yourself that what is now at issue is not your sin but my madness
148 *unction:* a soothing oil or ointment
150–52 *It . . . unseen:* if you neglect your real problem, which is your sinful state, you will be like someone applying an ointment that covers up a sore but does not heal it. Meanwhile, the infection will be working away untreated

154 *weeds:* Gertrude's sinful habits. He is telling her that if she persists in her association with her husband, she will be making a bad situation worse
155 *ranker:* more luxuriant and foul smelling
155–8 *Forgive . . . good:* forgive me for taking such a self-righteous tone with you; however, in times like these, remarkable for their grossness and moral degeneracy, good people are obliged to bow and beg ('curb and woo') in order to be allowed to help sinners to reform

QUEEN GERTRUDE
To whom do you speak this?

HAMLET
Do you see nothing there?

QUEEN GERTRUDE
Nothing at all; yet all that is, I see.

HAMLET
135 Nor did you nothing hear?

QUEEN GERTRUDE
No, nothing but ourselves.

HAMLET
Why, look you there! Look how it steals away!

My father in his habit as he lived.

Look, where he goes, even now, out at the portal.

Exit GHOST.

QUEEN GERTRUDE
140 This is the very coinage of your brain!

This bodiless creation ecstasy

Is very cunning in.

HAMLET
          Ecstasy?

My pulse, as yours, doth temperately keep time,

And makes as healthful music. It is not madness

145 That I have uttered; bring me to the test,

And I the matter will re-word, which madness

Would gambol from. Mother, for love of grace,

Lay not that flattering unction to your soul

That not your trespass but my madness speaks:

150 It will but skin and film the ulcerous place,

Whiles rank corruption, mining all within,

Infects unseen. Confess yourself to heaven.

Repent what's past; avoid what is to come;

And do not spread the compost on the weeds

155 To make them ranker. Forgive me this my virtue;

For in the fatness of these pursy times

Virtue itself of vice must pardon beg,

Yea, curb and woo for leave to do him good.

QUEEN GERTRUDE

O Hamlet, thou hast cleft my heart in twain.

HAMLET

O throw away the worser part of it,   160

And live the purer with the other half.

Good night, but go not to mine uncle's bed.

Assume a virtue, if you have it not.

That monster, custom, who all sense doth eat,

Of habits devil, is angel yet in this,   165

That to the use of actions fair and good

He likewise gives a frock or livery

That aptly is put on. Refrain tonight,

And that shall lend a kind of easiness

To the next abstinence; the next more easy;   170

For use almost can change the stamp of nature,

And either lodge the devil, or throw him out

With wondrous potency. Once more, good night,

And when you are desirous to be blest,

I'll blessing beg of you. For this same lord,   175

Points to POLONIUS.

I do repent; but heaven hath pleased it so,

To punish me with this, and this with me,

That I must be their scourge and minister.

I will bestow him, and will answer well

The death I gave him. So, again, good night.   180

I must be cruel only to be kind.

This bad begins, and worse remains behind.

One word more, good lady.

QUEEN GERTRUDE

                    What shall I do? — *weakness*

HAMLET

Not this, by no means, that I bid you do.   *Hamlet*

Let the bloat king tempt you again to bed,   *doesn't*   185

Pinch wanton on your cheek, call you his mouse,   *trust her*

And let him for a pair of reechy kisses,

Or paddling in your neck with his damned fingers,

Make you to ravel all this matter out,

That I essentially am not in madness,   190

But mad in craft. 'Twere good you let him know.

(handwritten note: if you...do this Ill restore my faith in you)

---

159 *cleft ... twain:* broken my heart in two

163 *Assume ... not:* if you have no self-control, acquire some, and practise it from now on

164–8 *That ... on:* habit ('custom') works in two ways: it can blind us to the evil of what we do from day to day, or it can confirm us in good practices that become easier to maintain with time

171–3 *For ... potency:* habit and custom can almost change the nature of a person, either confirming wicked tendencies ('lodge the devil') or eliminating them ('throw him out') with extraordinary effectiveness ('potency')

174–5 *And ... of you:* when you have repented and thereby earned God's blessing, I will ask you for your blessing. His duty to her depends on her proper behaviour

175 *this same lord:* Polonius

177 *with this:* by permitting me to slay Polonius (and so get myself into serious trouble)
and ... me: while at the same time I have been permitted to punish Polonius

178 *their ... minister:* the heavens' instrument of vengeance ('scourge') and executer of justice on the wicked ('minister')

179 *bestow:* dispose of
answer well: atone for, account for

182 *This ... behind:* the killing of Polonius ('This') is a bad beginning, but there is worse to come

184 *Not ... do:* whatever you do, do not do what I am now going to tell you to do

185 *bloat:* bloated

186 *Pinch wanton:* express his endearment by leaving pinch marks
mouse: a term of affection

187 *reechy:* filthy

188 *paddling:* playing lecherously

189–91 *Make ... craft:* persuade you to reveal the important information ('matter') I have given you, namely that I am not really mad, but am cunningly pretending to be so ('mad in craft')

191 *'Twere ... know:* Hamlet is being sarcastic

For who that's but a queen, fair, sober, wise,

Would from a paddock, from a bat, a gib,

Such dear concernings hide? Who would do so?

195   No, in despite of sense and secrecy,

Unpeg the basket on the house's top.

Let the birds fly, and like the famous ape,

To try conclusions, in the basket creep

And break your own neck down.

QUEEN GERTRUDE

200   Be thou assured, if words be made of breath,

And breath of life, I have no life to breathe

What thou hast said to me.

HAMLET

I must to England. You know that?

QUEEN GERTRUDE

                         Alack,

I had forgot, 'tis so concluded on.

HAMLET

205   There's letters sealed: and my two schoolfellows,

Whom I will trust as I will adders fanged,

They bear the mandate; they must sweep my way,

And marshal me to knavery. Let it work.

For 'tis the sport to have the engineer

210   Hoist with his own petar: and 't shall go hard

But I will delve one yard below their mines,

And blow them at the moon. O 'tis most sweet,

When in one line two crafts directly meet.

This man shall set me packing.

215   I'll lug the guts into the neighbour room. *shows disrespect*

Mother, good night indeed. This counsellor

Is now most still, most secret, and most grave,

Who was in life a foolish prating knave.

Come, sir, to draw towards an end with you.

220   Good night, mother.

Exeunt severally; HAMLET dragging POLONIUS.

---

193   *paddock:* toad
      gib: tomcat

194   *dear concernings:* matters of importance

195–9   *No ... down:* Hamlet reminds his mother of a well-known story about an ape that, having released some birds from a basket and observed their power to fly, tried to imitate them to see what would happen, and so crashed to the ground from a housetop, breaking its neck. Hamlet is warning Gertrude not to disclose his secret to Claudius if she wants to avoid disaster for herself

203   *Alack:* an expression of regret, sorrow

205   *my two schoolfellows:* Rosencrantz and Guildenstern

206   *as ... fanged:* as one might trust poisonous snakes

207   *bear the mandate:* carry the royal orders

207–8   *must ... knavery:* have been appointed to escort me into danger

208   *Let it work:* let them do their utmost

209–10   *For ... petar:* it is the best kind of game to have a maker of military devices blown into the air by his own bomb or mine ('petar')

210–12   *and't ... moon:* I shall consider myself unfortunate if I cannot dig ('delve') a tunnel and place an explosive charge under theirs, and blow them into the air. In other words, Hamlet is confident that he can somehow outwit them

213   *in ... meet:* two clever plots ('crafts') meet head on

214   *This ... packing:* Polonius will be responsible for having me sent off to England

215   *neighbour:* next

216–18   *This ... knave:* now that he is dead, Polonius has been transformed into an ideal counsellor – silent, grave and discreet, all attributes he lacked while he lived. There is an obvious pun on 'grave'

219   *draw ... you:* to finish my business with you and to end discussion of you. He is also thinking of the fact that this is the end of Polonius, and that he is about to draw his body across the stage
      severally: separately, in different directions

Key points

Hamlet forces Gertrude to see the truth about Claudius. In the process, Hamlet also stabs Polonius to death, an event that will have disastrous consequences for many of the characters.

- The interview between Hamlet and Gertrude takes an ironic twist almost as soon as it begins. She intends to rebuke him, but it is she who has to endure chastisement of a kind she can never have expected.

- It is possible to detect a number of motives for Hamlet's sustained outburst against Gertrude: (a) he is disgusted by her suspected adulterous affair with Claudius during the lifetime of her late husband; (b) he is appalled by her incestuous marriage to Claudius, a man he hates; (c) he feels that it is indecent for a middle-aged widow to give way to her feelings as she has done; and (d) he is fulfilling the ghost's command not to let 'the royal bed of Denmark be a couch for luxury and damned incest' (Act 1, Scene 5, lines 82–3).

- Gertrude does not appear to have known that Claudius murdered her first husband. For Hamlet, however, the fact that she married the murderer, even if unwittingly, is morally no different from complicity in the murder.

- Polonius is the unintended victim of Hamlet's anger. Hamlet stabs him to death through a tapestry, hoping he is killing Claudius. From the point of view of the plot, the death of Polonius is the single most significant moment, since it will have fateful consequences for Hamlet. All the subsequent deaths in the play will be largely a consequence of Hamlet's brief moment of rashness in killing Polonius.

- The slaying of Polonius is in obvious contrast to the sparing of Claudius in the previous scene. Hamlet is able to perform this 'rash and bloody deed' (line 27) because he does not have any time to think about it. It is significant that he thought he was killing Claudius. Hamlet realises that this act will inevitably have tragic consequences (line 182).

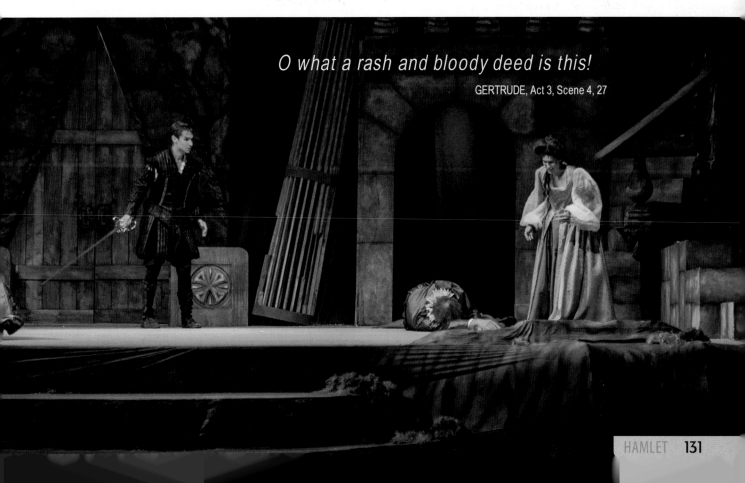

O what a rash and bloody deed is this!

GERTRUDE, Act 3, Scene 4, 27

Useful quotes

> Look you lay home to him,
> Tell him his pranks have been too broad to bear
>
> (Polonius, lines 1–2)

> O shame, where is thy blush? Rebellious hell,
> If thou canst mutine in a matron's bones,
> To flaming youth let virtue be as wax
> And melt in her own fire.
>
> (Hamlet, lines 82–5)

> Mother, you have my father much offended.
>
> (Hamlet, line 10)

> Thou wretched, rash, intruding fool, farewell!
> I took thee for thy better.
>
> (Hamlet, lines 31–2)

> O Hamlet, speak no more.
> Thou turn'st mine eyes into my very soul,
> And I see there such black and grainèd spots
> As will not leave their tinct.
>
> (Gertrude, lines 88–91)

> Here is your husband, like a mildewed ear,
> Blasting his wholesome brother.
>
> (Hamlet, lines 64–5)

> Do not forget. This visitation
> Is but to whet thy almost blunted purpose.
>
> (Ghost, lines 110–11)

? Questions

1 'I'll silence me even here. Pray you be round with him' (lines 4–5). There is a double irony here. Explain.

2 Hamlet feels that he has a task to perform in this scene. What is the nature of this task? Does he succeed in performing it?

3 What use does Gertrude hope to make of her interview with Hamlet?

4 Discuss the mother–son relationship depicted in this scene.

5 What effect has the ghost on Hamlet's treatment of Gertrude?

6 Does Hamlet regard the death of Polonius as a mere accident? Give evidence from the scene in support of your answer.

7 Hamlet says he repents for the killing of Polonius (line 176). Discuss whether or not he is sincere.

8 How is Hamlet feeling at the end of this scene? Do you think he is satisfied with what he has done? Give reasons for your answers.

9 Is it surprising that Hamlet does not tell Gertrude all the ghost told him in Act 1, Scene 5 about the circumstances of his death? Can you think of any good reason why Hamlet is silent about this?

10 Imagine you are Gertrude. Compose a diary entry in which you write about the events of this scene and how you feel about Claudius and about Hamlet as a result.

Elsinore. Another room in the castle.

Enter HAMLET.

HAMLET

Safely stowed.

ROSENCRANTZ, GUILDENSTERN [*within*]

Hamlet! Lord Hamlet!

HAMLET

What noise? Who calls on Hamlet? O here they come.

Enter ROSENCRANTZ, GUILDENSTERN, and ATTENDANTS.

ROSENCRANTZ

What have you done, my lord, with the dead body?

HAMLET

Compounded it with dust, whereto 'tis kin.   5

5 *Compounded . . . kin:* mingled it with the dust to which it is related

ROSENCRANTZ

Tell us where 'tis, that we may take it thence

And bear it to the chapel.

6 *thence:* from there

7 *bear:* carry

HAMLET

Do not believe it.

8 *Do . . . it:* Hamlet changes the subject

ROSENCRANTZ

Believe what?

HAMLET

That I can keep your counsel and not mine own. Besides,   10

to be demanded of a sponge, what replication should be

made by the son of a king?

10 *counsel:* secret. Their main secret, which Hamlet has not betrayed to Claudius, is their admission that they were 'sent for' (Act 2, Scene 2, line 281). His own secret is the location of the body of Polonius

11 *demanded of:* questioned by

replication: reply

ROSENCRANTZ

Take you me for a sponge, my lord?

HAMLET

Ay, sir, that soaks up the king's countenance, his rewards,

his authorities. But such officers do the king best service in   15

the end: he keeps them, like an ape an apple in the corner

of his jaw; first mouthed to be last swallowed. When he

needs what you have gleaned, it is but squeezing you,

and, sponge, you shall be dry again.

14 *countenance:* favour

15 *authorities:* influence and power

officers: servants

17 *mouthed:* taken into the mouth

18 *gleaned:* acquired, gathered

18–19 *it . . . again:* he squeezes it out of you, and you are left with nothing

ROSENCRANTZ

I understand you not, my lord.   20

21 *a knavish ... ear*: an unintelligent person like yourself cannot be expected to understand a clever, sarcastic speech like the one I have made

22–5 *My ... with the body*: Rosencrantz tells Hamlet to reveal where the body is and then to go under escort to the king. But Hamlet pretends to think that Rosencrantz means: 'You must come to where the body and the king are.' He replies that the corpse of Polonius is in the king's palace, but the king is not yet another corpse like Polonius

25 *The ... thing*: Hamlet is probably echoing a verse from Psalm 144: 'Man is a thing of nought. His time passeth away like a shadow.' In other words, the king's days are numbered

27 *Of nothing*: a thing of no importance
Hide ... after: let's play hide-and-seek. Hamlet runs away as he speaks, the others following

HAMLET

I am glad of it: a knavish speech sleeps in a foolish ear.

ROSENCRANTZ

My lord, you must tell us where the body is, and go with us to the king.

HAMLET

The body is with the king, but the king is not with the body. The king is a thing—

[handwritten: Claudius' kingship goes against God]

25

GUILDENSTERN

A thing, my lord?

HAMLET

Of nothing: bring me to him. Hide fox, and all after.

Exeunt.

[handwritten: Rosencrantz is not very clever]

Key points

Hamlet, knowing that he cannot trust Rosencrantz and Guildenstern, uses his 'antic disposition' to make them feel foolish.

- Now that Hamlet is almost an outlaw, Rosencrantz and Guildenstern feel that they have the upper hand. They soon find out how mistaken they are.

- Hamlet is far too clever for them and makes them feel utterly foolish. When they ask straight questions, he refuses to give them straight answers, or any answers at all. When, for example, Rosencrantz asks what Hamlet has done with the body, he tells them he has 'compounded it with dust' (line 5), meaning that he has sent Polonius to his death (ashes to ashes, dust to dust).

- Hamlet changes the subject to remind Rosencrantz that any benefits his corrupt servants manage to soak up are liable to be squeezed out of them again by the unscrupulous Claudius. In the end they will have served Claudius much better than they served themselves, and they will be left with nothing.

- Hamlet proceeds to speak in riddles, such as 'The body is with the king, but the king is not with the body' (lines 24–5). Hamlet is fond of such word play, which is a sign of his intelligent and reflective character. He often uses language as a weapon. Here, his words make no sense to Rosencrantz, but this does not bother Hamlet, whose purpose is to make him feel foolish.

- Finally, Hamlet runs off, making the others chase after him. The result on stage can have a macabre aspect, as Rosencrantz and Guildenstern lead a hue and cry by torchlight through the darkened castle in pursuit of Hamlet, and in search of the dead body of Polonius, which they must convey to the chapel.

Useful quote

> *When he needs what you have gleaned, it is but squeezing you, and, sponge, you shall be dry again.*
>
> (Hamlet, lines 17–19)

Questions ?

1 Explain Hamlet's attitude to Rosencrantz and Guildenstern.

2 Discuss whether Rosencrantz and Guildenstern deserve the treatment Hamlet metes out to them.

3 Hamlet behaves like a man who has lost his reason. Suggest why he does this.

4 Imagine you are Rosencrantz or Guildenstern. Write an account of the events of this scene.

Hide fox, and all after.

HAMLET, Act 4, Scene 2, 27

ACT 4 † Scene 3

Plot summary

Given what has happened to Polonius, Claudius fears for his own life. Rosencrantz informs him that Hamlet has been captured and waits outside under guard. Claudius sends for him and asks where the body of Polonius is. Hamlet uses his 'antic disposition' as a cloak to abuse his uncle. He indicates where the body may be found. Claudius informs Hamlet that he is being sent to England for his own safety. In a soliloquy, Claudius reveals his plan to have Hamlet put to death in England.

Follow him at foot; tempt him with speed aboard.
Delay it not; I'll have him hence tonight.

CLAUDIUS, Act 4, Scene 3, 52–3

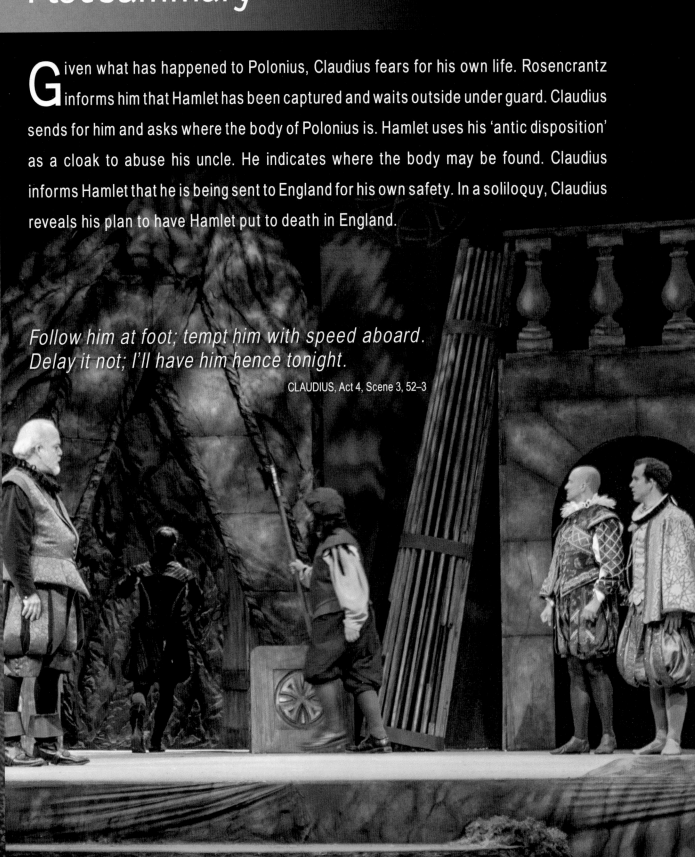

Elsinore. Another room in the castle.

Enter KING CLAUDIUS and ATTENDANTS.

KING CLAUDIUS

I have sent to seek him, and to find the body.

How dangerous is it that this man goes loose!

Yet must not we put the strong law on him: *Hamlet is beloved in Denmark*

He's loved of <u>the distracted multitude,</u>

Who like not in their judgement, but their eyes; 5

And where 'tis so, the offender's scourge is weighed,

But never the offence. To bear all smooth and even,

carefully considered This sudden sending him away must seem

<u>Deliberate pause.</u> Diseases desperate grown

By desperate appliance are relieved, 10

Or not at all.

Enter ROSENCRANTZ.

How now! What hath befall'n? *images of disease*

ROSENCRANTZ

Where the dead body is bestowed, my lord,

We cannot get from him.

KING CLAUDIUS

But where is he?

ROSENCRANTZ

Without, my lord; guarded, to know your pleasure.

KING CLAUDIUS

Bring him before us. 15

ROSENCRANTZ

Ho! Bring in the lord.

Enter HAMLET, GUILDENSTERN, and ATTENDANTS.

KING CLAUDIUS

Now, Hamlet, where's Polonius?

HAMLET

At supper.

KING CLAUDIUS

At supper? Where?

HAMLET

Not where he eats, but where he is eaten. A certain 20

convocation of politic worms are e'en at him. Your worm

Attendants: perhaps members of his council, but almost certainly his bodyguard

1 *to seek ... body:* people to find Hamlet and Polonius's body

2 *goes loose:* wanders freely

3 *strong law:* full rigours of the law, heaviest penalties

4 *of ... multitude:* by the irrational mob

5 *like ... eyes:* choose, not as a result of careful thought, but by outward appearances

6 *scourge:* punishment
 weighed: considered

7 *never the offence:* public opinion turns a blind eye to his offence
 bear ... even: avoid arousing opposition

8–9 *seem ... pause:* be made to appear the result of calm and careful consideration, not of panic

9–10 *Diseases ... relieved:* dangerous illnesses will be cured only by extreme remedies. Hamlet and the threat he represents to Claudius are here seen as diseases

11 *hath befall'n:* has happened

12 *bestowed:* hidden

14 *Without:* outside
 guarded: waiting under guard

20–21 *A ... him:* an assembly of crafty worms is at this very moment in session eating away at him

22–3 *is . . . maggots:* enjoys a better diet than any other creature: we fatten all sorts of animals in order to eat and make ourselves fat, so that after death our well-fed bodies will provide food for worms

23–5 *Your . . . table:* a well-fed king (like Claudius) and a skinny, half-starved beggar are merely different courses of the same meal that the worms will one day enjoy

30 *a progress:* on a formal royal journey

33 *send thither:* send someone there

34 *the other place:* hell

35 *nose:* smell

38 *stay:* wait

39 *thine especial:* your own

40 *do tender:* have a special regard for

43 *The . . . help:* the ship is waiting, and the wind is favourable

44–5 *The . . . England:* Rosencrantz and Guildenstern ('associates') are waiting, and everything is prepared for your voyage to England

---

is your only emperor for diet: we fat all creatures else to fat us, and we fat ourselves for maggots. Your fat king and your lean beggar is but variable service — two dishes, but

25 to one table — that's the end.

KING CLAUDIUS

Alas, alas!

HAMLET

A man may fish with the worm that hath eat of a king, and eat of the fish that hath fed of that worm.

KING CLAUDIUS

What dost thou mean by this?

HAMLET

30 Nothing but to show you how a king may go a progress through the guts of a beggar.

KING CLAUDIUS

Where is Polonius?

HAMLET

In heaven; send thither to see. If your messenger find him not there, seek him in the other place yourself. But if

35 indeed you find him not within this month, you shall nose him as you go up the stairs into the lobby.

KING CLAUDIUS

[*to ATTENDANTS*] Go seek him there.

HAMLET

He will stay till you come.

Exeunt some ATTENDANTS.

KING CLAUDIUS

Hamlet, this deed, for thine especial safety —

40 Which we do tender, as we dearly grieve

For that which thou hast done — must send thee hence

With fiery quickness. Therefore prepare thyself;

The bark is ready, and the wind at help,

The associates tend, and everything is bent

For England.

HAMLET

For England?

KING CLAUDIUS

Ay, Hamlet.

HAMLET

Good.　　　　　　　　　　　　　　　　　45

KING CLAUDIUS

So is it, if thou knew'st our purposes.

HAMLET

I see a cherub that sees them. But, come; for England!
Farewell, dear mother.

KING CLAUDIUS

Thy loving father, Hamlet.

HAMLET

My mother: father and mother is man and wife, man and　　50
wife is one flesh, and so: my mother. Come, for England!

Exit, attended.

KING CLAUDIUS

Follow him at foot; tempt him with speed aboard.
Delay it not; I'll have him hence tonight.
Away! For everything is sealed and done
That else leans on th'affair. Pray you make haste.　　　55

Exeunt all but KING CLAUDIUS.

And, England, if my love thou hold'st at aught —
As my great power thereof may give thee sense,
Since yet thy cicatrice looks raw and red
After the Danish sword, and thy free awe
Pays homage to us — thou mayst not coldly set　　　60
Our sovereign process; which imports at full,
By letters congruing to that effect,
The present death of Hamlet. Do it, England.
For like the hectic in my blood he rages,
And thou must cure me. Till I know 'tis done,　　　65
Howe'er my haps, my joys were ne'er begun.

Exit.

46　*So . . . purposes:* if you knew my reasons for sending you to England, you would approve

47　*a cherub:* an angel who is aware of everything, a guardian angel
48　*dear mother:* Claudius

52　*Follow . . . aboard:* stay close to him; encourage him to board the ship quickly
53　*hence:* away from here
54–5　*For . . . th'affair:* all the arrangements connected with this business have been completed

56　*England:* King of England
　　if . . . aught: if you place any value on my love
57　*As . . . sense:* since my great power may make you appreciate the importance of my love
58–9　*Since . . . sword:* since you still bear the battle-scars ('cicatrice') following your defeat by the Danes
59–60　*thy . . . us:* you continue to pay tribute to Denmark of your own free will
60　*coldly set:* undervalue
61　*sovereign process:* royal mandate
61–3　*imports . . . Hamlet:* contains full instructions, conveyed in letters, making it clear that my objective is the immediate ('present') death of Hamlet
62　*congruing:* agreeing
64　*hectic:* fever
65–6　*Till . . . begun:* whatever happens to me, I shall not be content until I learn that Hamlet is dead

[handwritten annotation:] It will reflect badly on Claudius if Hamlet is still in Denmark when Polonius is found

[handwritten annotation:] Cant rest until Hamlets dead

Key points

Hamlet is sent to England in this scene, and the audience learns that he will be put to death when he arrives there.

- Claudius shows his political nature when he reveals Hamlet's widespread popularity among the people and recognises that he must be seen to handle him sensitively.

- This scene contains some of the most macabre humour in the play and illustrates Hamlet's habit of dealing with profoundly serious topics using earthy and basic language. This time his topic is that death makes all men equal. He takes a morbid delight in choosing Claudius and Polonius as examples of how death humiliates even those who enjoyed power and prestige when alive. Polonius, he tells Claudius, is 'at supper' (line 18), where he is a dish being eaten by worms.

- Hamlet argues that people fatten animals in order to eat them, but they are really only fattening themselves for the worms that will eat them when they die. This line of argument enables Hamlet to degrade Claudius, telling him that kings will be at the same table as beggars when the worms dine on their remains.

- Hamlet offers Claudius an even more shocking and humiliating image of what death may have in store for him. A beggar might well eat a fish that had eaten a worm that had fed on a king's corpse, so that a bit of a king could go in a formal procession through that beggar's intestines.

- Claudius suggests that he is sending Hamlet to England for his 'especial safety' (line 39), with the best intentions in mind. Hamlet tells him that his guardian angel ('cherub'; line 47) is aware of all his uncle's intentions, which shows that he suspects Claudius of having sinister motives for sending him away.

- Hamlet's suspicions are immediately shown to be well founded. Claudius reveals that Rosencrantz and Guildenstern are carrying letters with orders for the King of England to have Hamlet put to death on his arrival.

- Claudius's decision to have Hamlet killed seems to be a hasty one, inspired by the thought that Hamlet meant to kill him, rather than Polonius.

Useful quotes

> How dangerous is it that this man goes loose!
> Yet must not we put the strong law on him:
> He's loved of the distracted multitude
>
> (Claudius, lines 2–4)

> Hamlet, this deed, for thine especial safety —
> Which we do tender, as we dearly grieve
> For that which thou hast done — must send thee hence
> With fiery quickness.
>
> (Claudius, lines 39–42)

? Questions

1 Discuss the instances of black humour in this scene.

2 Comment on Hamlet's behaviour as Claudius confronts him.

3 Does Hamlet deserve to be put to death in England? Give reasons for your answer.

4 Why does Claudius not have Hamlet's sentence of death for murder carried out in Denmark?

5 There is evidence in this scene that Claudius is a clever hypocrite. What is this evidence?

6 Imagine you are Claudius. Write the letter to the King of England in which you order him to have Hamlet killed.

Hamlet is on his way to the harbour, under guard. He meets a Norwegian army captain, who tells him about the expedition of Fortinbras to Poland. The object of the expedition is to capture a tiny patch of territory. Hamlet meditates on the contrast between Fortinbras and himself.

If that his majesty would aught with us,
We shall express our duty in his eye

FORTINBRAS, Act 4, Scene 4, 5–6

A plain in Denmark.

Enter FORTINBRAS with an army (CAPTAIN and SOLDIERS), marching over the stage.

[handwritten: the equivalent of Hamlet in Norway]

FORTINBRAS

Go, captain, from me greet the Danish king;

Tell him that, by his licence, Fortinbras

Craves the conveyance of a promised march

Over his kingdom. You know the rendezvous.

5   If that his majesty would aught with us,

We shall express our duty in his eye,

And let him know so.

[handwritten: looking for a safe passage across Denmark]

CAPTAIN

                              I will do't, my lord.

FORTINBRAS

[*to SOLDIERS*] Go softly on.

Exeunt all but CAPTAIN.

Enter HAMLET, ROSENCRANTZ, GUILDENSTERN, and ATTENDANTS.

HAMLET

Good sir, whose powers are these?

CAPTAIN

10   They are of Norway, sir.

HAMLET

How purposed, sir, I pray you?

CAPTAIN

Against some part of Poland.

HAMLET

Who commands them, sir?

CAPTAIN

The nephew to old Norway, Fortinbras.

HAMLET

15   Goes it against the main of Poland, sir,

Or for some frontier?

CAPTAIN

Truly to speak, and with no addition,

We go to gain a little patch of ground

That hath in it no profit but the name.

[handwritten: worthless piece of land]

Left margin glossary:

1   *captain:* an officer in the Norwegian army

2   *licence:* permission

3–4   *Craves . . . kingdom:* begs that his troops should be given safe passage through Denmark, as earlier agreed

4   *rendezvous:* prearranged meeting place

5–6   *If . . . eye:* should Claudius have any business with me, I will pay my respects to him personally ('in his eye')

8   *softly:* slowly, gently

9   *powers:* troops

11   *How purposed:* where are they marching to

14   *old Norway:* the elderly King of Norway

15–16   *Goes . . . frontier?* Is the army going to operate against Poland as a whole or against some outlying part?

17   *with no addition:* without exaggeration

19   *That . . . name:* its only value to us will lie in the fact that we will have the reputation of having conquered it

To pay five ducats, five, I would not farm it;   20

Nor will it yield to Norway or the Pole

A ranker rate, should it be sold in fee.

HAMLET

Why, then the Polack never will defend it.

CAPTAIN

Yes, it is already garrisoned.

HAMLET

Two thousand souls and twenty thousand ducats   25

Will not debate the question of this straw!

This is th'imposthume of much wealth and peace,

That inward breaks, and shows no cause without

Why the man dies. I humbly thank you, sir.

CAPTAIN

God buy you, sir.

Exit.

ROSENCRANTZ

               Will't please you go, my lord?   30

HAMLET

I'll be with you straight; go a little before.

Exeunt all but HAMLET.   SOLILOQUY

How all occasions do inform against me,

And spur my dull revenge! What is a man,

If his chief good and market of his time

Be but to sleep and feed? A beast, no more.   35

Sure He that made us with such large discourse,

Looking before and after, gave us not

That capability and godlike reason

To fust in us unused. Now, whether it be

Bestial oblivion, or some craven scruple   40

Of thinking too precisely on th'event —

A thought which, quartered, hath but one part wisdom

And ever three parts coward — I do not know

Why yet I live to say 'This thing's to do',

Sith I have cause, and will, and strength, and means   45

To do't. Examples gross as earth exhort me.

Witness this army of such mass and charge

Led by a delicate and tender prince,

---

20   *To . . . it:* I would not rent it from somebody to farm, even if the rent was only five ducats

22   *ranker . . . fee:* richer amount (than five ducats), even if it were sold outright

23   *Polack:* King of Poland

24   *garrisoned:* occupied by the defending army

26   *debate . . . straw:* decide the ownership of this worthless piece of land
27   *th'imposthume:* an abscess, an ulcer. Norway and Poland have enjoyed so much peace and prosperity that they have become corrupt
28–9   *inward . . . dies:* bursts inside, but there is no external evidence of its activity

30   *God buy you:* good bye to you

31   *straight:* straightaway, immediately
    before: ahead of me

32   *How . . . me:* it seems that all chance happenings discredit me
33   *spur:* urge on

34   *market . . . time:* the activity in which he employs his time

36–9   *Sure . . . unused:* surely God, who gave us our impressive reasoning powers, the capacity to contemplate the past as well as the future, did not intend such abilities to go rusty from lack of use

40   *Bestial oblivion:* the kind of forgetfulness one associates with animals
40–41   *craven . . . th'event:* cowardly doubt arising from thinking too carefully about the outcome
42–3   *A . . . coward:* my anxious doubts about the consequences of taking action are three-quarters due to cowardice and only one-quarter due to prudence
45   *Sith:* since

46   *gross:* obvious

47   *mass and charge:* size and cost

48   *delicate and tender:* sensitive and youthful

50	*Makes ... event:* displays contempt and indifference for the unforeseeable outcome
51–3	*Exposing ... eggshell:* risking his own life, and the lives of his men, and challenging fate, death and danger, in pursuit of a trivial prize
53–6	*Rightly ... stake:* a truly great man is not one who will fight ('stir') for every trivial cause, but one who will fight over a trifle when his honour is involved
58	*Excitements ... blood:* causes to excite both my reason and my passions
61	*a fantasy and trick:* an illusion and a trifle
62–3	*plot ... cause:* territory that is not big enough to hold all those who are fighting for it
64	*continent:* container, receptacle
65	*hide:* bury

> Whose spirit, with divine ambition puffed,
> 50 Makes mouths at the invisible event,
> Exposing what is mortal and unsure
> To all that fortune, death and danger dare,
> Even for an eggshell. Rightly to be great
> Is not to stir without great argument,
> 55 But greatly to find quarrel in a straw
> When honour's at the stake. How stand I then,
> That have a father killed, a mother stained,
> Excitements of my reason and my blood,
> And let all sleep? While, to my shame, I see
> 60 The imminent death of twenty thousand men,
> That, for a fantasy and trick of fame,
> Go to their graves like beds, fight for a plot
> Whereon the numbers cannot try the cause,
> Which is not tomb enough and continent
> 65 To hide the slain? O, from this time forth,
> My thoughts be bloody, or be nothing worth!
>
> *Exit.*

Key points

The outstanding feature of this scene is the soliloquy with which it ends. In this bitterly self-critical speech, Hamlet contrasts the vigorous activity of Fortinbras with his own inactivity.

- Fortinbras is the personification of the strong, unthinking man of action, who is prepared to risk the lives of thousands of soldiers 'for a fantasy and trick of fame' (line 61). Hamlet, with a much greater and nobler cause to fight for, remains the passive spectator of his own tardiness. Impressed, at least for the moment, by the spirited activity of Fortinbras, Hamlet resolves to perform bloody deeds.

- Hamlet is aware of the limitations of the military ideal that Fortinbras stands for. He finds it absurd that Fortinbras will go to war to gain what his own officer admits is 'a little patch of ground' (line 18) and what Hamlet calls 'this straw' (line 26). He observes that Norway and Poland have enjoyed so much peace and prosperity that they have become corrupt.

- Nevertheless, Hamlet contrasts his slowness to take action against Claudius with the energetic activity of Fortinbras, who is leading an army to invade a worthless piece of Polish territory. Hamlet rebukes himself and uses the example of Fortinbras to spur himself on to fulfil the task the ghost has given him. But can we be sure that Shakespeare is exalting Fortinbras at the expense of Hamlet?

I do not know
Why yet I live to say 'This thing's to do'

HAMLET, Act 4, Scene 4, 43–4

Useful quotes

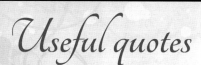

I do not know
Why yet I live to say 'This thing's to do',
Sith I have cause, and will, and strength, and means
To do't.

(Hamlet, lines 43–6)

How stand I then,
To have a father killed, a mother stained,
Excitements of my reason and my blood,
And let all sleep?

(Hamlet, lines 56–9)

Questions ?

1 Is Hamlet being fair to himself in his soliloquy (lines 32–66)? Give reasons for your answer.

2 On the evidence of this scene, which character do you admire more, Hamlet or Fortinbras? Give reasons for your answer.

3 If you were directing a theatrical production of *Hamlet*, would your choice of actors, costumes, etc. highlight the differences or the similarities between Hamlet and Fortinbras? Give reasons for your answer.

ACT 4 † Scene 5

Plot summary

Ophelia, completely insane, confronts Claudius and Gertrude, and sings love songs. Laertes, leading a rebellious army of followers, forces his way into the presence of Claudius and demands to know how his father died. Claudius calms him, and promises him satisfaction. Ophelia re-enters, singing and distributing flowers. Claudius again promises Laertes that his father's death will not go unpunished.

I cannot choose but weep to think they should lay him in the cold ground. My brother shall know of it.

OPHELIA, Act 4, Scene 5, 67–9

Elsinore. A room in the castle.

Enter QUEEN GERTRUDE, HORATIO and a GENTLEMAN.

QUEEN GERTRUDE

I will not speak with her.

GENTLEMAN

She is importunate, indeed distract:

Her mood will needs be pitied.

QUEEN GERTRUDE

What would she have?

GENTLEMAN

She speaks much of her father; says she hears   5

There's tricks i' th' world, and hems, and beats her heart,

Spurns enviously at straws, speaks things in doubt

That carry but half sense. Her speech is nothing,

Yet the unshapèd use of it doth move

The hearers to collection: they aim at it,   10

And botch the words up fit to their own thoughts;

Which, as her winks and nods and gestures yield them,

Indeed would make one think there might be thought,

Though nothing sure, yet much unhappily.

HORATIO   *Horatio is sensible*

'Twere good she were spoken with, for she may strew   15

Dangerous conjectures in ill-breeding minds.

QUEEN GERTRUDE

Let her come in.

Exit GENTLEMAN.

[*aside*] To my sick soul, as sin's true nature is,

Each toy seems prologue to some great amiss:

So full of artless jealousy is guilt,   20

It spills itself in fearing to be spilt.

Enter OPHELIA.

OPHELIA

Where is the beauteous majesty of Denmark?

QUEEN GERTRUDE

How now, Ophelia?

---

1 *her:* Ophelia

2 *importunate:* persistent
   distract: out of her mind
3 *mood:* state of mind

4 *What . . . have?* What does she want?

6 *hems:* sighs, says 'hmm'

7 *Spurns . . . straws:* is offended by the most trivial things
   speaks . . . doubt: says ambiguous things
9 *unshapèd:* formless, incoherent

10 *collection:* try to deduce meaning
10–11 *aim . . . thoughts:* interpret her words to suit their own idea of what she means
12 *yield:* enhance

13 *thought:* meaning

14 *much unhappily:* much of this meaning appears harmful

15–16 *strew . . . minds:* inspire dangerous speculations in the minds of mischief-makers

18–19 *To . . . amiss:* because my soul is sick from sin, I fear that every trivial event foretells some disaster

20–21 *So . . . spilt:* guilty people are so full of uncontrollable suspicion ('artless jealousy') that their fears about potential disasters cause them more misery than the disasters themselves would
21 *spills:* destroys, ruins

OPHELIA

[*sings*] How should I your true love know

25   From another one?

     By his cockle hat and staff,

     And his sandal shoon.

QUEEN GERTRUDE

Alas, sweet lady, what imports this song?

[handwritten note: Ophelia has gone mad because of Hamlet's actions]

OPHELIA

Say you? Nay, pray you mark.

30 [*sings*] He is dead and gone, lady,

     He is dead and gone.

     At his head a grass-green turf,

     At his heels a stone.

O, ho!

QUEEN GERTRUDE

     Nay, but, Ophelia—

OPHELIA

                   Pray you mark.

35 [*sings*] White his shroud as the mountain snow—

Enter KING CLAUDIUS.

QUEEN GERTRUDE

Alas, look here, my lord.

OPHELIA

[*sings*] Larded all with sweet flowers

     Which bewept to the grave did not go

     With true-love showers.

KING CLAUDIUS

40 How do you, pretty lady?

OPHELIA

Well, God dild you! They say the owl was a baker's daughter. Lord, we know what we are, but know not what we may be. God be at your table!

KING CLAUDIUS

Conceit upon her father—

OPHELIA

45 Pray let's have no words of this; but when they ask you what it means, say you this:

26–7   *By ... shoon:* the cockle-shell on the hat, the staff and the sandals are all associated with pilgrims. Lovers were often depicted as pilgrims worshipping at the shrine of the beloved

27   *shoon:* old plural of 'shoe'

28   *imports this song:* does this song mean

29   *mark:* observe, listen

38   *Larded:* covered, dressed

39   *bewept:* wept over, wet with tears

41   *dild:* reward, thank

41–2   *They ... daughter:* Ophelia is recalling a folktale in which a baker's daughter gave too little bread to Christ for the price paid, and was changed into an owl

43   *God ... table:* a hospitable greeting, but also a troubled reflection on the lack of hospitality shown by the baker's daughter when Christ called to her shop

44   *Conceit upon:* her thoughts (the song and her words) are inspired by

[*sings*] Tomorrow is Saint Valentine's day,

> All in the morning betime,
>
> And I a maid at your window,
>
> To be your Valentine.   50
>
> Then up he rose, and donned his clothes,
>
> And dupped the chamber door;
>
> Let in the maid, that out a maid
>
> Never departed more.

KING CLAUDIUS

Pretty Ophelia!   55

OPHELIA

Indeed, la, without an oath, I'll make an end on't:

[*sings*] By Gis and by Saint Charity,

> Alack and fie for shame!
>
> Young men will do't if they come to't;
>
> By Cock, they are to blame.   60
>
> Quoth she, 'Before you tumbled me,
>
> You promised me to wed.'

He answers:

> 'So would I ha' done, by yonder sun,
>
> An thou hadst not come to my bed.'   65

KING CLAUDIUS

How long hath she been thus?

OPHELIA

I hope all will be well. We must be patient, but I cannot
choose but weep to think they should lay him in the cold
ground. My brother shall know of it. And so I thank you for
your good counsel. Come, my coach! Good night, ladies,   70
good night. Sweet ladies, good night, good night.

Exit.

KING CLAUDIUS

Follow her close; give her good watch, I pray you.

Exit HORATIO.

O this is the poison of deep grief; it springs

All from her father's death — and now, behold!

O Gertrude, Gertrude!   75

When sorrows come, they come not single spies,

But in battalions. First, her father slain.

---

48 *betime:* early

49 *maid:* young woman, virgin

51 *donned:* put on

52 *dupped:* opened

56 *without … on't:* I'll finish the song without including the strong oaths
57 *By … Charity:* by Jesus and Holy Charity (Ophelia has substituted relatively mild oaths here)

59 *do't … to't:* have sex when the opportunity presents itself
60 *Cock:* God. This corruption was devised to avoid mentioning the name of God in an oath
61 *tumbled:* had sex with

65 *An thou:* if you

68 *choose but weep:* avoid weeping

70 *counsel:* advice

72 *Follow … watch:* go after her and keep an eye on her

76–7 *When … battalions:* troubles tend to come not singly, but all together

78–9 *he . . . remove:* his own violent behaviour was responsible for his being sent away

79 *muddied:* confused

80–81 *Thick . . . For:* harbouring dangerous suspicions, and indulging in malicious gossip about

81 *greenly:* foolishly

82 *In . . . him:* to bury Polonius secretly and in haste

83 *Divided . . . judgement:* she is no longer herself

84 *Without . . . beasts:* when we lose our judgement we are not true people

85 *much . . . these:* important as all of the threats or troubles facing us

87 *Feeds . . . clouds:* allows his bewilderment and uncertainty to grow

88–9 *wants . . . speeches:* does not lack whisperers to fill his ears with rumours and poisonous descriptions. This is ironic, given that Claudius killed King Hamlet by pouring poison into his ear

90–92 *Wherein . . . and ear:* facts may be scarce in the stories told to Laertes, and deprived of facts, they may not hesitate to accuse me of complicity in the death of Polonius, and pour their accusations into one ear after another

92–4 *this . . . death:* these troubles, like a cannon loaded not with a single ball but with shot that is able to scatter more widely, may kill me. 'Superfluous' suggests that any one of his troubles, like any one of the cannon-shots, would be enough to kill him

96 *Switzers:* Swiss guards (the king's bodyguard)

98–101 *The . . . officers:* Laertes and his rebellious armed followers are overpowering the king's soldiers, like a sea rising above its normal level ('list') and quickly flooding low-lying land

99 *impetuous:* violent

101 *rabble:* mob

102 *as . . . begin:* as if civilisation were only now being created

103 *Antiquity . . . known:* as if ancient tradition had been forgotten, and long-established norms of conduct had never been heard of

104 *ratifiers and props:* supporters

109 *counter:* the wrong path

Next, your son gone, and he most violent author

Of his own just remove; the people muddied,

80 Thick and unwholesome in their thoughts and whispers

For good Polonius' death — and we have done but greenly

In hugger-mugger to inter him — poor Ophelia

Divided from herself and her fair judgement,

Without the which we are pictures, or mere beasts.

85 Last, and as much containing as all these,

Her brother is in secret come from France,

Feeds on his wonder, keeps himself in clouds,

And wants not buzzers to infect his ear

With pestilent speeches of his father's death,

90 Wherein necessity, of matter beggared,

Will nothing stick our person to arraign

In ear and ear. O my dear Gertrude, this,

Like to a murdering-piece, in many places

Gives me superfluous death.

Noise within.

QUEEN GERTRUDE

Alack, what noise is this?

KING CLAUDIUS

95   Attend!

Enter ATTENDANT.

Where are my Switzers? Let them guard the door.

What is the matter?

ATTENDANT

                       Save yourself, my lord!

The ocean, overpeering of his list,

Eats not the flats with more impetuous haste

100 Than young Laertes, in a riotous head,

O'erbears your officers. The rabble call him lord;

And, as the world were now but to begin,

Antiquity forgot, custom not known,

The ratifiers and props of every word,

105 They cry: 'Choose we, Laertes shall be king!'

Caps, hands and tongues applaud it to the clouds:

'Laertes shall be king! Laertes king!'

Noise within.

QUEEN GERTRUDE — *avoids taking situations into her own hands*

How cheerfully on the false trail they cry!

O this is counter, you false Danish dogs!

ACT 4 ✝ Scene 6

Horatio gets a letter from Hamlet, describing his adventures since he left for England, and revealing that he is now back in Denmark. Hamlet wants Horatio first to arrange for letters to be delivered to Claudius and Gertrude, and second to come to meet him as soon as possible.

Let the king have the letters I have sent; and repair thou to me with as much speed as thou wouldest fly death.

HORATIO *(reading)*, Act 4, Scene 6, 20–21

Elsinore. Another room in the castle.

Enter HORATIO and an ATTENDANT.

HORATIO

What are they that would speak with me?

ATTENDANT

Sailors, sir. They say they have letters for you.

HORATIO

Let them come in.

Exit ATTENDANT.

I do not know from what part of the world

5   I should be greeted, if not from Lord Hamlet.

Enter SAILORS.

FIRST SAILOR

God bless you, sir.

HORATIO

Let Him bless thee, too.

FIRST SAILOR

He shall, sir, an't please Him. There's a letter for you, sir — it
came from th'ambassador that was bound for England —

10   if your name be Horatio, as I am let to know it is.

HORATIO

[*reads, aside*] 'Horatio, when thou shalt have overlooked
this, give these fellows some means to the king. They
have letters for him. Ere we were two days old at sea, a
pirate of very warlike appointment gave us chase. Finding

15   ourselves too slow of sail, we put on a compelled valour,
and in the grapple I boarded them. On the instant they
got clear of our ship; so I alone became their prisoner.
They have dealt with me like thieves of mercy; but they
knew what they did: I am to do a good turn for them.

20   Let the king have the letters I have sent; and repair thou
to me with as much speed as thou wouldest fly death. I
have words to speak in thine ear will make thee dumb; yet
are they much too light for the bore of the matter. These
good fellows will bring thee where I am. Rosencrantz and

25   Guildenstern hold their course for England; of them I have
much to tell thee. Farewell.

    He that thou knowest thine, Hamlet.'

---

5   *greeted:* have a letter addressed to me

8   *an't:* if it

9   *th'ambassador:* Hamlet (who must be claiming that he is on a diplomatic mission to England)

10   *let to know:* led to believe

11   *overlooked:* read

12   *means:* means of access

13   *Ere:* before

14   *pirate:* pirate ship
    appointment: appearance

15   *put ... valour:* were forced to put up a fight

16   *in ... them:* during the combat I boarded the pirate ship
    On the instant: at that moment

18   *thieves of mercy:* thieves acting like angels of mercy

19   *did:* were doing (i.e. that Hamlet might be of use to them)

20   *repair:* come

21   *thou ... death:* you would if you were trying to escape death

22   *speak ... dumb:* to tell you that will astonish you

23   *much ... matter:* unable to convey the terrible gravity of the case

25   *hold their course:* continue on their journey

Come, I will give you way for these your letters,
And do't the speedier that you may direct me
To him from whom you brought them. 30

Exeunt.

28 *give … letters:* provide you with the means of delivering your letters
29–30 *do't … them:* I will do this all the more quickly so that you may lead me to Hamlet

Key points

The news of Hamlet's return to Denmark raises the dramatic tempo, and the economical account of his adventures with the pirates will save explanation later when he appears in person.

- The tone of Hamlet's letter is upbeat. His escape from Rosencrantz and Guildenstern, or perhaps simply spending some time away from the royal court, appears to have energised him.

- Up to this point in the play, fate seemed to be working against Hamlet. His letter suggests that at last, in the guise of chance and accident, it may be working in his favour.

- Nevertheless, while Horatio is reading Hamlet's letter, Claudius is conferring elsewhere with Laertes and assuring him that Hamlet will soon be dead.

Questions ?

1 Hamlet's letter is an answer to those who think of him as an indecisive dreamer. Develop this idea.

2 Why, do you think, have the pirates treated Hamlet well?

3 Hamlet says he has something to tell Horatio that will shock him (line 22). What has he in mind here?

4 Hamlet tells Horatio to make sure the sailors have access to Claudius, since they have letters for him. Suggest what these letters may be about. Who has written them?

5 Do the events described in Hamlet's letter suggest that his luck may have changed? Explain your answer.

6 If you were making a film version of Hamlet, how might you handle this scene?

ACT 4 ✝ Scene 7

Plot summary

Claudius has convinced Laertes that Hamlet not only killed his father, but also wanted to kill Claudius. He did not take public action against Hamlet because it would hurt Gertrude, and turn public opinion against Claudius. A letter from Hamlet is delivered to Claudius. Hamlet promises to be in Elsinore on the following day. Claudius is puzzled, but proceeds to devise a plot, in collaboration with Laertes, against Hamlet's life. In a fencing match, which can easily be arranged, Claudius suggests that Laertes will use an unbated sword to kill Hamlet. Laertes adds a further deadly detail to the plan: he will poison the tip of his sword. Claudius, not to be outdone, will make the success of the plan even more certain by adding poison to the wine Hamlet will drink during the fencing match. Gertrude brings news of Ophelia's death by drowning. Laertes is grief-stricken.

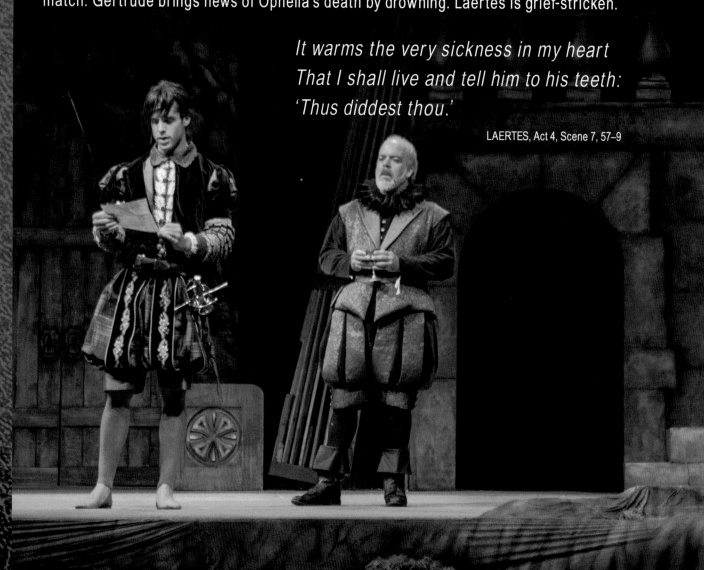

It warms the very sickness in my heart
That I shall live and tell him to his teeth:
'Thus diddest thou.'

LAERTES, Act 4, Scene 7, 57–9

Elsinore. Another room in the castle.

Enter KING CLAUDIUS and LAERTES.

KING CLAUDIUS
Now must your conscience my acquittance seal,
And you must put me in your heart for friend,
Sith you have heard, and with a knowing ear,
That he which hath your noble father slain
Pursued my life.

LAERTES
              It well appears. But tell me   5
Why you proceeded not against these feats
So crimeful and so capital in nature,
As by your safety, greatness, wisdom, all things else,
You mainly were stirred up.

KING CLAUDIUS
O for two special reasons,   10
Which may to you, perhaps, seem much unsinewed,
But yet to me they are strong. The queen his mother
Lives almost by his looks; and for myself —
My virtue or my plague, be it either which —
She's so conjunctive to my life and soul   15
That, as the star moves not but in his sphere,
I could not but by her. The other motive
Why to a public count I might not go
Is the great love the general gender bear him,
Who, dipping all his faults in their affection,   20
Would like the spring that turneth wood to stone,
Convert his gyves to graces; so that my arrows,
Too slightly timbered for so loud a wind,
Would have reverted to my bow again,
And not where I had aimed them.   25

LAERTES
And so have I a noble father lost;
A sister driven into desperate terms,
Whose worth, if praises may go back again,
Stood challenger on mount of all the age
For her perfections. But my revenge will come.   30

1 *Now . . . seal:* you must now be satisfied of my innocence
2 *put . . . friend:* think of me as a friend
3 *Sith:* since
  knowing ear: Claudius is flattering Laertes, telling him he (Laertes) is sufficiently intelligent to understand the meaning of what he has heard

6 *proceeded . . . feats:* did not take action in response to these evil deeds
7 *So . . . nature:* which were criminal to the point of meriting capital punishment
8–9 *by . . . up:* concern for your own safety and the preservation of your authority, not to mention other considerations, should have strongly ('mainly') encouraged you, in your wisdom, to do something

11 *unsinewed:* unconvincing, weak

14 *My . . . which:* whether this is a good thing or a bad thing in me
15 *conjunctive:* intimately linked
16 *as . . . sphere:* in Ptolemaic astronomy, each of the planets was carried around the earth by a revolving sphere. Claudius thinks of himself as a planet ('star') depending for his welfare on Gertrude (his 'sphere')
17 *but by her:* exist without Gertrude
18 *count:* trial (of Hamlet)
19 *general gender:* common people
20–22 *dipping . . . graces:* in their love for Hamlet, they would regard the fetters ('gyves') he wore while a prisoner as emblems of honour rather than of shame. The spring that turns wood to stone is an image of the people's power to transform a criminal into a hero, as Claudius sees it
22 *arrows:* legal action
23 *Too . . . wind:* would be totally ineffective in the face of strong public opinion

27 *terms:* circumstances

28–30 *Whose . . . perfections:* if one may think of Ophelia as she was, her virtues entitle her to be considered equal to any of her contemporaries
29 *on mount:* in an obvious way, for everybody to see

31 Break . . . that: do not lose any sleep over that

32 flat and dull: unenterprising and stupid

33–4 we . . . pastime: I can allow such menacing and insulting behaviour to occur so close to me and regard it as mere sport

34 shortly: Claudius is expecting news from England that Hamlet has been executed. What follows immediately (the message from the newly returned Hamlet) is bitterly ironic for Claudius

35 we love ourself: I love myself

44 Laertes . . . them: Claudius is taking Laertes fully into his confidence

45 High and mighty: this is a sarcastic form of address
naked: this can mean: (a) without belongings, destitute; (b) ready to confront you openly, without further concealment; or (c) carrying a drawn sword

47 your kingly eyes: you face to face

48 recount . . . of: relate to you the reason for

51 all the rest: especially Rosencrantz and Guildenstern

52 abuse: trick, deception

53 hand: handwriting

53 character: handwriting

55 devise: explain to

56 I'm . . . it: I have no idea of its significance

KING CLAUDIUS

Break not your sleeps for that. You must not think

That we are made of stuff so flat and dull

That we can let our beard be shook with danger

And think it pastime. You shortly shall hear more.

35   I loved your father, and we love ourself

And that, I hope, will teach you to imagine—

Enter a MESSENGER with letters.

How now? What news?

MESSENGER

Letters, my lord, from Hamlet:

These to your majesty; these to the queen.

KING CLAUDIUS

40   From Hamlet! Who brought them?

MESSENGER

Sailors, my lord, they say; I saw them not.

They were given me by Claudio. He received them

Of him that brought them.

KING CLAUDIUS

Laertes, you shall hear them. [*to MESSENGER*] Leave us.

Exit MESSENGER.

45   [*reads*] 'High and mighty, You shall know I am set naked on your kingdom. Tomorrow shall I beg leave to see your kingly eyes, when I shall (first asking your pardon thereunto) recount the occasion of my sudden and more strange return.

50   Hamlet.'

What should this mean? Are all the rest come back?

Or is it some abuse, and no such thing?

LAERTES

Know you the hand?

KING CLAUDIUS

                    'Tis Hamlet's character.

'Naked'! And in a postscript here, he says:

55   'Alone'. Can you devise me?

LAERTES

I'm lost in it, my lord. But let him come!

It warms the very sickness in my heart

That I shall live and tell him to his teeth:

'Thus diddest thou.'

KING CLAUDIUS

            If it be so, Laertes —

As how should it be so? How otherwise? —   60

Will you be ruled by me?

LAERTES

            Ay, my lord,

So you will not o'errule me to a peace.

KING CLAUDIUS

To thine own peace. If he be now returned,

As checking at his voyage, and that he means

No more to undertake it, I will work him   65

To an exploit now ripe in my device,

Under the which he shall not choose but fall.

And for his death no wind of blame shall breathe,

But even his mother shall uncharge the practice

And call it accident. → *claudius is cruel*

LAERTES

            My lord, I will be ruled;   70

The rather if you could devise it so

That I might be the organ.

KING CLAUDIUS

            It falls right.

You have been talked of since your travel much,

And that in Hamlet's hearing, for a quality

Wherein they say you shine. Your sum of parts   75

Did not together pluck such envy from him

As did that one, and that, in my regard,

Of the unworthiest siege.

LAERTES

What part is that, my lord?

KING CLAUDIUS

A very riband in the cap of youth,   80

Yet needful too; for youth no less becomes

The light and careless livery that it wears

Than settled age his sables and his weeds,

Importing health and graveness. Two months since,

Here was a gentleman of Normandy —   85

59 *be so:* is true that Hamlet has come back

60 *As ... otherwise?* How can Hamlet have come back? How could he have sent this letter without coming back?

62 *So ... peace:* provided that you won't force me to make peace with Hamlet

63 *To ... peace:* what I will advise will give you peace of mind

64 *As checking at:* because he has broken off

65–6 *work ... device:* get him to take part in an enterprise ('exploit'), the details of which are now matured in my mind ('device')

67 *Under ... fall:* it will inevitably lead to his death

68 *for ... breathe:* nobody will be blamed for his death

69 *uncharge:* exonerate, make no accusation against *practice:* treacherous plot, underhand trick

70–72 *be ... organ:* do what you ask, and will be even more ready to do it if your plan involves my being the instrument or agent of Hamlet's death

72 *It falls right:* my plan happens to coincide with your wish

75–8 *Your ... siege:* Hamlet envies one talent of yours more than all the others combined, although I must say that I regard this talent as being less significant than any of your other ones

78 *siege:* rank

80 *very riband:* mere ornament, something superficial

81 *becomes:* is suited to

82 *light ... livery:* bright, colourful clothes

83–4 *settled ... graveness:* people past their youth are suited to sober and conservative clothes, signifying health and gravity

84 *since:* ago

85 *Here:* at the court of Denmark

I've seen myself, and served against, the French,
And they can well on horseback, but this gallant
Had witchcraft in't. He grew unto his seat,
And to such wondrous doing brought his horse,

90 As he had been incorpsed and demi-natured
With the brave beast. So far he topped my thought,
That I, in forgery of shapes and tricks,
Come short of what he did.

LAERTES
                                A Norman was't?

KING CLAUDIUS
A Norman.

LAERTES
Upon my life, Lamord.

KING CLAUDIUS
95   The very same.

LAERTES
I know him well. He is the brooch indeed
And gem of all the nation.

KING CLAUDIUS
He made confession of you,
And gave you such a masterly report

100 For art and exercise in your defence,
And for your rapier most especial,
That he cried out 'twould be a sight indeed
If one could match you: the scrimers of their nation,
He swore, had had neither motion, guard, nor eye,

105 If you opposed them. Sir, this report of his
Did Hamlet so envenom with his envy
That he could nothing do but wish and beg
Your sudden coming o'er, to play with him.
Now, out of this—

LAERTES
                                What out of this, my lord?

KING CLAUDIUS
110 Laertes, was your father dear to you?
Or are you like the painting of a sorrow,
A face without a heart?

---

87   *can well:* have much skill
87–8 *gallant . . . in't:* this gentleman had magical skills in horsemanship
88–91 *He . . . beast:* riding a horse was so natural to him, and he made his horse perform such wonders that it seemed as if he shared the horse's body, the combination of horse and rider resembling the mythological centaur (half-man and half-beast)
90   *incorpsed:* made into one body with
      demi-natured: having half the nature of
91–3 *So . . . did:* what he was able to do was so remarkable that even the most exaggerated descriptions of his movements and feats of skill that I might compose would fail to match the reality
95   *Lamord:* the Norman's name may suggest death (French *la mort*)
96–7 *brooch . . . nation:* jewel (or star) of France
98   *made . . . you:* testified to, or acknowledged, your abilities
99–100 *gave . . . defence:* paid tribute to your expertise in both the theoretical ('art') and practical ('exercise') aspects of fencing ('defence')
101   *for . . . especial:* particularly for your sword
103   *one could match:* someone could be found who was capable of competing with
      scrimers: fencers
104   *motion, guard:* attack, defence
106   *envenom:* poison
108   *play:* fence

LAERTES

Why ask you this?

KING CLAUDIUS

Not that I think you did not love your father;

But that I know love is begun by time,

And that I see, in passages of proof,   115

Time qualifies the spark and fire of it.

There lives within the very flame of love

A kind of wick or snuff that will abate it;

And nothing is at a like goodness still;

For goodness, growing to a pleurisy,   120

Dies in his own too much. That we would do

We should do when we would, for this 'would' changes

And hath abatements and delays as many

As there are tongues, are hands, are accidents.

And then this 'should' is like a spendthrift sigh,   125

That hurts by easing. But, to the quick of th'ulcer:

Hamlet comes back. What would you undertake

To show yourself your father's son in deed

More than in words?

LAERTES

To cut his throat i' th' church.

KING CLAUDIUS

No place indeed should murder sanctuarise;   130

Revenge should have no bounds. But, good Laertes,

Will you do this: keep close within your chamber;

Hamlet returned shall know you are come home.

We'll put on those shall praise your excellence,

And set a double varnish on the fame   135

The Frenchman gave you, bring you in fine together

And wager on your heads. He, being remiss,

Most generous, and free from all contriving,

Will not peruse the foils, so that, with ease,

Or with a little shuffling, you may choose   140

A sword unbated, and in a pass of practice

Requite him for your father.

LAERTES

I will do't.

And for that purpose I'll anoint my sword:

I bought an unction of a mountebank,

---

114 *is . . . time:* has its beginning in time

115 *passages of proof:* instances for which there is good evidence

116 *qualifies . . . it:* can modify and reduce its intensity

118 *abate:* diminish. Claudius is suggesting that love is ultimately self-consuming and self-destructive

119 *is . . . still:* remains at a constant level of goodness

120 *a pleurisy:* superabundance

121 *Dies . . . much:* destroys itself by its own excess

121–6 *That . . . easing:* if we have the will to do something, we should do it there and then. If we do not, our resolution will diminish. We will find our will to act weakened by words, actions and random events ('accidents'). Our recognition of our duty ('should'), without the will to perform it, may ease our minds for a moment, but in the end enfeebles ('hurts') our moral natures

125–6 *spendthrift . . . easing:* sighing was believed to drain the blood and waste the vital powers

126 *to . . . th'ulcer:* returning to the painful cause of our trouble

129 *More than:* not merely

129 *To . . . church:* Hamlet has recently shown himself incapable of killing the murderer of his father at prayer. The contrast is deliberate

130 *sanctuarise:* provide immunity from, protect

131 *have no bounds:* not answer to any law. Claudius is telling Laertes that he is morally justified in killing Hamlet anywhere, even in a church

132 *keep . . . chamber:* confine yourself to your room

134 *We'll . . . excellence:* I shall see to it that certain people will pay tribute to your skill in fencing

135 *set . . . fame:* add a further gloss to the reputation

136 *in fine:* finally

137 *wager . . . heads:* place bets on you (in a fencing match)
     remiss: careless, negligent

138 *Most . . . contriving:* noble in mind, and incapable of underhanded plotting (of the kind Claudius and Laertes are now engaged in)

139 *peruse:* examine
     foils: blunt fencing swords with a button on the point

140 *shuffling:* trickery, sleight of hand

141 *unbated:* sharp, with no button on the point
     pass of practice: treacherous sword-thrust

142 *Requite him:* pay him back

143 *anoint:* here, apply poison to

144 *unction . . . mountebank:* ointment from a travelling quack doctor

<table>
<tr><td>145</td><td>mortal: fatal</td></tr>
<tr><td>146</td><td>cataplasm: plaster, poultice</td></tr>
<tr><td>147–8</td><td>Collected . . . moon: composed of all the medicinal herbs that gain extra power from being gathered by moonlight</td></tr>
<tr><td>149</td><td>withal: with it
touch my point: contaminate the point of my sword</td></tr>
<tr><td>150</td><td>contagion: poison</td></tr>
<tr><td>150–51</td><td>gall . . . death: graze him even a little his death is assured</td></tr>
<tr><td>152–3</td><td>Weigh . . . shape: consider what may be the most appropriate time and opportunity for us to act out our scheme</td></tr>
<tr><td>154–5</td><td>that . . . assayed: if our intention ('drift') were to become obvious through our own mismanagement, it would be better not to have tried the plan at all</td></tr>
<tr><td>156</td><td>back or second: something to fall back on</td></tr>
<tr><td>156–7</td><td>hold . . . proof: succeed if the first plan fails the test</td></tr>
<tr><td>158</td><td>cunnings: skills</td></tr>
<tr><td>159</td><td>ha't: have it</td></tr>
<tr><td>160</td><td>When . . . dry: when you are warm and thirsty from your exercise</td></tr>
<tr><td>161</td><td>bouts . . . end: exchanges more vigorous than usual to bring this about</td></tr>
<tr><td>163</td><td>chalice . . . nonce: drinking goblet for a special occasion</td></tr>
<tr><td>164</td><td>venomed stuck: poisoned sword-thrust</td></tr>
<tr><td>165</td><td>Our . . . there: we will still achieve our aim</td></tr>
<tr><td>169</td><td>willow: the emblem of disappointed love
askant: slanting over</td></tr>
<tr><td>170</td><td>That . . . stream: which reflects its silvery-grey leaves</td></tr>
<tr><td>171</td><td>Therewith: with the willow branches
fantastic: ingenious, intricate</td></tr>
<tr><td>172</td><td>crow-flowers: buttercups or ragged robins
long purples: purple orchids</td></tr>
<tr><td>173</td><td>liberal . . . name: free-spoken shepherds call by a coarser word</td></tr>
<tr><td>174</td><td>cold: chaste</td></tr>
<tr><td>175–6</td><td>There . . . broke: while she was climbing along the hanging boughs to hang her wreath made of weeds, a malicious branch gave way</td></tr>
<tr><td>177</td><td>weedy trophies: floral wreath</td></tr>
</table>

145 So mortal that, but dip a knife in it,
Where it draws blood, no cataplasm so rare,
Collected from all simples that have virtue
Under the moon, can save the thing from death
That is but scratched withal. I'll touch my point
150 With this contagion, that if I gall him slightly
It may be death.

KING CLAUDIUS
Let's further think of this;
Weigh what convenience both of time and means
May fit us to our shape. If this should fail,
And that our drift look through our bad performance,
155 'Twere better not assayed. Therefore this project
Should have a back or second, that might hold
If this should blast in proof. Soft, let me see . . .
We'll make a solemn wager on your cunnings . . .
I ha't!
160 When in your motion you are hot and dry —
As make your bouts more violent to that end —
And that he calls for drink, I'll have prepared him
A chalice for the nonce, whereon but sipping,
If he by chance escape your venomed stuck,
165 Our purpose may hold there— but stay, what noise?

Enter QUEEN GERTRUDE.

QUEEN GERTRUDE
One woe doth tread upon another's heel,
So fast they follow. Your sister's drowned, Laertes.

LAERTES
Drowned! O where?

QUEEN GERTRUDE
There is a willow grows askant the brook,
170 That shows his hoar leaves in the glassy stream;
Therewith fantastic garlands did she make
Of crow-flowers, nettles, daisies, and long purples
That liberal shepherds give a grosser name,
But our cold maids do dead men's fingers call them.
175 There, on the pendent boughs her crownet weeds
Clambering to hang, an envious sliver broke;
When down her weedy trophies and herself
Fell in the weeping brook. Her clothes spread wide,

And, mermaid-like, a while they bore her up,   *Ophelias*

Which time she chanted snatches of old tunes,   *flowers* 180

As one incapable of her own distress,   *represent innocence*

Or like a creature native and indued

Unto that element. But long it could not be,   *incapable of saving herself*

Till that her garments, heavy with their drink,

Pulled the poor wretch from her melodious lay   185

To muddy death.   *clothes weighed her down*

LAERTES

          Alas, then she is drowned?

QUEEN GERTRUDE

Drowned, drowned.   *more reason for Laertes revenge*

LAERTES

Too much of water hast thou, poor Ophelia,

And therefore I forbid my tears. But yet

It is our trick, nature her custom holds,   190

Let shame say what it will [*weeps*] when these are gone,

The woman will be out. Adieu, my lord,

I have a speech of fire that fain would blaze,

But that this folly drowns it.

Exit.

KING CLAUDIUS   *— thinks only of himself*

Let's follow, Gertrude.   195

How much I had to do to calm his rage!

Now fear I this will give it start again,

Therefore let's follow.

Exeunt.

179 *bore her up:* kept her afloat

180 *Which … tunes:* during which time she sang fragments of old songs

181 *As … distress:* like someone unable to grasp her own miserable plight

182–3 *native … element:* adapted by nature to live in water

184 *heavy … drink:* sodden with water

185 *melodious lay:* sweet-sounding song

190 *trick:* habit

190–92 *nature … out:* in the face of such grief as this, it is natural to give way to tears, whatever embarrassment ('shame') this may cause; but when I finish crying, the womanly sentiment in me will be gone

193 *I … blaze:* I would love to express my burning anger

194 *this folly:* my foolish tears

196–8 *How … follow:* these comments show the hypocrisy, self-interest and callousness of Claudius. It is his only response to Ophelia's death

One woe doth tread upon another's heel,
So fast they follow. Your sister's drowned, Laertes.

GERTRUDE, Act 4, Scene 7, 166–7

Key points

The murder of Polonius has led to the emergence of Laertes as Hamlet's mortal enemy, and to Ophelia's madness, which culminates in her drowning. Claudius intends to exploit this situation by using Laertes to destroy Hamlet.

- Although Laertes is now convinced that Claudius was not involved in the death of Polonius, he still has nagging doubts. Why, for example, did Claudius not act against Hamlet, when he was certain of his nephew's guilt? Claudius is at his impressive best in dealing with this obvious difficulty. He greatly flatters Laertes by taking him into his confidence and confessing to him how much he depends on Gertrude's good will towards him. He implies that action against Hamlet might threaten his relationship with Gertrude. He further explains that if he brought Hamlet to a public trial, he might face a revolt by the common people, who love Hamlet.

- Claudius makes Laertes a willing ally in his plot against Hamlet. This does not prove very difficult, as each of them is determined to kill Hamlet.

- News of Hamlet's imminent return to Denmark brings cheer to Laertes, making him desperately anxious to confront Hamlet. This would not suit Claudius, because if challenged, Hamlet might well inform Laertes of the king's own deadly secrets.

- Claudius is briefly thrown off-balance by Hamlet's letter announcing his unexpected return, but recovers quickly. He hatches a plan that will enable Laertes to be the means of Hamlet's death, as a result of what will seem to be an accident.

- Before revealing the details of his plan, Claudius flatters Laertes by telling him that he is widely recognised as a master of fencing with the rapier, and that Hamlet was jealous of this and wished he could test his own skill against that of Laertes. He also provokes Laertes by questioning his love for his father. These manipulations are designed to test Laertes' commitment, and to incite his desire for revenge.

- It is worth noting that Laertes has no moral scruples about the treacherous activity Claudius wants to involve him in. It turns out that Laertes has brought poison with him, intending some such evil purpose as the one under discussion. His talk of poisoning the rapier prompts Claudius to think of a poisoned chalice: two unscrupulous minds reinforce each other's villainy.

- Claudius has only one further fear: that Laertes and Hamlet may meet before their fencing match. To prevent this, he tells Laertes to remain in his room (and he will later order Gertrude to place Hamlet under restraint).

- Gertrude provides a poetic account of the death of Ophelia. The description suggests an accidental death, free of pain and distress, but apparently witnessed by someone who did not attempt to save her. Ophelia, remaining passive to the end, made no attempt to save herself. Death by suicide seems more likely.

Useful quotes

> The queen his mother
> Lives almost by his looks; and for myself —
> My virtue or my plague, be it either which —
> She's so conjunctive to my life and soul
> That, as the star moves not but in his sphere,
> I could not but by her.
>
> (Claudius, lines 12–17)

> No place indeed should murder sanctuarise;
> Revenge should have no bounds.
>
> (Claudius, lines 130–31)

> My lord, I will be ruled;
> The rather if you could devise it so
> That I might be the organ.
>
> (Laertes, lines 70–72)

> He, being remiss,
> Most generous, and free from all contriving,
> Will not peruse the foils, so that, with ease,
> Or with a little shuffling, you may choose
> A sword unbated, and in a pass of practice
> Requite him for your father.
>
> (Claudius, lines 137–42)

Questions ?

1 Discuss the methods used by Claudius in this scene to make Laertes the agent of his schemes.

2 Claudius proffers not only his love for Gertrude, but also his total dependence on her (lines 12–17). Explain why you do or do not think he is sincere in this.

3 Claudius describes Hamlet as 'generous, and free from all contriving' (line 138). Is this an accurate description in your opinion? Give reasons for your answer.

4 Hamlet agonises over the possible consequences of seeking revenge for his father's death. Is there any evidence in this scene that Laertes is troubled by similar thoughts? Explain.

5 Why has Hamlet very little prospect of coming out of the planned fencing match alive?

6 Describe the character of Laertes, based on the evidence of this scene.

7 Gertrude's account of Ophelia's slow death by drowning raises a problem of credibility. What is this problem?

8 What reasons might Gertrude have for pretending that Ophelia's death was accidental, if it was not?

9 If you were making a film version of *Hamlet*, how would you handle Ophelia's death? Discuss the pros and cons of showing her death on screen.

10 Discuss whether Claudius's words to Laertes about acting without hesitation (lines 121–6) can be applied to Hamlet's situation.

11 Imagine you are Claudius. Compose a diary entry in which you discuss the key events of this scene.

ACT 4 ⚔ Key moments

Scene 1
- Gertrude gives Claudius a benign account of the killing of Polonius, to protect Hamlet.
- Claudius decides to send Hamlet to England immediately.

Scene 2
- Hamlet treats Rosencrantz and Guildenstern with contempt, refusing to tell them the location of the body of Polonius.

Scene 3
- Claudius feels that Hamlet is a serious threat to his life, and decides to order the King of England to have Hamlet put to death without delay when he arrives in England.
- During a meeting with Claudius, Hamlet exposes him to a disturbing account of how worms are eating Polonius, and how worms also eat dead kings.

Scene 4
- Fortinbras, another avenger, is leading a large army in an invasion of a tiny piece of Polish territory.
- Hamlet, impressed by how active Fortinbras can be in pursuit of such a trivial goal, feels contempt for his own slowness in pursuing his task of avenging his father's death.

Scene 5
- Ophelia has lost her sanity, and sings bawdy love songs in front of the king and queen.
- Laertes, at the head of a group of rebellious Danes who want to make him king, confronts Claudius and Gertrude.
- Claudius skilfully quells the rebellion by convincing Laertes that his father's killer will be dealt with.

Scene 6
- Horatio is given a letter from Hamlet, which reveals that Hamlet has escaped and is back in Denmark.

Scene 7
- Claudius wins the confidence of Laertes and they plot to kill Hamlet by poisoning him.
- Gertrude reveals that Ophelia has drowned.

ACT 4 ⚔ Speaking and listening

1 Assign the part of Claudius. He will be interviewed by members of the class chosen at random. Questions put to him might include: how he feels about his successful handling of the problems presented by Laertes, his opinions on Hamlet, his current relationship with Gertrude, his plans for the future, and whether his conscience ever troubles him.

2 In pairs, assign the roles of Rosencrantz and Guildenstern. Discuss your experiences since you were first summoned to Elsinore by Claudius and Gertrude. Give your opinions on the different members of the royal family and on recent events. Are you happy about your present situation? What are your hopes and fears?

Plot summary

Two gravediggers discuss the burial of suicide cases, and other subjects. Their ignorance of proper legal terminology makes their comments laughable. Hamlet and Horatio enter the churchyard and observe one of the gravediggers. Hamlet reflects on life and death. A mourning procession approaches. Hamlet soon realises that he is observing Ophelia's funeral. Laertes publicly curses Hamlet, who emerges from hiding, struggles with Laertes, and declares his love for Ophelia. After Hamlet's departure with Horatio, Claudius reminds Laertes that he will soon have his opportunity to deal with Hamlet.

Sweets to the sweet, farewell!
I hoped thou shouldst have been my Hamlet's wife;
I thought thy bride-bed to have decked, sweet maid,
And not t'have strewed thy grave.

GERTRUDE, Act 5, Scene 1, 229–32

Elsinore. A churchyard. *comic relief*

Enter two GRAVEDIGGERS (clowns) with spades.

FIRST GRAVEDIGGER

Is she to be buried in Christian burial when she wilfully seeks her own salvation?

Gets a christian burial because she's from a rich family

SECOND GRAVEDIGGER

I tell thee she is, and therefore make her grave straight. The crowner hath sat on her, and finds it Christian burial.

FIRST GRAVEDIGGER

5 How can that be, unless she drowned herself in her own defence?

SECOND GRAVEDIGGER

Why, 'tis found so.

FIRST GRAVEDIGGER

It must be *se offendendo*; it cannot be else. For here lies the point: if I drown myself wittingly, it argues an act, and 10 an act hath three branches: it is to act, to do, to perform; *argal*, she drowned herself wittingly.

SECOND GRAVEDIGGER

Nay, but hear you, Goodman Delver—

FIRST GRAVEDIGGER

Give me leave. Here lies the water — good: here stands the man — good. If the man go to this water, and drown 15 himself, it is, will he nill he, he goes; mark you that. But if the water come to him, and drown him, he drowns not himself; *argal*, he that is not guilty of his own death, shortens not his own life.

SECOND GRAVEDIGGER

But is this law?

FIRST GRAVEDIGGER

20 Ay, marry, is't — crowner's quest law.

SECOND GRAVEDIGGER

Will you ha' the truth on't? If this had not been a gentlewoman, she should have been buried out o' Christian burial.

1–2 *wilfully ... salvation:* deliberately ended her own life. In Shakespeare's time, and for long after, suicides were denied Christian funeral rites and were buried out of consecrated ground. The gravedigger's assumption that Ophelia died by suicide contradicts Gertrude's account, which suggested that her death was accidental

3 *straight:* immediately. There is a pun on both 'straight' meaning 'aligned' and 'strait' meaning 'narrow'

4 *The ... burial:* the coroner's inquest concluded that she is to have a Christian burial (i.e. did not return a verdict of suicide)

5–6 *in ... defence:* he is thinking of homicide in self-defence, which is not a crime

7 *'tis found so:* the coroner has so decided

8 *se offendendo:* he means *se defendendo*, the legal term for self-defence, but uses its opposite *else:* otherwise

9 *wittingly:* consciously, knowingly

11 *argal:* he means *ergo* (Latin for 'therefore')

12 *but ... Delver:* just listen, Mr Digger

13 *Give me leave:* let me finish

15 *will he nill he:* willy-nilly, whether he likes it or not

20 *crowner's quest:* coroner's inquest

21 *Will ... on't?* Do you want to know the truth about it?

22 *gentlewoman:* well-born lady

FIRST GRAVEDIGGER

Why, there thou say'st, and the more pity that great folk should have count'nance in this world to drown or hang themselves, more than their even-Christen. Come, my spade. There is no ancient gentleman but gard'ners, ditchers, and grave-makers: they hold up Adam's profession.

25

SECOND GRAVEDIGGER

Was he a gentleman?

30

FIRST GRAVEDIGGER

He was the first that ever bore arms.

SECOND GRAVEDIGGER

Why, he had none.

FIRST GRAVEDIGGER

What, art a heathen? How dost thou understand the Scripture? The Scripture says Adam digged. Could he dig without arms? I'll put another question to thee. If thou answerest me not to the purpose, confess thyself—

35

SECOND GRAVEDIGGER

Go to.

FIRST GRAVEDIGGER

What is he that builds stronger than either the mason, the shipwright or the carpenter?

SECOND GRAVEDIGGER

The gallows-maker; for that frame outlives a thousand tenants.

40

FIRST GRAVEDIGGER

I like thy wit well, in good faith. The gallows does well; but how does it well? It does well to those that do ill. Now thou dost ill to say the gallows is built stronger than the church. *Argal*, the gallows may do well to thee. To't again, come.

45

SECOND GRAVEDIGGER

Who builds stronger than a mason, a shipwright or a carpenter?

FIRST GRAVEDIGGER

Ay, tell me that, and unyoke.

24 *there thou say'st:* you're talking sense there

25 *count'nance:* privilege

26 *even-Christen:* fellow Christians

26–7 *Come, my spade:* hand me my spade. The shape of the spade may remind him of a coat of arms, and account for the references to gentlemen that follows

27 *ancient:* going back to ancient times

28 *ditchers:* diggers of ditches
hold up: uphold, continue to practise

28–9 *Adam's profession:* Adam was the first digger

31 *that ... arms:* to have the arms to carry a spade with. But this gravedigger wants his companion to think he is referring to Adam's possession of a coat of arms, the badge of a gentleman

32 *none:* no coat of arms

33 *art:* are you

35–6 *If ... purpose:* if you don't give the proper answer

36 *confess thyself:* the full saying was 'confess thyself and be hanged'

37 *Go to:* get to work

40 *that frame:* the gallows (device used to hang people)

41 *tenants:* victims of the gallows

42 *I ... well:* that's an intelligent answer

43–5 *It ... to thee:* the gallows does a good job for criminals, but you are doing wrong by saying that the gallows is built stronger than the church. Talk like that could get you hanged

45–6 *To't again, come:* come on, try again

49 *unyoke:* get this over with

SECOND GRAVEDIGGER

50 Marry, now I can tell.

FIRST GRAVEDIGGER

To't.

SECOND GRAVEDIGGER

Mass, I cannot tell.

Enter HAMLET and HORATIO, afar off.

FIRST GRAVEDIGGER

Cudgel thy brains no more about it, for your dull ass will not mend his pace with beating; and when you are asked
55 this question next, say: 'a grave-maker' — the houses that he makes last till doomsday. Go, get thee to Yaughan, and fetch me a stoup of liquor.

Exit SECOND GRAVEDIGGER.

FIRST GRAVEDIGGER digs and sings.

> In youth, when I did love, did love,
> Methought it was very sweet,
60 > To contract — o — the time — a — my behove,
> O methought there — a —was nothing — a — meet.

used to digging graves

HAMLET

Has this fellow no feeling of his business, that he sings in grave-making?

HORATIO

Custom hath made it in him a property of easiness.

HAMLET

65 'Tis e'en so, the hand of little employment hath the daintier sense.

FIRST GRAVEDIGGER

[*sings*] But age, with his stealing steps,
> Hath clawed me in his clutch,
> And hath shipped me into the land,
70 > As if I had never been such.

Throws up a skull.

HAMLET *the gravedigger has no respect*

That skull had a tongue in it, and could sing once. How the knave jowls it to the ground, as if it were Cain's jaw-

Glosses (left margin):
51 *To't:* come on, tell me
52 *Mass:* by the Mass (an oath)
53–4 *Cudgel … beating:* don't overwork your brains any longer in trying to solve it, for all the beating in the world won't make a stupid ass go any faster
55 *houses:* graves
56 *Yaughan:* a local alehouse keeper
57 *stoup:* tankard, pitcher
60 *contract … behove:* shorten the time pleasantly to my advantage
61 *methought … meet:* it seemed to me that there was nothing appropriate
62 *feeling of:* sensitivity for
64 *Custom … easiness:* habit makes it possible for him to do his job with indifference
65–6 *'Tis … sense:* I agree, those of us who work little have softer and more delicate feelings
69 *hath … land:* has ended my mortal journey
70 *such:* young
72 *jowls:* flings, hurls; with a pun on 'jowl', a jawbone *Cain:* the first man to kill his brother (the same crime as Claudius)

bone, that did the first murder! This might be the pate of a politician, which this ass now o'erreaches; one that would circumvent God, might it not? 75

HORATIO

It might, my lord.

HAMLET

Or of a courtier, which could say: 'Good morrow, sweet lord! How dost thou, good lord?' This might be my Lord Such-a-one, that praised my Lord Such-a-one's horse when he meant to beg it, might it not? 80

HORATIO

Ay, my lord.

HAMLET

Why, e'en so: and now my Lady Worm's, chopless and knocked about the mazzard with a sexton's spade; here's fine revolution an we had the trick to see't. Did these bones cost no more the breeding, but to play at loggets 85 with them? Mine ache to think on't.

FIRST GRAVEDIGGER

[*sings*] A pick-axe and a spade, a spade,

    For and a shrouding sheet,

    O, a pit of clay for to be made

    For such a guest is meet. 90

Throws up another skull.

HAMLET

There's another. Why may not that be the skull of a lawyer? Where be his quiddities now, his quillets, his cases, his tenures, and his tricks? Why does he suffer this rude knave now to knock him about the sconce with a dirty shovel, and will not tell him of his action of battery? Hum! This 95 fellow might be in's time a great buyer of land, with his statutes, his recognisances, his fines, his double vouchers, his recoveries. Is this the fine of his fines, and the recovery of his recoveries, to have his fine pate full of fine dirt? Will his vouchers vouch him no more of his purchases, 100 and double ones too, than the length and breadth of a pair of indentures? The very conveyances of his lands will scarcely lie in this box, and must the inheritor himself have no more, ha?

---

73   *pate:* head

74   *politician:* schemer, conspirator
    o'erreaches: both 'reaches over' in the physical sense, and 'rises to a higher rank'. A pun in which the humble gravedigger who bends over the skull of the ambitious schemer is now the superior of one who spent his life plotting for high office
75   *circumvent:* get around

77   *morrow:* morning

80   *beg:* borrow

82   *my Lady Worm's:* belongs to the worms
    chopless: without a jaw
83   *knocked . . . spade:* beaten about the head with a gravedigger's spade
83–4 *here's . . . see't:* this is an impressive example of a change of fortune wrought by time if we had the art to see it
84–6 *Did . . . them?* Were these human beings brought up at such cost and trouble, only to have their bones used in a game played by gravediggers?
85   *loggets:* a game in which pieces of wood are thrown at a fixed object
86   *Mine . . . on't:* my bones hurt at the thought of it. Hamlet is appalled
88   *For and:* and in addition
90   *meet:* appropriate

92   *quiddities . . . quillets:* dubious arguments based on fine distinctions and quibbles
93   *tenures:* titles for the holding of property
    suffer: put up with, allow
94   *sconce:* head
95   *will . . . battery:* does not say he is taking a case against him for assault

97–8 *statutes . . . recoveries:* various legal procedures for acquiring, transferring and holding land
98–9 *the fine . . . dirt:* four different meanings of the word 'fine' are played upon to mean 'end', 'legal document', 'handsome' and 'powdered'
100 *vouchers vouch him:* contracts guarantee him
101–2 *than . . . indentures:* than a piece of land (i.e. his grave) that is the size of a couple of his written contracts ('indentures')
102–4 *The . . . more:* he had so much land that the title deeds to it would scarcely fit in this grave, and must he now have no more space for himself than that occupied by his documents

106 *parchment:* the material on which legal documents were written

108–9 *They ... that:* people who think that the possession of legal documents will give them permanent possession of land are fools ('sheep and calves')

110 *sirrah:* term of address spoken by a superior

114 *liest in't:* a pun on two meanings of 'lie in it'

115 *out on't:* out of it

118 *quick:* living

119 *quick:* fast-moving

HORATIO

105 Not a jot more, my lord.

HAMLET

Is not parchment made of sheepskins?

HORATIO

Ay, my lord, and of calves' skins too.

HAMLET

They are sheep and calves which seek out assurance in that. I will speak to this fellow. — Whose grave's this,

110 sirrah?

FIRST GRAVEDIGGER

Mine, sir.

[*sings*] O, a pit of clay for to be made

For such a guest is meet.

HAMLET

I think it be thine, indeed; for thou liest in't.

FIRST GRAVEDIGGER

115 You lie out on't, sir, and therefore 'tis not yours; for my part, I do not lie in't, and yet it is mine.

HAMLET

Thou dost lie in't, to be in't and say it is thine: 'tis for the dead, not for the quick; therefore thou liest.

FIRST GRAVEDIGGER

'Tis a quick lie, sir; 'twill away again, from me to you.

HAMLET

120 What man dost thou dig it for?

FIRST GRAVEDIGGER

For no man, sir.

Hamlet is annoyed that the grave digger doesn't speak clearly – ironic

HAMLET

What woman, then?

FIRST GRAVEDIGGER

For none, neither.

HAMLET

Who is to be buried in't?

FIRST GRAVEDIGGER

125 One that was a woman, sir; but, rest her soul, she's dead.

HAMLET

How absolute the knave is! We must speak by the card, or equivocation will undo us. By the Lord, Horatio, these three years I have took note of it; the age is grown so picked that the toe of the peasant comes so near the heel of the courtier, he galls his kibe. — How long hast thou been a grave-maker?   130

FIRST GRAVEDIGGER

Of all the days i' th'year, I came to't that day that our last King Hamlet overcame Fortinbras.

HAMLET

How long is that since?

FIRST GRAVEDIGGER

Cannot you tell that? Every fool can tell that. It was the   135
very day that young Hamlet was born — he that is mad and sent into England.

HAMLET

Ay, marry, why was he sent into England?

FIRST GRAVEDIGGER

Why, because he was mad: he shall recover his wits there; or, if he do not, 'tis no great matter there.   140

HAMLET

Why?

FIRST GRAVEDIGGER

'Twill not be seen in him there. There, the men are as mad as he.

HAMLET

How came he mad?

FIRST GRAVEDIGGER

Very strangely, they say.   145

HAMLET

How strangely?

FIRST GRAVEDIGGER

Faith, e'en with losing his wits.

HAMLET

Upon what ground?

126 *absolute:* strict and precise in his language
126–7 *by ... us:* very carefully and accurately, or we will be made fools of by his double-meaning talk ('equivocation')
128–30 *age ... kibe:* people have grown so refined ('picked') in their manners and habits of speech that peasants imitate the habits of courtiers
130 *galls his kibe:* chafes the chilblain (on the courtier's heel), i.e. he is following in his superior's footsteps very closely

134 *since:* ago

148 *Upon what ground?* For what reason?

FIRST GRAVEDIGGER

Why, here in Denmark. I have been sexton here, man and

150   boy, thirty years.

HAMLET

How long will a man lie in the earth ere he rot?

FIRST GRAVEDIGGER

Faith, if he be not rotten before he die (as we have many

pocky corpses nowadays, that will scarce hold the laying

in), he will last you some eight year or nine year. A tanner

155   will last you nine year.

HAMLET

Why he more than another?

FIRST GRAVEDIGGER

Why, sir, his hide is so tanned with his trade that he will

keep out water a great while; and your water is a sore

decayer of your whoreson dead body. Here's a skull now;

160   this skull has lain i' th'earth three-and-twenty years.

HAMLET

Whose was it?

FIRST GRAVEDIGGER

A whoreson mad fellow's it was. Whose do you think it

was?

HAMLET

Nay, I know not.

FIRST GRAVEDIGGER

165   A pestilence on him for a mad rogue! He poured a flagon

of Rhenish on my head once. This same skull, sir, was

Yorick's skull, the king's jester.

HAMLET

This?

FIRST GRAVEDIGGER

E'en that.

HAMLET

170   Let me see.

Takes the skull.

149   *in Denmark:* the gravedigger takes Hamlet's question literally

150   *thirty years:* as the gravedigger began his occupation on the day Hamlet was born, Hamlet must be thirty years old

151   *ere:* before

153   *pocky corpses:* corpses suffering the effects of the pox (syphilis)

153–4   *scarce . . . in:* scarcely last long enough to be buried

154   *tanner:* one who works in a tannery, converting skins and hides into leather

158   *sore:* serious, severe

159   *whoreson:* wretched, vile

162   *A . . . was:* it belonged to a notoriously unruly character

165   *pestilence:* plague

166   *Rhenish:* wine from the Rhine valley, Germany

169   *E'en that:* that very one

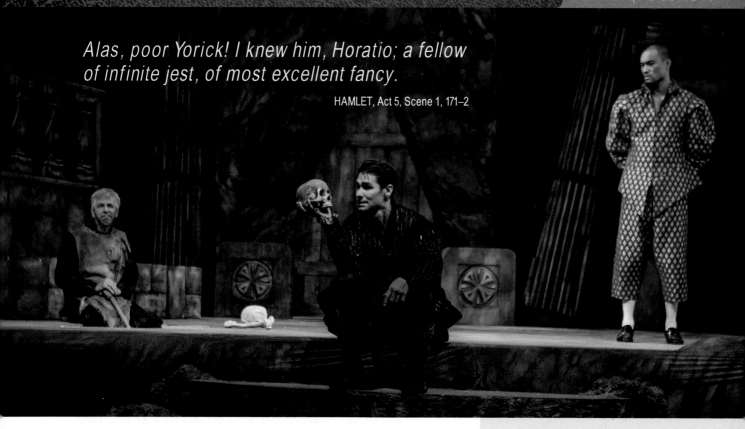

Alas, poor Yorick! I knew him, Horatio; a fellow of infinite jest, of most excellent fancy.

HAMLET, Act 5, Scene 1, 171–2

Alas, poor Yorick! I knew him, Horatio; a fellow of infinite jest, of most excellent fancy. He hath borne me on his back a thousand times. And now, how abhorred in my imagination it is! My gorge rises at it. Here hung those lips that I have kissed I know not how oft. — Where be your gibes now? Your gambols? Your songs? Your flashes of merriment that were wont to set the table on a roar? Not one now, to mock your own grinning? Quite chop-fallen? Now get you to my lady's chamber, and tell her, let her paint an inch thick, to this favour she must come. Make her laugh at that. — Prithee, Horatio, tell me one thing.

HORATIO
What's that, my lord?

HAMLET
Dost thou think Alexander looked of this fashion in the earth?

HORATIO
E'en so.

HAMLET
And smelt so? Puh!

Puts down the skull.

HORATIO
E'en so, my lord.

171–2 *of infinite jest:* having an endless capacity for making fun
172 *fancy:* imagination
173 *abhorred:* filled with horror, distasteful (to think I was once carried on his back)
174 *My . . . it:* I feel sick at the thought of it

176 *gibes:* jeers, sarcasm
gambols: capers
177 *were . . . roar:* usually had everyone laughing loudly
178 *grinning . . . chop-fallen:* the skull appears dejected, down in the mouth (the lower jaw has fallen off)
179–80 *Now . . . come:* go to the dressing-room of any fashionable lady today and tell her that, however well she paints her face, she will ultimately have a facial appearance like that of the skull. Hamlet may be thinking of Ophelia here, not knowing that she is, ironically, already dead
180–81 *Make . . . that:* see if she finds that amusing

183–4 *Dost . . . earth?* Do you think Alexander the Great looked like this after he had been buried a while? In Shakespeare's time, Alexander, the king of kings, was seen as the exemplar of human splendour and achievement, and was thought to have been extremely handsome in appearance
185 *E'en so:* exactly like that

186 *smelt:* Alexander was said to have perfumed the air as he passed by

[handwritten margin note:] sickened by death

180

185

HAMLET

To what base uses we may return, Horatio! Why, may not imagination trace the noble dust of Alexander till he find

190 it stopping a bung-hole?

HORATIO

'Twere to consider too curiously, to consider so.

HAMLET

No, faith, not a jot; but to follow him thither with modesty enough, and likelihood to lead it, as thus: Alexander died, Alexander was buried, Alexander returneth to dust; the

195 dust is earth; of earth we make loam; and why of that loam whereto he was converted, might they not stop a beer-barrel? *He is making little of poles*

Imperious Caesar, dead and turned to clay,

Might stop a hole to keep the wind away.

200 O, that that earth, which kept the world in awe,

Should patch a wall t'expel the winter's flaw!

But soft, but soft a while — here comes the king.

Enter, in funeral procession, ATTENDANTS carrying OPHELIA's corpse, PRIEST, LAERTES, KING CLAUDIUS, QUEEN GERTRUDE, and LORDS.

The queen, the courtiers. Who is this they follow?

And with such maimèd rites? This doth betoken

205 The corpse they follow did with desperate hand

Fordo its own life. 'Twas of some estate.

Couch we a while, and mark.

Retires, with HORATIO.

LAERTES

What ceremony else?

HAMLET [*aside*]

That is Laertes, a very noble youth: mark.

LAERTES

210 What ceremony else?

PRIEST

Her obsequies have been as far enlarged

As we have warranty. Her death was doubtful; *suspicious*

And but that great command o'ersways the order,

She should in ground unsanctified have lodged

Glossary (left column)

188 *base:* low, unworthy

190 *bung-hole:* hole in a cask of wine or beer

191 *'Twere . . . so:* such speculations are too minute and ingenious

192–3 *No . . . thus:* I disagree. I'm simply following Alexander in my imagination in a moderate way, taking account of where probability may have taken him, in the following way

195 *loam:* a mixture containing clay, used for plastering

195–7 *of that . . . beer-barrel:* might not Alexander's dust, having turned to loam, be used as a stopper for a beer-barrel

198 *Imperious:* imperial

200 *earth:* piece of clay that Caesar has become

201 *t'expel . . . flaw:* to keep out a gust of winter wind

202 *soft:* wait

204 *maimèd rites:* incomplete ceremony
betoken: indicate

206 *Fordo:* take
'Twas . . . estate: it was somebody of fairly high rank in society

207 *Couch . . . mark:* let us hide ourselves for a while and watch
Retires: withdraws to the back or side of the stage (still visible to the audience)

208 *What ceremony else?* What further ceremony will there be?

211–12 *Her . . . warranty:* the funeral rites have been made as complete as we have sanction to make them

212 *Her . . . doubtful:* the cause of her death is suspicious

213 *great . . . order:* the authority of the king has altered the established practice

214 *in . . . lodged:* remain in unconsecrated ground

Till the last trumpet; for charitable prayers,   215

Shards, flints and pebbles should be thrown on her.

Yet here she is allowed her virgin crants,

Her maiden strewments and the bringing home

Of bell and burial.

LAERTES

Must there no more be done?

PRIEST

                    No more be done!   220

We should profane the service of the dead

To sing sage requiem and such rest to her

As to peace-parted souls.

LAERTES *— genuine sorrow*

                Lay her i' th'earth:

And from her fair and unpolluted flesh *flower imgery*

May violets spring! *— innocence like Ophelia*

The coffin is lowered into the grave.

              I tell thee, churlish priest,   225

A ministering angel shall my sister be,

When thou liest howling.

HAMLET [*aside*]

What, the fair Ophelia!

QUEEN GERTRUDE

Sweets to the sweet, farewell!

Scatters flowers.

I hoped thou shouldst have been my Hamlet's wife;   230

I thought thy bride-bed to have decked, sweet maid,

And not t'have strewed thy grave.

LAERTES

                 O, treble woe

Fall ten times treble on that cursèd head,

Whose wicked deed thy most ingenious sense

Deprived thee of! Hold off the earth a while,   235

Till I have caught her once more in mine arms.

Leaps into the grave. *very dramatic*

Now pile your dust upon the quick and dead,

Till of this flat a mountain you have made,

T'o'ertop old Pelion, or the skyish head

Of blue Olympus.

215 *last trumpet; for:* Day of Judgement; instead

216 *Shards:* broken pieces of pottery

217 *crants:* garlands

218 *strewments:* flowers strewn on the coffin

218–19 *bringing . . . burial:* going to her last resting place in a proper funeral with the tolling of the bell

221–3 *We . . . souls:* it would be treating the burial service with disrespect if we were to sing a solemn ('sage') Requiem Mass for the repose of her soul, as we do for those who died at peace with God

225 *churlish:* rude, ungracious, grudging

227 *howling:* in hell

229 *Sweets:* beautiful flowers

231 *decked:* decorated, covered with flowers

233 *that cursèd head:* Hamlet

234 *deed:* murder of Polonius
ingenious sense: alert mind

235 *the earth:* filling in the grave with earth

237 *quick:* living. Laertes is asking to be buried alive with Ophelia

238–40 *Till . . . Olympus:* until this level ground becomes a mountain that is higher than Mount Pelion and Mount Olympus (home of the Greek gods)

HAMLET

240 [*comes forward*] What is he whose grief

Bears such an emphasis? Whose phrase of sorrow

Conjures the wand'ring stars, and makes them stand

Like wonder-wounded hearers? This is I,

Hamlet the Dane.

LAERTES

The devil take thy soul!

Leaps out of the grave and grapples with Hamlet.

HAMLET

245 Thou pray'st not well.

I prithee take thy fingers from my throat;

For though I am not splenitive and rash,

Yet have I something in me dangerous,

Which let thy wisdom fear. Hold off thy hand.

KING CLAUDIUS

Pluck them asunder.

QUEEN GERTRUDE

250 Hamlet, Hamlet!

ALL

Gentlemen—

HORATIO

Good my lord, be quiet.

HAMLET

Why, I will fight with him upon this theme

Until my eyelids will no longer wag.

QUEEN GERTRUDE

O my son, what theme?

HAMLET

255 I loved Ophelia. Forty thousand brothers

Could not, with all their quantity of love,

Make up my sum. What wilt thou do for her?

KING CLAUDIUS

O he is mad, Laertes.

QUEEN GERTRUDE

For love of God, forbear him.

241 *Bears ... emphasis:* is expressed in such strong language

241–3 *Whose ... hearers?* Whose method of expressing his sorrow casts a spell on the moving stars and causes them to stand still like awe-struck listeners?

244 *Hamlet the Dane:* Hamlet, King of Denmark

247 *splenitive and rash:* hot-tempered and impulsive

250 *Pluck them asunder:* separate them

251 *be quiet:* calm down

252 *theme:* subject

253 *wag:* stir (regarded as one of the last visible indications of life)

256 *quantity:* small sum. Hamlet is expressing contempt for Laertes' tendency to exaggerate (see lines 232–3)

258 *O ... Laertes:* Claudius does not want Laertes to act prematurely and ruin their plan

259 *forbear him:* leave him (Hamlet) alone; do not provoke him

HAMLET

'Swounds, show me what thou't do: 260

Woo't weep? Woo't fight? Woo't fast? Woo't tear thyself?

Woo't drink up eisel? Eat a crocodile?

I'll do't. Dost thou come here to whine?

To outface me with leaping in her grave?

Be buried quick with her, and so will I. 265

And if thou prate of mountains, let them throw

Millions of acres on us, till our ground,

Singeing his pate against the burning zone,

Make Ossa like a wart! Nay, an thou'lt mouth,

I'll rant as well as thou.

QUEEN GERTRUDE

                This is mere madness. 270

And thus a while the fit will work on him.

Anon, as patient as the female dove,

When that her golden couplets are disclosed,

His silence will sit drooping.

HAMLET

              Hear you, sir;

What is the reason that you use me thus? 275

I loved you ever. But it is no matter.

Let Hercules himself do what he may,

The cat will mew, and dog will have his day.

Exit.

KING CLAUDIUS

I pray thee, good Horatio, wait upon him.

Exit HORATIO.

[*aside to LAERTES*] Strengthen your patience in our last

  night's speech; 280

We'll put the matter to the present push —

Good Gertrude, set some watch over your son —

This grave shall have a living monument.

An hour of quiet shortly shall we see;

Till then, in patience our proceeding be. 285

Exeunt.

260 *'Swounds:* by God's wounds (an oath)

261 *Woo't:* will you

262 *drink up eisel:* swallow vinegar greedily

264 *outface:* outdo

265 *quick:* alive

266 *prate:* boast, brag

268 *Singeing . . . zone:* scorching its head in the heat of the upper air

269 *Make . . . wart:* make Mount Ossa seem utterly insignificant. In Greek mythology, the giants, warring with the gods, piled Mount Pelion on the nearby Mount Ossa in order to reach the top of Mount Olympus. Hamlet is mocking the mountain imagery Laertes used in lines 238–40

269–70 *an . . . as thou:* if you want to shout and rave like a bad actor, I'll compete with you

270 *mere:* absolute, complete

272–4 *Anon . . . drooping:* he will soon become as calm and composed as a female dove does at the sight of her pair of newly hatched nestlings

275 *use:* treat

276 *ever:* always

277–8 *Let . . . day:* you may rave like Hercules, but I will be victorious in the end

279 *wait upon him:* Claudius hopes that Horatio will persuade Hamlet not to confront Laertes again

280 *Strengthen . . . speech:* let the thought of what we planned last night make you more patient

281 *matter . . . push:* plan into instant action

282 *watch:* guard, observer

283 *living:* Claudius is using 'living' in a double sense. The queen will take it to mean 'enduring' or 'lasting'. Laertes will see Hamlet's life as being the most appropriate memorial to Ophelia

285 *Till . . . be:* until the time of peace, let us behave with patience

Key points

Death, burial and the deteriorating condition of corpses are dominant themes in the first part of this scene. Then attention turns to Ophelia's funeral. An encounter between Hamlet and Laertes gives the latter a further incentive to kill Hamlet.

- Before the funeral procession arrives at the graveyard, the tone of the scene is largely humorous, but behind the jokes of the gravediggers there is a strong emphasis on the permanence of the grave as the dwelling place of human beings.

- Hamlet's conversation with the First Gravedigger raises the subject of his own birth. When Hamlet asks him how long he has been at his trade, it turns out that he took it up on the day that Hamlet was born (line 136). The terrible inevitability of death, Hamlet's in particular, is brought into a new focus for the audience. We know that Hamlet's early death is already planned, and that the gravediggers preparing Ophelia's grave may soon be digging his. To add a further chilling emphasis to the point, the procession entering the graveyard includes Claudius and Laertes, the very men who plan to end Hamlet's life.

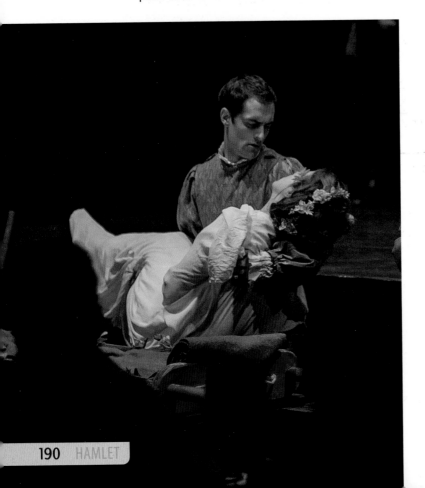

- Hamlet has returned from his sea-voyage a changed man. He is more calm and self-assured than he was before. He has a new air of confidence. However, in this scene, his self-possession is disturbed by his discovery that the newly opened grave is Ophelia's and by her brother's exaggerated displays of grief.

- Laertes' tasteless conduct includes a request to be buried alive with his dead sister, and for the gravediggers to cover them both with a mountain of soil. This kind of hyperbole and melodramatic gesture are typical of Laertes, and are an index of his superficial nature.

- Hamlet's behaviour at the graveside is often misinterpreted. The comments of Claudius and Gertrude suggest that Hamlet is behaving like a madman (lines 258, 270). These comments are misleading. It suits Claudius to dismiss Hamlet's conduct as insane in order to prevent Laertes from acting prematurely against him, and Gertrude uses the plea of insanity as a defence of her son.

- When Hamlet is using wild and extravagant language (such as challenging Laertes to drink vinegar or eat crocodile, line 262), he is not losing his head, but showing that if Laertes can express grief in this hysterical manner, he can do the same. Thus, Hamlet is using the style and manner of Laertes as a weapon with which to ridicule him.

- It is worth noting that when Hamlet steps forward to reveal himself to the funeral party, he announces himself as 'Hamlet the Dane' (line 244). This is Hamlet's first assumption of the title King of Denmark. His claim to royal dignity is spoken with solemn authority.

Useful quotes

Alexander died, Alexander was buried, Alexander returneth to dust; the dust is earth; of earth we make loam; and why of that loam whereto he was converted, might they not stop a beer-barrel?

(Hamlet, lines 193–7)

What is he whose grief
Bears such an emphasis? Whose phrase of sorrow
Conjures the wand'ring stars, and makes them stand
Like wonder-wounded hearers? This is I,
Hamlet the Dane.

(Hamlet, lines 240–44)

I loved Ophelia. Forty thousand brothers
Could not, with all their quantity of love,
Make up my sum.

(Hamlet, lines 255–7)

Dost thou come here to whine?
To outface me with leaping in her grave?
Be buried quick with her, and so will I.

(Hamlet, lines 263–5)

Questions ?

1 The talk of the gravediggers is not a mere comic irrelevance. How is it connected to the larger themes of the play?

2 The gravediggers indulge in an amusing parody of technical language. Discuss this aspect of the scene.

3 Choose and discuss some examples of irony in this scene.

4 The scene is full of black humour. Discuss some examples of this.

5 The scene as a whole is a profound meditation on death. Examine the ways in which death is treated.

6 Hamlet declares that he 'loved Ophelia' (line 255). Do you believe him? Give reasons for your answer.

7 Describe Hamlet's treatment of Laertes in this scene.

8 Consider the events in this scene from the point of view of Claudius and of Laertes. Compare and contrast their two perspectives.

9 Imagine you are Horatio. Compose a diary entry in which you discuss the events of this scene.

10 What do you expect to happen in the one remaining scene of this play?

ACT 5 † Scene 2

Plot summary

Hamlet tells Horatio of his adventures at sea, where he discovered that his uncle's commission to the King of England contained orders for his immediate execution. Hamlet changed these orders, substituting the names of Rosencrantz and Guildenstern for his own.

Osric, a foppish courtier who uses flamboyant language, arrives, bringing details of the proposed fencing match between Hamlet and Laertes. Hamlet takes up the challenge.

Hamlet wins the first two bouts and the third is a draw. Laertes resorts to foul play, attacks Hamlet off guard and wounds him with the poisoned rapier. They exchange weapons and Hamlet wounds Laertes. Gertrude drinks from a poisoned cup intended for Hamlet. The dying Laertes reveals the truth about Claudius. Hamlet stabs his uncle with the poisoned rapier. Laertes and Hamlet exchange forgiveness. Hamlet prevents Horatio from taking his own life. With his dying breath, Hamlet nominates Fortinbras as King of Denmark. Fortinbras arrives and claims the throne.

> *Let four captains*
> *Bear Hamlet, like a soldier, to the stage;*
> *For he was likely, had he been put on,*
> *To have proved most royal.*

FORTINBRAS, Act 5, Scene 2, 386–9

Elsinore. A hall in the castle.

Hamlet has returned a decisive character (handwritten annotation)

Enter HAMLET and HORATIO.

HAMLET

So much for this, sir, now shall you see the other;

You do remember all the circumstance?

HORATIO

Remember it, my lord?

HAMLET

Sir, in my heart there was a kind of fighting

That would not let me sleep; methought I lay   5

Worse than the mutines in the bilboes. Rashly,

And praised be rashness for it, let us know,

Our indiscretion sometime serves us well,

When our deep plots do pall: and that should learn us

There's a divinity that shapes our ends,   10

Rough-hew them how we will.

HORATIO

That is most certain.

HAMLET

                    Up from my cabin,

My sea-gown scarfed about me, in the dark

Groped I to find out them, had my desire,

Fingered their packet, and in fine withdrew   15

To mine own room again, making so bold

(My fears forgetting manners) to unseal

Their grand commission; where I found, Horatio —

Ah royal knavery! — an exact command,

Larded with many several sorts of reasons,   20

Importing Denmark's health and England's too,

With, ho, such bugs and goblins in my life,

That, on the supervise, no leisure bated,

No, not to stay the grinding of the axe,

My head should be struck off.

End rosencrantz and guildenstern letters (handwritten annotation)

HORATIO

                    Is't possible?   25

HAMLET

Here's the commission. Read it at more leisure.

But wilt thou hear me how I did proceed?

---

1 *So ... other:* you have heard the early part of my story, now I'll tell you the rest

2 *circumstance:* details

6 *mutines ... bilboes:* mutineers confined in stocks or fetters (on board ship)
Rashly: on impulse. Hamlet does not tell Horatio what he did on impulse until line 12

7–11 *And ... we will:* thank goodness for my impetuosity; let us recognise that actions we undertake spontaneously and without planning can sometimes prove successful, while carefully made plans prove worthless. That should teach us that there is a divine power that gives final shape to our affairs, however inexpertly we ourselves try to plan them

13 *scarfed about:* loosely wrapped around

14 *them:* Rosencrantz and Guildenstern
had my desire: got what I wanted

15 *Fingered their packet:* stole their papers
in fine: finally

17 *manners:* the convention that one does not read letters belonging to others

18 *grand commission:* royal warrant or mandate

19 *knavery:* wickedness

20 *Larded ... reasons:* fortified with a variety of justifications

21 *Importing:* concerning
health: welfare

22 *bugs and goblins:* bugbears and hobgoblins. These belong to childhood horror fiction and are Hamlet's way of dismissing the threat he represents as an imaginary one

23 *on the supervise:* as soon as the King of England had read the letter

23–4 *no leisure ... axe:* no time to elapse, not even to wait for the sharpening of the axe

28 *I beseech you:* I beg you to continue

29 *be-netted ... villainies:* caught in the toils of a wicked plot

30–31 *Ere ... play:* my brains began instinctively to act before I could frame a plan

32 *Devised:* composed
fair: in a clear hand, the kind used by professional scribes, clerks

33–6 *I ... service:* there was a time when I held the opinion, in common with our statesmen ('statists'), that proper handwriting was a mark of low breeding, and did all I could to forget my handwriting skills, but I can tell you that on this occasion good handwriting did me good and faithful service

37 *Th'effect:* the gist, the substance

38 *conjuration:* request

39 *faithful tributary:* one who faithfully pays the tribute he owes

40 *the palm:* a sign of prosperity

41 *wheaten garland:* an emblem of the fruitfulness generated by peace

42 *comma:* here, something trivial and insignificant
amities: friendship

43 *many ... charge:* Hamlet is referring in a mocking way to the clauses in his letter that begin with 'as' and contain matters of great weight ('charge'). There is a clever pun in this line since it can also mean 'many similar asses carrying great loads'

45 *debatement:* consideration

46 *those bearers:* Rosencrantz and Guildenstern

47 *Not ... allowed:* no time to be given to them to confess their sins and make their peace with God. They thus die unprepared, as Hamlet's father did

47 *How ... sealed?* How did you seal the letter? Without the personal seal of the sender (in this case Claudius), the authenticity of a letter would be in doubt

48 *ordinant:* directing or controlling events

49 *signet:* a ring bearing a personal seal

50 *model:* exact likeness

51 *writ ... th'other:* document in the same way as the original one had been folded

52 *Subscribed ... impression:* signed and sealed it

53 *changeling:* exchange. The word originally described a child substituted by fairies for a stolen one

54 *to ... sequent:* followed this

56 *to't:* to their deaths

HORATIO

I beseech you.

HAMLET

Being thus be-netted round with villainies,

30   Ere I could make a prologue to my brains,

They had begun the play. I sat me down,

Devised a new commission, wrote it fair —

I once did hold it, as our statists do,

A baseness to write fair, and laboured much

35   How to forget that learning, but, sir, now

It did me yeoman's service. Wilt thou know

Th'effect of what I wrote?

HORATIO

                              Ay, good my lord.

HAMLET

An earnest conjuration from the king,

As England was his faithful tributary,

40   As love between them like the palm might flourish,

As peace should still her wheaten garland wear

And stand a comma 'tween their amities,

And many such-like 'as's of great charge,

That, on the view and knowing of these contents,

45   Without debatement further, more or less,

He should those bearers put to sudden death,

Not shriving-time allowed.

HORATIO

                              How was this sealed?

HAMLET

Why, even in that was heaven ordinant.

I had my father's signet in my purse,

50   Which was the model of that Danish seal,

Folded the writ up in form of th'other,

Subscribed it, gave't the impression, placed it safely,

The changeling never known. Now, the next day

Was our sea-fight; and what to this was sequent

55   Thou knowest already.

HORATIO

So Guildenstern and Rosencrantz go to't.

HAMLET

Why, man, they did make love to this employment.

They are not near my conscience; their defeat

Does by their own insinuation grow.

'Tis dangerous when the baser nature comes

Between the pass and fell incensèd points

Of mighty opposites.

HORATIO

Why, what a king is this!

HAMLET

Does it not, think'st thee, stand me now upon —

He that hath killed my king and whored my mother,

Popped in between th'election and my hopes,

Thrown out his angle for my proper life,

And with such cozenage — is't not perfect conscience,

To quit him with this arm? And is't not to be damned,

To let this canker of our nature come

In further evil?

HORATIO

It must be shortly known to him from England

What is the issue of the business there.

HAMLET

It will be short. The interim is mine;

And a man's life's no more than to say 'one'.

But I am very sorry, good Horatio,

That to Laertes I forgot myself.

For by the image of my cause, I see

The portraiture of his, I'll court his favours.

But sure the bravery of his grief did put me

Into a towering passion.

HORATIO

Peace, who comes here?

Enter OSRIC.

OSRIC

Your lordship is right welcome back to Denmark.

HAMLET

I humbly thank you, sir. [*aside to HORATIO*] Dost know this waterfly?

Handwritten notes (margin):
- Hamlet is a much colder character than he was
- logical
- reasons why Hamlet should kill Claudius
- logical Hamlet
- ironic

Glosses:
57–9 did … grow: were willing agents of Claudius in the plot to kill me. I don't feel morally responsible for their deaths, which they brought upon themselves by their intrusion into the crooked affairs of Claudius ('their own insinuation')
60–62 baser … opposites: inferior people get caught up in the deadly struggle between powerful antagonists
61 pass: sword-thrust / fell incensèd points: swords wielded by angry men
63 stand … upon: put an obligation on me
64 king: father
65 Popped … hopes: got himself elected king before my claim could be properly considered
66 angle: fishing-hook and line / proper: own
67 cozenage: trickery, deception / perfect conscience: absolutely right
68 quit him: repay him by getting rid of him / be damned: deserve damnation
69–70 this … evil: Claudius, this spreading infection ('canker') of human nature, continue his evil existence
72 issue: outcome
73–4 It … 'one': the time at my disposal will indeed be short, but at least I will be able to use the intervening time ('interim'), and anyway, it will take a mere moment to kill Claudius
74 'one': a swordsman shouted 'one' to show he had hit his opponent
77–8 For … his: Hamlet recognises that Laertes, like himself, has a just cause for seeking vengeance; Hamlet must appear to Laertes as Claudius does to Hamlet (i.e. as the murderer of a beloved father)
79 bravery: ostentatious display
84 waterfly: vain, trivial creature with brightly flapping wings

HORATIO [*aside to HAMLET*]

85 No, my good lord.

HAMLET [*aside to HORATIO*]

Thy state is the more gracious, for 'tis a vice to know him. He hath much land, and fertile: let a beast be lord of beasts, and his crib shall stand at the king's mess. 'Tis a chough, but, as I say, spacious in the possession of dirt.

OSRIC

90 Sweet lord, if your lordship were at leisure, I should impart a thing to you from his majesty.

HAMLET

I will receive it, sir, with all diligence of spirit. Put your bonnet to his right use: 'tis for the head.

OSRIC

I thank your lordship, it is very hot.

HAMLET

95 No, believe me, 'tis very cold; the wind is northerly.

OSRIC

It is indifferent cold, my lord, indeed.

HAMLET

But yet methinks it is very sultry and hot for my complexion.

OSRIC

Exceedingly, my lord; it is very sultry as 'twere — I cannot tell how. But, my lord, his majesty bade me signify to you

100 that he has laid a great wager on your head. Sir, this is the matter—

HAMLET

I beseech you, remember—

Signs to OSRIC to put on his hat.

OSRIC

Nay, good my lord, for mine ease, in good faith. Sir, here is newly come to court Laertes — believe me, an absolute

105 gentleman, full of most excellent differences, of very soft society and great showing: indeed, to speak feelingly of him, he is the card or calendar of gentry, for you shall find in him the continent of what part a gentleman would see.

HAMLET

Sir, his definement suffers no perdition in you; though, I know to divide him inventorially would dizzy the arithmetic of memory, and yet but yaw neither in respect of his quick sail. But, in the verity of extolment, I take him to be a soul of great article and his infusion of such dearth and rareness, as, to make true diction of him, his semblable is his mirror; and who else would trace him, his umbrage, nothing more.

OSRIC

Your lordship speaks most infallibly of him.

HAMLET

The concernancy, sir? Why do we wrap the gentleman in our more rawer breath?

OSRIC

Sir?

HORATIO

Is't not possible to understand in another tongue? You will do't, sir, really.

HAMLET

What imports the nomination of this gentleman?

OSRIC

Of Laertes?

HORATIO [aside to HAMLET]

His purse is empty already; all's golden words are spent.

HAMLET

Of him, sir.

OSRIC

I know you are not ignorant—

HAMLET

I would you did, sir; yet, in faith, if you did, it would not much approve me. Well, sir?

OSRIC

You are not ignorant of what excellence Laertes is—

HAMLET

I dare not confess that, lest I should compare with him in excellence. But to know a man well were to know himself.

110

115

120

125

130

109–16 *his ... more:* he loses nothing through your description of him; although, to list all his qualities separately will utterly confuse the memory, because these qualities are so numerous, and it would make one's memory stagger ('yaw') because he is so far ahead of everybody else. But, to praise him truly, I find him to be a man whose perfections would require an extensive catalogue to list them, a man filled with such a rich and rare spirit that, to speak truthfully of him, the only one like him is his own reflection in the mirror; the only thing that can do him justice is his own shadow ('umbrage')

117 *most infallibly:* with absolute truth

118–19 *The ... breath?* How does all this talk concern us? Why are we talking of this refined man in our poor uncouth way? Hamlet really means: 'Why are we talking about Laertes in the first place?'

121 *understand ... tongue:* communicate in plainer language

121–2 *You ... really:* if you try, you will surely manage it. It is not clear whether Horatio is talking to Hamlet or to Osric

123 *imports ... of:* is your purpose in mentioning

125 *His ... spent:* Osric has run out of his store of fine words

128–9 *I ... me:* I wish you did recognise the fact that I am not ignorant; but then, even if you did, I would not take that as much of a compliment, because I value your judgement very little

131–2 *confess ... himself:* say that Laertes is excellent, because only excellent people can see the excellence of others, and I don't wish to claim to be excellent. However, it is only when a man knows himself that he can know another man well

OSRIC

I mean, sir, for his weapon. But in the imputation laid on him by them, in his meed, he's unfellowed.

HAMLET

135 What's his weapon?

OSRIC

Rapier and dagger.

HAMLET

That's two of his weapons. But well.

OSRIC

The king, sir, hath wagered with him six Barbary horses, against the which he has impawned, as I take it, six French

140 rapiers and poniards, with their assigns, as girdle, hangers and so. Three of the carriages, in faith, are very dear to fancy, very responsive to the hilts, most delicate carriages, and of very liberal conceit.

HAMLET

What call you the carriages?

HORATIO [aside to HAMLET]

145 I knew you must be edified by the margent ere you had done.

OSRIC

The carriages, sir, are the hangers.

HAMLET

The phrase would be more germane to the matter if we could carry cannon by our sides. I would it might be

150 'hangers' till then. But on! Six Barbary horses against six French swords, their assigns and three liberal-conceited carriages — that's the French bet against the Danish. Why is this 'impawned', as you call it?

OSRIC

The king, sir, hath laid, sir, that in a dozen passes between

155 yourself and him, he shall not exceed you three hits. He hath laid on twelve for nine; and it would come to immediate trial, if your lordship would vouchsafe the answer.

HAMLET

How if I answer 'no'?

---

133 *for his weapon:* as a swordsman

133–4 *But ... unfellowed:* and that those in his service ('meed') consider him without equal

138–41 *The ... so:* Claudius has bet six prize horses on Hamlet, against which Laertes has staked ('impawned') six fine swords and daggers ('poinards'), complete with all accessories

141–3 *carriages ... conceit:* hangers are pleasing to the imagination, of a design similar to that of the hilts, finely made and ornate ('of very liberal conceit')

144 *call you:* do you mean by

145–6 *must ... done:* would have to ask him what he meant before you had finished. To be 'edified by the margent' is to get instruction from the margin of a book, which, in Shakespeare's time, often explained the text

148–50 *The ... then:* it might be appropriate ('germane') to refer to hangers as carriages if we could carry cannon guns; until we can, I would prefer to use the term 'hanger' (for the device by which the scabbard is attached to the belt)

150 *But on!* But go ahead!

154–5 *hath ... hits:* has bet that in twelve bouts, Laertes will not make three more hits than you

156 *He ... nine:* Laertes wants twelve hits as the winning score, and is prepared to wager that he will have achieved that score by the time you score nine

156–8 *it ... answer:* the fencing match could take place immediately if you accept the challenge

OSRIC

I mean, my lord, the opposition of your person in trial.

160

the ... trial: accepting the challenge to a duel

HAMLET

Sir, I will walk here in the hall. If it please his majesty, it is the breathing time of day with me. Let the foils be brought, the gentleman willing, and the king hold his purpose, I will win for him an I can; if not, I will gain nothing but my shame and the odd hits.

165

162 *breathing ... me:* my time for exercise or recreation
foils: blunt fencing swords, rapiers
164 *an:* if

165 *odd hits:* extra three hits Laertes will have inflicted on me

OSRIC

Shall I re-deliver you e'en so?

166 *Shall ... so?* Shall I report what you have said?

HAMLET

To this effect, sir; after what flourish your nature will.

167 *To ... will:* yes, report what I have said, and frame your report in the kind of language that suits you

OSRIC

I commend my duty to your lordship.

168 *commend my duty:* offer my respects. Osric bows

HAMLET

Yours, yours.

Exit OSRIC.

He does well to commend it himself; there are no tongues else for's turn.

170

169 *Yours, yours:* at your service. Hamlet is impatient

170–1 *He ... turn:* it is well that he praises his duty himself, since no one else will praise it for him. Hamlet deliberately misunderstands 'commend' to mean 'praise' and not 'offer'

HORATIO

This lapwing runs away with the shell on his head.

172 *lapwing:* a bird that leaves the nest within a few hours of being hatched; hence the reference to a hasty departure with a shell on its head

HAMLET

He did comply with his dug, before he sucked it. Thus has he (and many more of the same bevy that I know the drossy age dotes on) only got the tune of the time and, out of an habit of encounter, a kind of yeasty collection, which carries them through and through the most fanned and winnowed opinions; and do but blow them to their trial, the bubbles are out.

Enter a LORD.

175

173 *did ... it:* paid his respects to his mother's nipple before sucking
174 *bevy:* flock of birds
175 *drossy age:* frivolous world we live in
only ... time: merely aped fashionable modes of speech and thought
176 *out ... encounter:* as a result of constant association
kind ... collection: frothy, empty lot
177–8 *most ... winnowed:* well-tested and well-sifted
178–9 *do ... out:* once you put them to the test, their emptiness is exposed

LORD

My lord, his majesty commended him to you by young Osric, who brings back to him that you attend him in the hall. He sends to know if your pleasure hold to play with Laertes, or that you will take longer time.

180

180 *commended him:* sent his greetings, and his request
181 *brings ... attend:* has brought back your message to him that you wait upon
182 *your pleasure hold:* you are still willing

184–6 *I am ... as now:* in remaining firm in my intention to fence with Laertes, I am ready to fulfil the king's desire. If he says he is ready, then so am I, now or at any time when I shall be as well prepared as I am now. Hamlet is ready to confront Claudius at last, to bring their deadly feud to a head

188 *In happy time:* at a most opportune moment

189 *gentle entertainment:* sign of friendliness or courtesy

194 *at the odds:* considering the advantage the bet has given me
194–5 *thou ... heart:* you can't imagine how troubled in spirit I feel

198 *gain-giving:* misgiving, foreboding

200 *If ... it:* follow your instincts, listen to your intuition
200–1 *forestall ... hither:* prevent their coming here

202 *Not a whit:* not at all
We defy augury: I shall treat superstitious forebodings with contempt
202–3 *there's ... sparrow:* divine providence is expressed in every individual event, whether that event be the fall of a sparrow or the confrontation of Hamlet with Claudius
203–4 *it:* death. Hamlet is saying that death is inevitable and we need to be prepared for it
205–6 *aught ... betimes:* anything of the time he is leaving behind him, what does it matter if I leave the world early
206 *Let be:* I will say no more

HAMLET

I am constant to my purposes, they follow the king's pleasure. If his fitness speaks, mine is ready; now or whensoever, provided I be so able as now.

LORD

The king and queen and all are coming down.

HAMLET

In happy time.

LORD

The queen desires you to use some gentle entertainment to Laertes before you fall to play.

HAMLET

She well instructs me.

Exit LORD.

HORATIO

You will lose this wager, my lord.

HAMLET

I do not think so. Since he went into France, I have been in continual practice; I shall win at the odds. But thou wouldst not think how ill all's here about my heart — but it is no matter.

HORATIO

Nay, good my lord—

HAMLET

It is but foolery; but it is such a kind of gain-giving, as would perhaps trouble a woman.

HORATIO

If your mind dislike anything, obey it. I will forestall their repair hither and say you are not fit.

HAMLET

Not a whit. We defy augury; there's a special providence in the fall of a sparrow. If it be now, 'tis not to come; if it be not to come, it will be now; if it be not now, yet it will come. The readiness is all. Since no man has aught of what he leaves, what is't to leave betimes? Let be.

Enter KING CLAUDIUS, QUEEN GERTRUDE, LAERTES, OSRIC, LORDS, MUSICIANS, and ATTENDANTS with cushions, foils, daggers, gauntlets and wine.

185

190

195

200

205

KING CLAUDIUS

Come, Hamlet, come, and take this hand from me.

Puts LAERTES' hand into HAMLET's.

HAMLET

Give me your pardon, sir: I've done you wrong;

But pardon't, as you are a gentleman.

This presence knows, and you must needs have heard,   210

How I am punished with sore distraction.

What I have done,

That might your nature, honour and exception

Roughly awake, I here proclaim was madness.

Was't Hamlet wronged Laertes? Never Hamlet.   215

If Hamlet from himself be ta'en away,

And when he's not himself does wrong Laertes,

Then Hamlet does it not, Hamlet denies it.

Who does it, then? His madness. If't be so,

Hamlet is of the faction that is wronged;   220

His madness is poor Hamlet's enemy.

Sir, in this audience,

Let my disclaiming from a purposed evil

Free me so far in your most generous thoughts,

That I have shot my arrow o'er the house,   225

And hurt my brother.

LAERTES

I am satisfied in nature,

Whose motive, in this case, should stir me most

To my revenge. But in my terms of honour

I stand aloof; and will no reconcilement   230

Till by some elder masters of known honour,

I have a voice and precedent of peace

To keep my name ungored. But till that time,

I do receive your offered love like love,

And will not wrong it.

HAMLET

                      I embrace it freely;   235

And will this brother's wager frankly play.

Give us the foils. Come on.

LAERTES

                      Come, one for me.

---

210 *presence:* royal assembly

211 *sore distraction:* extreme confusion of mind

212 *What:* whatever

213–14 *That ... awake:* to offend your natural love and your sense of honour, and to provoke your justified dislike

216 *from ... away:* is no longer himself

220 *faction:* party

222–6 *Sir ... brother:* Laertes, in the presence of this assembly, I declare that what I did to you and your family was not motivated by evil intent. I rely on your generosity of mind to see me as one who has accidentally injured someone dear to him, like a man whose arrow was misdirected

227–8 *in nature ... most:* as far as my natural feelings are concerned, which should be spurring me on

229 *in my terms:* as a man

230–33 *I ... ungored:* I must reserve my position; and do not desire to be reconciled to you until I have been able to get the advice of experts in matters of honour, who can quote me precedents for my case, so that I may preserve my reputation from harm

233 *ungored:* unwounded, undamaged

234 *receive:* accept

235 *And ... it:* this is a treacherous, lying promise

235 *embrace it freely:* welcome without reservation what you have said

236 *frankly:* without bitterness or ill feeling

237 *foils:* blunt fencing swords

238 *foil:* also means the background against which
a jewel shines more brightly. Hamlet is about to
make a pun on the word, saying that the skills of
Laertes will appear most impressive by contrast
with his own lack of skill

240 *Stick fiery off:* show to advantage

244 *Your . . . side:* your majesty has bet on the weaker
side

246 *since . . . odds:* as Laertes is generally considered
better, Hamlet has to have the odds

247 *This . . . another:* Laertes is looking for the
poisoned, unprotected rapier, which is difficult
to distinguish from the others without a close
inspection

248 *likes:* pleases
These . . . length? Are these foils all the same
length?

250 *stoups:* flagons, tankards

252 *quit . . . exchange:* draw level in the third bout

253 *ordnance:* cannons

254 *breath:* fitness

255 *an union:* a large pearl, presumably containing the
poison intended for Hamlet

258 *kettle:* drum

259 *cannoneer without:* cannon operator outside

HAMLET
I'll be your foil, Laertes: in mine ignorance
Your skill shall, like a star i' th' darkest night,
Stick fiery off indeed.

LAERTES

240   You mock me, sir.

HAMLET
No, by this hand.

KING CLAUDIUS
Give them the foils, young Osric. Cousin Hamlet,
You know the wager?

HAMLET
                         Very well, my lord.
Your grace hath laid the odds o' th' weaker side.

KING CLAUDIUS

245   I do not fear it; I have seen you both.
But since he is bettered, we have therefore odds.

LAERTES
This is too heavy, let me see another.

HAMLET
This likes me well. These foils have all a length?

OSRIC
Ay, my good lord.

They prepare to play.

KING CLAUDIUS

250   Set me the stoups of wine upon that table.
If Hamlet give the first or second hit,
Or quit in answer of the third exchange,
Let all the battlements their ordnance fire.
The king shall drink to Hamlet's better breath;

255   And in the cup an union shall he throw,
Richer than that which four successive kings
In Denmark's crown have worn. Give me the cups;
And let the kettle to the trumpet speak,
The trumpet to the cannoneer without,

260   The cannons to the heavens, the heaven to earth,
'Now the king drinks to Hamlet.' Come, begin.

Drinks; trumpets sound.

And you, the judges, bear a wary eye.

HAMLET
Come on, sir.

LAERTES
Come, my lord.

They play.

They play: each round of the fencing match may last for more than one minute, and sometimes for several minutes, on stage or screen

HAMLET
One.   265

LAERTES
No.

HAMLET
Judgement.

OSRIC
A hit, a very palpable hit.

268 *palpable:* obvious

Drums, trumpets; cannon shot off within.

LAERTES
Well, again.

KING CLAUDIUS
Stay, give me drink. Hamlet, this pearl is thine.   270
Here's to thy health! — Give him the cup.

HAMLET
I'll play this bout first; set it by a while. — Come.

They play.

Another hit. What say you?

LAERTES
A touch, a touch, I do confess.

KING CLAUDIUS
Our son shall win.

QUEEN GERTRUDE
                    He's fat, and scant of breath.   275
Here, Hamlet, take my napkin, rub thy brows.
The queen carouses to thy fortune, Hamlet.

275 *fat ... breath:* sweaty and breathless
276 *napkin:* handkerchief
277 *carouses:* drinks a toast

HAMLET
Good madam!

279 *do not drink:* Gertrude has taken the goblet
intended for Hamlet

286 *third:* third bout
286–8 *you . . . me:* you're only trifling with me; I wish
you would make your sword-thrusts with all the
energy you are capable of; I fear that you are
playing the fool with me

290 *Nothing, neither way:* a draw

292 *are incensed:* have lost their tempers. Claudius may
realise that Hamlet has the lethal weapon

294 *ho:* this is Osric's call to stop the duel

KING CLAUDIUS
Gertrude, do not drink.

QUEEN GERTRUDE
280 I will, my lord; I pray you pardon me.

KING CLAUDIUS [*aside to LAERTES*]
It is the poisoned cup; it is too late.

HAMLET
I dare not drink yet, madam; by and by.

QUEEN GERTRUDE
Come, let me wipe thy face.

LAERTES [*aside to KING CLAUDIUS*]
My lord, I'll hit him now.

KING CLAUDIUS
                              I do not think't.

LAERTES [*aside*]
285 And yet 'tis almost against my conscience.

HAMLET
Come, for the third, Laertes: you but dally;

I pray you pass with your best violence;

I am afeard you make a wanton of me.

LAERTES
Say you so? Come on.

They play.

OSRIC
290 Nothing, neither way.

They break off.

LAERTES
Have at you now!

*LAERTES wounds HAMLET; then in scuffling, they change
rapiers, and HAMLET wounds LAERTES.*

KING CLAUDIUS
Part them; they are incensed.

HAMLET
Nay, come again!
QUEEN GERTRUDE falls.

OSRIC
Look to the queen there, ho!

HORATIO

They bleed on both sides. How is it, my lord? 295

OSRIC

How is't, Laertes?

LAERTES

Why, as a woodcock to mine own springe, Osric.

I am justly killed with mine own treachery.

HAMLET

How does the queen?

KING CLAUDIUS

She swoons to see them bleed.

QUEEN GERTRUDE

No, no, the drink, the drink — O my dear Hamlet! — 300

The drink, the drink! I am poisoned.

Dies.

HAMLET

O villainy! Ho! Let the door be locked.

Treachery! Seek it out.

LAERTES falls.

LAERTES

It is here, Hamlet. Hamlet, thou art slain;

No medicine in the world can do thee good. 305

In thee there is not half an hour of life.

The treacherous instrument is in thy hand,

Unbated and envenomed. The foul practice

Hath turned itself on me. Lo, here I lie,

Never to rise again. Thy mother's poisoned. 310

I can no more. The king, the king's to blame.

HAMLET

The point envenomed too?

Then, venom, to thy work.

Strikes KING CLAUDIUS.

ALL

Treason! treason!

KING CLAUDIUS

O yet defend me, friends; I am but hurt. 315

---

297 *woodcock:* a foolish bird that is easily trapped
springe: snare

299 *swoons:* faints. The self-composed Claudius wants to save himself by concealing his criminal activities

308 *Unbated and envenomed:* unprotected and poisoned
practice: treachery, plot

311 *can:* can do

315 *but hurt:* merely wounded. Claudius may be assuming that the poison on the rapier has been used up on Hamlet and Laertes

HAMLET

Here, thou incestuous, murderous, damned Dane,

Forces KING CLAUDIUS to drink.

Drink off this potion. Is thy union here?

Follow my mother.

KING CLAUDIUS dies.

LAERTES

                He is justly served;

It is a poison tempered by himself.

320   Exchange forgiveness with me, noble Hamlet.

Mine and my father's death come not upon thee,

Nor thine on me.

Dies.

HAMLET

Heaven make thee free of it! I follow thee.

I am dead, Horatio. Wretched queen, adieu!

325   You that look pale and tremble at this chance,

That are but mutes or audience to this act,

Had I but time (as this fell sergeant, death,

Is strict in his arrest), O, I could tell you—

But let it be. Horatio, I am dead,

330   Thou livest, report me and my cause aright

To the unsatisfied.

HORATIO

                Never believe it.

I am more an antique Roman than a Dane.

Here's yet some liquor left.

HAMLET

                As thou'rt a man,

Give me the cup. Let go, by heaven, I'll have't!

335   O God, Horatio, what a wounded name,

Things standing thus unknown, shall live behind me!

If thou didst ever hold me in thy heart,

Absent thee from felicity a while,

And in this harsh world, draw thy breath in pain,

To tell my story.

A march afar off, and shout within.

340   What warlike noise is this?

---

317 *potion:* the poison in the cup
thy union: the pearl you placed in the cup, but also the union of Claudius and Gertrude in death

319 *tempered:* prepared, mixed

321–2 *Mine . . . me:* may we not be held morally guilty of what we have done to each other

323 *make . . . it:* forgive you

324 *Wretched:* pitiful

325 *chance:* unfortunate event

327 *fell:* cruel

328 *Is . . . arrest:* takes its victims strictly at the appointed time

330–31 *report . . . unsatisfied:* give an accurate account of the true circumstances of my life and actions to those who are not properly informed

332 *antique:* ancient. In ancient Rome, when life appeared to have lost its meaning, suicide was considered an honourable tradition. The prospect of outliving Hamlet leads the classically educated Horatio to contemplate suicide

335–6 *wounded . . . unknown:* damaged reputation, if the truth about me is not known

337 *hold . . . heart:* love me

338 *Absent . . . while:* remain on earth a while longer, do not embrace the happiness ('felicity') of death

339–40 *in . . . story:* endure the miseries of this life while you explain my case

OSRIC

Young Fortinbras, with conquest come from Poland,

To the ambassadors of England gives

This warlike volley.

HAMLET

              O, I die, Horatio!

The potent poison quite o'ercrows my spirit,

I cannot live to hear the news from England,   345

But I do prophesy th'election lights

On Fortinbras. He has my dying voice.

So tell him, with th'occurrents, more and less,

Which have solicited. The rest is silence.

Dies.

HORATIO

Now cracks a noble heart. Good night, sweet prince,   350

And flights of angels sing thee to thy rest.

March within.

Why does the drum come hither?

Enter FORTINBRAS, the English AMBASSADORS, and
ATTENDANTS, with drums and colours.

FORTINBRAS

Where is this sight?

HORATIO

              What is it you would see?

If aught of woe or wonder, cease your search.

FORTINBRAS

This quarry cries on havoc. O proud death,   355

What feast is toward in thine eternal cell,

That thou so many princes at a shot

So bloodily hast struck?

FIRST AMBASSADOR

             The sight is dismal;

And our affairs from England come too late.

The ears are senseless that should give us hearing,   360

To tell him his commandment is fulfilled,

That Rosencrantz and Guildenstern are dead.

Where should we have our thanks?

---

341 *conquest:* victory

342 *ambassadors of England:* the King of England has sent courtiers to report that Rosencrantz and Guildenstern have been put to death

344 *potent:* powerful
quite o'ercrows: completely triumphs over

346–7 *do … voice:* predict that Fortinbras will be elected king. He has my dying vote

348–9 *So … solicited:* let him know that I give him my vote, and also tell him the circumstances, great and small, that have prompted ('solicited') me to do so

353 *this sight:* Fortinbras has heard news of what has happened and has come to see for himself

354 *If … search:* if you are looking for some dire calamity, you have found it

355 *quarry … havoc:* pile of corpses loudly proclaims mass slaughter. This is a hunting metaphor: 'quarry' was a heap of deer slain in the hunt; 'cries on havoc' means 'announces indiscriminate slaughter'
356 *toward:* in preparation
eternal cell: grave
357 *shot:* stroke

358 *dismal:* horrifying, dreadful

363 *Where … thanks?* To whom should we look for our reward? They are wondering who is to succeed Claudius as king

363 *his:* Claudius's

366 *so ... question:* at the very moment of this bloody business

367 *You ... wars:* Fortinbras and his men are returning from their Polish expedition

369 *stage:* platform

372 *carnal:* the adultery of Claudius and Gertrude, and their incestuous marriage
bloody: the various murders
unnatural acts: murder and incest

373 *accidental judgements:* judgements handed down by divine providence in the form of apparent accidents (e.g. the deaths of Polonius, Gertrude and Laertes)
casual slaughters: killings that appear accidental

374 *cunning ... cause:* cleverly planning (e.g. the deaths of Hamlet, Rosencrantz and Guildenstern)

375 *this upshot:* the concluding events of the tragedy, whose results are now visible on the stage

375–6 *purposes ... heads:* schemes that went astray and harmed those who planned and perpetrated them

377 *deliver:* report

379–81 *embrace ... invite me:* accept what fortune has given me. I have claims here that I have not forgotten, and will take this opportunity to demand the title King of Denmark

383 *And ... more:* Horatio is referring to Hamlet's dying vote for Fortinbras, which will encourage the other electors to support Fortinbras

384 *same ... performed:* matter of the succession to the throne be dealt with immediately

385–6 *Even ... happen:* especially now that people are in a dangerous state of unrest and agitation, in case further conspiracies and wrongdoings ('errors') bring about further misfortunes

388 *put on:* put to the test

389 *for his passage:* to mark his passing

391 *Speak ... him:* sound his praises loudly

393 *Becomes ... amiss:* would be appropriate to a battlefield, but looks very much out of place here

HORATIO

Not from his mouth,

Had it th'ability of life to thank you:

365 He never gave commandment for their death.

But since, so jump upon this bloody question,

You from the Polack wars, and you from England,

Are here arrived, give order that these bodies

High on a stage be placèd to the view;

370 And let me speak to th'yet unknowing world

How these things came about. So shall you hear

Of carnal, bloody and unnatural acts,

Of accidental judgements, casual slaughters,

Of deaths put on by cunning and forced cause,

375 And, in this upshot, purposes mistook

Fallen on the inventors' heads. All this can I

Truly deliver.

FORTINBRAS

Let us haste to hear it,

And call the noblest to the audience.

For me, with sorrow I embrace my fortune.

380 I have some rights of memory in this kingdom,

Which now to claim my vantage doth invite me.

HORATIO

Of that I shall have also cause to speak,

And from his mouth whose voice will draw on more.

But let this same be presently performed,

385 Even while men's minds are wild, lest more mischance

On plots and errors, happen.

FORTINBRAS

Let four captains

Bear Hamlet, like a soldier, to the stage;

For he was likely, had he been put on,

To have proved most royal. And, for his passage,

390 The soldiers' music and the rites of war

Speak loudly for him.

Take up the bodies. Such a sight as this

Becomes the field, but here shows much amiss.

Go, bid the soldiers shoot.

Exeunt with a dead march; after which a peal of ordnance is shot off.

Key points

This final scene sees the deaths of many of the main characters. Horatio is left to speak for Hamlet, and Fortinbras claims the Danish throne.

- Hamlet has adopted a new attitude to death. He no longer sees it as a desirable release from life's ills, or something to be dreaded for what may follow it. He now accepts it as part of human destiny, to be looked upon serenely.

- Hamlet reveals that he has been able to change the orders for his execution and substitute the names of Rosencrantz and Guildenstern for his own. This appears callous, but he argues that they were leading him to his death, and therefore he could avoid that fate only by having them killed in his place, without giving them the opportunity to talk, even to a confessor.

- Hamlet has a new sense of the mysterious operations of providence. He senses that a guiding hand has influenced all that has happened to him, particularly during his sea-voyage. He no longer reproaches himself for his delay in punishing Claudius, since he now has a deep conviction that he will get his opportunity in due course. When Osric invites him to partake in a fencing match with Laertes, Hamlet sees it as his chance to confront his uncle and bring their deadly feud to a head.

- Hamlet has a premonition of disaster, perhaps even of his own death. However, he is comforted by his new faith in the universal operation of divine influence. The outcome of events may be seen as justifying this faith. Claudius, by murdering Hamlet's father, created the initial situation. Claudius is now also the one who resolves it, by providing Hamlet with his opportunity for vengeance. The villain thus becomes the unwitting agent of his own destruction.

- The death of Claudius appears to come at last by sheer accident, with Hamlet acting on the spur of the moment; but in Hamlet's new scheme of things, it is one of the many examples of the operation of divine justice. The sense of providence working through apparently chance events is well conveyed in Horatio's term 'accidental judgements' (line 373), in other words judgements that show themselves at work in seeming accidents, the best examples being the deaths of Claudius and Laertes. He also refers to 'purposes mistook' (line 375), meaning plans that backfire fatally on the planners.

- Claudius seems most concerned with self-preservation in this scene. He makes only a half-hearted attempt to stop Gertrude from drinking the poisoned wine, and later tries to pretend that she has merely fainted. However, there is a strong sense of poetic justice conveyed by the final deeds of the play. The murderous king is himself murdered; the man who sent his brother to death and possible damnation (because he was unprepared) is now sent to his death, and to his damnation, in the midst of his crimes. Hamlet stabs Claudius with the sword that has been used to bring about his own imminent death, while Laertes also meets the fate that he himself planned for Hamlet. Claudius is forced to drink the poison he intended Hamlet to drink; he is made to share at the same time in the manner of Gertrude's death, a death that he helped to bring about and that he could have prevented.

- Unlike the unrepentant Claudius, Laertes dies in a spirit of peace and reconciliation. He and Hamlet exchange forgiveness.

- As the end approaches, Hamlet recovers much of the moral ground he may have lost earlier in the play. His treatment of Laertes is frank and generous. Horatio, the character who knows him best, has no doubt that Hamlet dies a good death (lines 350–51).

- Hamlet's final thoughts are not of himself, but of the welfare of Denmark. He intervenes to prevent Horatio from taking his own life. He needs Horatio to tell the world his story and to ensure that Fortinbras becomes King of Denmark.

Useful quotes

There's a divinity that shapes our ends,
Rough-hew them how we will.

(Hamlet, lines 10–11)

They are not near my conscience; their defeat
Does by their own insinuation grow.

(Hamlet, lines 58–9)

But I am very sorry, good Horatio,
That to Laertes I forgot myself.
For by the image of my cause, I see
The portraiture of his, I'll court his favours.

(Hamlet, lines 75–8)

It is the poisoned cup; it is too late.

(Claudius, line 281)

And yet, 'tis almost against my conscience.

(Laertes, line 285)

The foul practice
Hath turned itself on me. Lo, here I lie,
Never to rise again. Thy mother's poisoned.
I can no more. The king, the king's to blame.

(Laertes, lines 308–11)

Exchange forgiveness with me, noble Hamlet.
Mine and my father's death come not upon thee,
Nor thine on me.

(Laertes, lines 320–22)

Now cracks a noble heart. Good night, sweet prince,
And flights of angels sing thee to thy rest.

(Horatio, lines 350–1)

So shall you hear
Of carnal, bloody and unnatural acts,
Of accidental judgements, casual slaughters,
Of deaths put on by cunning and forced cause,
And, in this upshot, purposes mistook,
Fallen on the inventors' heads.

(Horatio, lines 371–6)

? Questions

1 Some commentators have written of Hamlet's 'murder' of Rosencrantz and Guildenstern. Is it murder? Explain your answer.

2 Hamlet claims that Claudius 'popped in between th'election' and his own 'hopes' of succeeding his father as king (line 65). Is Hamlet justified in saying this? Explain.

3 News of the proposed fencing match is brought to Hamlet by Osric. Suggest reasons why Shakespeare introduces this new character at this stage of the play.

4 Show how this scene brings into sharp focus the moral contrast between Hamlet and Laertes.

5 Describe Claudius's response as his plans go astray. What do his instincts suggest to him?

6 Discuss the part played by Gertrude in this scene. What is your final impression of her?

7 Do you think Laertes is to be pitied in this scene? Give reasons for your answer.

8 Can you find any significance in the fact that the major characters all die by poisoning?

9 Does Horatio give an accurate summary of the events of the play (lines 371–6)? Explain.

10 In your opinion, does the play end satisfactorily? Does the future look bright for Denmark? Give reasons for your answers.

- Ophelia's grave is being dug and the gravediggers discuss her death.
- Hamlet considers death and how it is a great leveller.
- Ophelia's funeral takes place. Laertes is overcome by grief.
- There is an angry encounter between Hamlet and Laertes.

Scene 2

- Hamlet gives Horatio an account of what has happened to him during his sea-voyage.
- Osric, a foppish courtier, is the target of Hamlet's mockery as he delivers Claudius's invitation to engage in a fencing match with Laertes, which Hamlet accepts.
- During a break in the fencing, Claudius offers Hamlet a poisoned cup from which to drink. Hamlet refuses, but Gertrude drinks from the cup.
- Laertes wounds Hamlet with the poisoned sword, and Hamlet wounds him with the same sword.
- When Laertes, on the point of death, reveals Claudius's guilt, Hamlet stabs Claudius with the poisoned sword, and forces him to drink from the poisoned cup. Hamlet and Laertes forgive each other.
- Hamlet, concerned about Denmark's future, asks Horatio to tell his story and, with his dying breath, nominates Fortinbras as the next King of Denmark.

ACT 5 Speaking and listening

1 Assign the roles of Hamlet and Horatio. Imagine that at the end of Act 5, Scene 1, they meet to reflect on what they have experienced in the graveyard. In groups of four, discuss what these two characters might be saying to each other. Prepare the text of their conversation. Choose a representative of each group to read the text aloud. A discussion follows, involving all members of the class, on the merits of each version.

2 In groups, select a significant moment from Act 5 and discuss how it might be interpreted on stage. Assign the roles and portray your chosen moment in a freeze-frame. Consider what your character may be thinking and feeling at that moment in the play and try to convey this through your frozen stance and expression. The class should then discuss the significance of what has been portrayed, and comment on how your group has presented it.

Genre

*H*amlet is a **tragedy**. In works that we call tragic, certain features seem to recur with unfailing regularity, and these features may be considered to be the essential elements of the genre.

In tragedies we usually see the random interaction of **external forces** (such as fate, chance or accident) and **human weakness** (such as vice, folly or stupidity). The result threatens the well-being of the individual and of society. In *Hamlet*, however, the force operating to bring about Hamlet's tragic situation is solely external: the ghost's demand that he take on the role of avenger as a matter of duty. Shakespeare did not give him a specific tragic flaw or defect.

The **essential** elements of **tragedy:**

Tragic drama focuses on a single individual, whom we call the **tragic hero** or the tragic protagonist. The hero should enjoy the audience's earnest good will. The tragic hero in this play is Hamlet, who speaks 37 per cent of the lines in the play.

The hero in Shakespearean tragedy is always **a person of status**, a noble personality who is involved in great events. Hamlet is a prince, and heir to the throne of Denmark.

The tragic hero must be motivated by a serious purpose or undertake a **serious course of action**. For Hamlet, this action involves avenging the murder of his father.

Through that purpose or action, the tragic hero **inevitably** meets with grave physical and/or spiritual **suffering**. The direction of his career in the play is always **from good to bad fortune**. If Shakespeare had caused Claudius to repent of his crime and abdicate as king in favour of Hamlet, the play would not be a tragedy.

In Shakespearean tragedy it is difficult to avoid the impression that **fate** is working against the hero from the beginning. Hamlet's situation seems to be so arranged that he has **no chance of a happy outcome**.

The **audience must identify with the tragic hero** in his sufferings. He must remind us strongly of our humanity, so that we can see him as in some way standing for us. He must be vulnerable to extreme suffering, as Hamlet is, and we should feel some degree of **pity and fear** for him.

For the tragic hero, **recognition** is the essential tragic experience. It occurs when he finally understands his character and his situation. Hamlet's recognition becomes obvious after his return from the sea-voyage to England, when he has accepted that a power greater than himself is directing the course of events and states that there is a divine purpose behind human activity.

The tragic hero grows in stature, and in the audience's estimation, as he **faces up to his destiny** and confronts it. Hamlet's speeches in Act 5 reflect his increased self-awareness and his realisation that his role is that of an instrument of providence and of justice. He knows that the fencing match with Laertes is a trap, but takes part willingly, ready to accept whatever fate has in store for him.

Shakespearean tragedy depicts **first the violation, and then the restoration, of order** and health in society. The corruption of Claudius, the main agent of social and moral disorder in *Hamlet*, destroys other characters and disrupts the state. A semblance of order is restored at the play's conclusion: the villainies are exposed, and Fortinbras will take control of Denmark.

Shakespearean tragedy is not concerned with punishing evil and rewarding virtue. Eight people perish in the **tragic catastrophe** (conclusion) of *Hamlet*, and the idea that unites all their deaths is that evil forces, once released (in this case by Claudius), work their destructive way and inflict punishment out of all proportion to any offence (as in the case particularly of Ophelia). The evil forces ultimately annihilate themselves as well as whatever forces of good they encounter. This notion of evil as a self-destructive force is illustrated in the undoing of Claudius as the play ends. Hamlet is engulfed by the same evil, and becomes the cause of further ruin in his dealings with Polonius, Ophelia, Laertes, Rosencrantz and Guildenstern.

Revenge tragedy

Hamlet is specifically a revenge tragedy. It is one of the many plays written by dramatists during Shakespeare's lifetime that deals with the theme of revenge.

All revenge tragedies follow a similar five-part structure:

1 A revelation is made to the chosen avenger by the victim of a murder, usually a ghost. The revelation consists of an account of a past event that needs to be avenged.
2 The avenger plans the revenge.
3 The avenger confronts the intended victim.
4 The avenger partially executes the plan.
5 The avenger completes the act of vengeance.

The avenger's role is essentially a waiting one. If he or she did not delay, the play would be over too quickly. One of the major conventions of revenge tragedy is that the villain eventually provides the avenger with an opportunity to take revenge. Thus, the villain becomes the agent of his or her own destruction. This is what happens in *Hamlet*. Claudius arranges a fencing match to destroy Hamlet, but is himself destroyed (along with Laertes and Gertrude), while Hamlet, without planning it, becomes the agent of his uncle's doom.

Hamlet is not the only avenger in this play. Shakespeare considers the idea of vengeance from several angles: Hamlet, Laertes, Fortinbras and Pyrrhus have similar missions, which they fulfil in different ways. The 'common theme', as Claudius says in another context, 'is death of fathers' (Act 1, Scene 2, lines 103–4). Laertes seeks revenge for the deaths of his father and sister; Fortinbras, for the death of his father and the loss of Norwegian territory to Denmark; and the mythological Pyrrhus, for the death of his father at the hands of the Trojans. Shakespeare presents these three avengers in sharp contrast to Hamlet the avenger.

Pyrrhus, the 'hellish' avenger who slays an old man, the 'reverend Priam', in a dubious act of vengeance, is presented as evil, 'dread and black', steeped in the 'blood of fathers, mothers, daughters, sons'. He is 'a painted tyrant', who enjoys 'mincing with his sword' the limbs of

Priam (Act 2, Scene 2, lines 437, 453, 429, 432, 454, 487). The contrast between Pyrrhus and Hamlet is plain.

Unlike Pyrrhus, Hamlet struggles to take revenge, even against the man who has secretly murdered his father and destroyed his mother's honour. There is even a telling parallel situation involving the two characters as would-be avengers. Pyrrhus suspends his sword for a moment over his victim until 'arousèd vengeance sets him new a-work' (line 462) and he slays old Priam. Hamlet stands behind the kneeling Claudius in Act 3, Scene 3 and puts up his sword, but unlike Pyrrhus, he then spares his target.

The Pyrrhus episode mirrors the central action of the main play. Pyrrhus can be seen as a reflection of both Hamlet and Claudius; Priam represents both Claudius and the late King Hamlet; and Hecuba is Gertrude. This makes the player's speech about Pyrrhus both a history of Elsinore's recent past and a piece of wish-fulfilment for Hamlet.

Hamlet's *Mousetrap* play has similarly subtle implications. This insert-play features a murder that resembles the murder of King Hamlet. However, by making the poisoner, **Lucianus**, the nephew of the murdered king, Hamlet presents the ultimate revenge of his father's murder as well as the original crime of Claudius. Lucianus, then, is both Hamlet and Claudius, avenger and killer in one.

In the context of the revenge theme, there is a close parallel between Hamlet and **Fortinbras** as Hamlet's father killed the father of Fortinbras. The most significant contrast between the two is that while Hamlet is deeply conscious of the moral issues involved in taking vengeance, there is no evidence that Fortinbras is troubled by any such concerns.

In the earliest references to him, Fortinbras appears to be a reckless adventurer at the head of a band of brigands. His war on Poland is one of aggression. He may be puffed up with ambition and dreams of honour, and he seems to pay very little attention to the justice or otherwise of his cause. Hamlet admires Fortinbras for his absolute dedication to his role, and criticises himself for his own inactivity.

Laertes is the most obvious contrast to Hamlet. This is made explicit by Hamlet himself when he tells Horatio that 'by the image of my cause, I see the portraiture of his' (Act 5, Scene 2, lines 77–8). He then repeats this idea just before the fencing match: 'I'll be your foil, Laertes' (line 238).

Laertes and Hamlet both have strong motives for revenge, but there the resemblance ends. When Laertes hears of his father's death, he quickly raises a rebellion against Claudius. He is prepared to cast the moral law aside:

> To hell, allegiance! Vows, to the blackest devil!
> Conscience and grace, to the profoundest pit!
>
> (Act 4, Scene 5, lines 130–31)

When Claudius asks him how far he is willing to go to show himself a true son of his father, Laertes declares that he would 'cut his throat i' th' church' (Act 4, Scene 7, line 129). This remark reminds us of Hamlet's inability to do the same to Claudius when he found him at prayer.

Claudius hints at another contrast between Hamlet and Laertes when he proposes that Laertes should use an unprotected fencing sword. He makes this proposal knowing that Hamlet would never dream of being so underhand, or even suspect that Laertes would do such a thing. Indeed, Claudius can assure Laertes that Hamlet, being 'most generous, and free from all contriving, will not peruse the foils' (Act 4, Scene 7, lines 138–9).

Laertes reveals the full force of his vicious nature when he intensifies the plot to kill Hamlet by stealth. He has already procured poison in case he might find a use for it, and now he intends to envenom the unguarded blade. Laertes has dedicated himself fully to the barbaric code of vengeance (as proposed by the ghost), something which Hamlet cannot do.

Laertes has another function that deserves attention. His revenge for his father has Hamlet as its object, so that Hamlet becomes for Laertes what Claudius is for Hamlet. In this most subtle and complex of plots, Hamlet, on the road to avenge the murder of his own father, has become the slayer of another man's father (Polonius). To add a further subtlety, each son, while killing his father's killer, forgives, and is forgiven by, his own killer.

Social, cultural and intellectual contexts

Shakespeare paid little attention to the facts of history or geography in his settings or in his plots. We can assume that the action of *Hamlet* is set in tenth-century Denmark. Denmark had significant influence over England at that time, and Claudius clearly has command over the King of England in the play (see Act 4, Scene 3, lines 56–63). However, there is nothing distinctively Danish about the atmosphere of the play. Indeed, the setting of *Hamlet* is firmly influenced by Elizabethan England and its beliefs, concerns and interests.

The play has references to many things with which Shakespeare's audiences would have been familiar, but which modern audiences or students of the play must inevitably find puzzling. *Hamlet* is in many respects a learned play, but the learning it displays is of a kind not generally familiar in twenty-first-century Ireland.

William Shakespeare (1564–1616)

Renaissance England

Shakespeare wrote *Hamlet* during the English Renaissance, a cultural movement based on a rediscovery of ancient Greek and Roman culture, which in turn led to a renewed interest in artistic and intellectual pursuits. This background is reflected in the play's references to classical literature and mythology, and in Hamlet's speculations on issues of life, death and human conduct.

Hamlet is based on an existing story about the barbaric revenge exacted by a son for the murder of his father. However, Shakespeare greatly refined the story. Most notably, he made the son a highly accomplished Renaissance prince, the noble and respected courtier, soldier and scholar described by Ophelia (Act 3, Scene 1, lines 148–52), and the sort of character his contemporary audience was interested in.

The most celebrated speech in the play, that beginning 'To be, or not to be' (Act 3, Scene 1, lines 56–88), is a means of revealing Hamlet's interest in abstract ideas and his ability to marshal these ideas into a coherent argument. This accomplishment is in the tradition of the ancient philosophers.

Several of the characters have classical names: Claudius, Laertes, Ophelia, Horatio, Cornelius and Marcellus. Telling details often remind us of the classical heritage of the characters. When Hamlet reminisces about his late father, he instinctively thinks of Hyperion, the god of the sun, and then likens Claudius to one of the most repulsive creatures of Greek mythology, the satyr, who is half-man and half-beast, ugly and lustful (Act 1, Scene 2, lines 139–40).

Classical references are characteristic of the educated Horatio, who, for example, invokes the death of Julius Caesar as a reminder of what can happen to the world when rulers die violently, and calls the sea 'Neptune's empire' (Act 1, Scene 1, lines 117, 122). The influence of a classical education has a profound effect on Horatio's outlook. This is especially apparent when the prospect of outliving Hamlet prompts him to contemplate suicide, a course of action widely approved by ancient Romans when it appeared to them that life had lost its meaning, but condemned by Christian teachers. Horatio sees himself as 'more an antique Roman than a Dane' (Act 5, Scene 2, line 332).

One of the visiting players entertains Hamlet with a dramatic speech about the Trojan War (Act 2, Scene 2, lines 442–91), a major event in Greek mythology and literature. Polonius recalls his own days as an actor and how he once played the part of Julius Caesar (Act 3, Scene 2, lines 92–5), an ancient Roman general and dictator. Such interests are typical of the Renaissance period.

Christianity

Hamlet is set in the Christian era, and its characters, in spite of their frequently un-Christian behaviour, are conceived by Shakespeare as practising Christians. The play refers to Christian practices, ideas and expressions, and is influenced by Christian morality.

The ghost is portrayed as a saved soul returning from the purgatory of traditional Catholic belief, where he will be confined until his earthly crimes 'are burnt and purged away' (Act 1, Scene 5, line 13). He was killed in a state of sin, 'with all my imperfections on my head', and deprived of the consolation of the Last Sacraments: 'unhouseled, disappointed, unaneled' (lines 76–9).

Both Hamlet and Claudius express sentiments that underline their belief in some of the central teachings of Christianity. The prayer scene (Act 3, Scene 3) provides an excellent illustration. Claudius considers the possibility of repentance and consequent pardon for his crime. He thinks of the great power of divine mercy, but is sufficiently aware of Christian teaching to understand that it is pointless to ask for forgiveness while he still enjoys the fruits of his crime: his crown and his wife.

Hamlet, seeing Claudius at prayer and concluding that he is in a state of grace and therefore fit for heaven, refrains from killing him. He would prefer to wait until he finds Claudius engaged in some wicked deed that will damn his soul forever. Only a believer in Christian teachings on sin, repentance and salvation could have, or even pretend to have, Hamlet's motives for delaying vengeance. Later, Hamlet urges his mother to confess her sins: 'Repent what's past, avoid what is to come' (Act 3, Scene 4, line 153).

The significance of Christian burial is debated in relation to Ophelia's funeral (Act 5, Scene 1); and Laertes imagines the priest who refuses Ophelia a full Christian burial enduring the torments of hell while she enjoys heaven: 'A ministering angel shall my sister be, when thou liest howling' (lines 226–7). Similarly, Horatio envisages Hamlet accompanied to heaven by 'flights of angels' (Act 5, Scene 2, line 351).

Superstition

The Elizabethan world was a superstitious place, where people readily believed in magic and witchcraft, fairies and ghosts. In *Hamlet* we see a ghost appear between midnight and dawn, as Elizabethans believed was the case. The play also features Elizabethan beliefs on why ghosts appear and how they should be addressed.

Modern audiences may struggle with the idea of a ghost appearing and talking to a live human being, but this aspect of the play would not have posed such a problem for Shakespeare's audience. Their primary concern would have been whether this supernatural apparition was in fact the devil in disguise.

Astrology was also part of the general structure of belief among all classes of Elizabethan society. People believed that the stars and the planets influenced life on earth. Horatio makes reference to comets and an eclipse, 'disasters in the sun; and the moist star' (moon), as a signal

of 'feared events' to come (Act1, Scene 1, lines 120–27). Such remarks would have enhanced the atmosphere of fear and foreboding created in the play's opening scene.

Suffering and cruelty

Shakespeare and his contemporaries, whether aristocrats or ordinary people, lived in a much harsher environment than we do today. They were also accustomed to experiences and events that we would find intolerably cruel.

Life was precarious for Shakespeare's audience. They had to contend with the widespread dangers presented by poor sanitation and infectious diseases such as the plague, smallpox and syphilis. Medical treatments were often gruelling, such as bleeding the patient or using leeches to suck the patient's blood. The average life expectancy was just thirty-five years.

There was also the threat posed by a heavy-handed and violent state system. Torture was used routinely as a method of interrogation. Tyburn Hill was the scene of public executions involving hanging, drawing and quartering. These gruesome spectacles would attract large crowds. On London Bridge, the heads of executed criminals were exposed to public view on pikes. Opposite the Globe theatre stood the bear pit, in which chained animals were mauled to death by savage dogs.

Daily exposure to such adversity and cruelty made Elizabethans less sensitive to suffering, and conditioned them to the bloody scenes we find in Shakespeare's tragedies. Indeed, such scenes were very popular and theatre audiences expected and demanded them.

Theatre

Hamlet's encounter with the touring company of players features some elements that can be understood only as references to the theatre scene in Shakespeare's London. Such topical references are found in many of Shakespeare's plays, whatever their supposed location or time period.

When Rosencrantz tells Hamlet that the boy actors carry away 'Hercules and his load too' (Act 2, Scene 2, line 341), he is suggesting that the popularity of a company of boy actors is such that they have captured audiences from the Globe theatre in London. This was the theatre that *Hamlet* was written for, and the sign outside it depicted Hercules carrying a globe representing the world.

When Polonius tells Hamlet that he once played the part of Julius Caesar (Act 3, Scene 2, line 94), the actor is making a subtle reference to Shakespeare's own play on the subject, performed in 1599, just a year or so before *Hamlet*. The actor playing Polonius might well have been known to Shakespeare's audience for his role as Caesar.

Shakespeare makes references to the structure of the theatre in which the plays were first performed (see p. 3). When Hamlet assures the ghost that he will remember him 'while memory holds a seat in this distracted globe'

(Act 1, Scene 5, lines 96–7), he is saying that he will remain faithful to what the ghost has commanded as long as his disturbed mind (his 'globe') retains the power of memory. The audience in the Globe theatre would also have recognised and enjoyed the pun on 'seat' and 'globe'.

A more complex and significant example occurs when Hamlet is telling Rosencrantz and Guildenstern of his depressive state of mind:

> …it goes so heavily with my disposition that this goodly frame, the earth, seems to me a sterile promontory; this most excellent canopy, the air, look you, this brave o'erhanging firmament, this majestical roof fretted with golden fire, why it appears no other thing to me but a foul and pestilent congregation of vapours.

(Act 2, Scene 2, lines 286–91)

The actor playing Hamlet delivered this speech on the rectangular stage of the Globe theatre, which projected into the audience like a 'promontory' or a headland jutting out into the sea. He looked up at the 'canopy' (or 'the heavens') that covered the stage, the underside of which was a ceiling painted with golden stars ('fretted with golden fire') and which represented the 'firmament' or sky. By having Hamlet point to the canopy ('look you'), Shakespeare used his theatre, which was part of the immediate experience of his audience, to underline his character's depressed withdrawal from everyday life. Hamlet was thus able to suggest that the poison injected by Claudius into his life had rendered the earth no more significant than a bare stage, and the sky no more majestic than the gaudy stars that decorate a stage canopy.

Shakespeare's tendency to break down the barrier between illusion and reality is even more strikingly conveyed towards the end of the play. Most of the main characters are dead. The bodies of Claudius, Gertrude and Laertes lie on the stage. Then, with only moments to live, Hamlet turns his attention to the remaining members of the court and says: 'You that look pale and tremble at this chance, that are but mutes or audience to this act' (Act 5, Scene 2, lines 325–6).

Shakespeare wrote plays to suit the tastes, expectations and attitudes of his varied audience. This audience comprised people from every level of society, from aristocratic patrons to the uneducated majority, from those who enjoyed coarse or crude spectacle to those with more sophisticated tastes. Shakespeare had to satisfy every kind of spectator, and *Hamlet*, like his other plays, represents his response to this problem.

For the cultured minority, he provides learned references to mythology and ancient history and discusses the nature of acting and the politics of the theatre. These spectators would also have appreciated Hamlet's philosophical cast of mind, as well as the frequent subtlety of the play's language with its elaborate figures of speech and word play.

The less cultured majority would have derived particular enjoyment from comic episodes such as the conversation of the gravediggers, as well as the moments of spectacle such as the ghost's appearances, the killings and the displays of swordsmanship.

Shakespeare's audiences were highly trained listeners. They relied on conversation, discussion and listening as the means of acquiring information. Weekly attendance at the local Church of England was compulsory, and sermons were elaborate and highly rhetorical, requiring the same kind of close attention as the complex speeches in *Hamlet*. Many sermons lasted for two or three hours. Even the least sophisticated of *Hamlet*'s early audiences had developed powers of concentration that were superior to those of today's audiences.

The Globe 1614

25

General vision and viewpoint

To understand *Hamlet*, we must keep in mind some of the principles that governed Shakespeare's view of the world and of the place of human beings in it.

Elizabeth I (1533–1603)

Shakespeare and most of his contemporaries took it for granted that God had created a world in which nature, including human nature, was governed by universal and divine laws. They believed that keeping those laws was essential to the welfare of human beings, and that breaking them, especially in significant ways, would lead to disastrous consequences for those involved and for society as a whole. These laws are expressed in the Ten Commandments and teachings of Christianity.

We also have to bear in mind that monarchy was the common form of government when Shakespeare wrote. Monarchs were regarded as God's representatives on earth, and as sacred persons, on whom the welfare of the entire population depended. This idea is conveyed in the play when Guildenstern and Rosencrantz remind Claudius that the fortunes and welfare of his subjects depend on his survival, and that a king's death or overthrow can be part of a massive process of destruction (Act 3, Scene 3, lines 8–23).

The first law of nature is that it will punish violations of its laws. In *Hamlet* it is Claudius who first violates natural law, and who sets nature's revenge for this in motion. Claudius kills his brother, a deed that has 'the primal eldest curse upon't' (Act 3, Scene 3, line 38). Since his brother was a king, Claudius has also killed God's anointed deputy on earth. To these two appalling crimes are added adultery, incest and the moral corruption of Gertrude.

Shakespeare uses the ghost to suggest that nature is in revolt against these massive breaches of the natural order by Claudius. The soldiers are terrified by the supernatural apparition, and Horatio claims that it 'bodes some strange eruption to our state' (Act 1, Scene 1, line 72). They see the ghost as a messenger, bringing evil news. Hamlet also recognises this as soon as he is told about the ghost: 'Foul deeds will rise, though all the earth o'erwhelm them, to men's eyes' (Act 1, Scene 2, lines 259–60).

The point here is that there are deeds so evil that nature will not tolerate them. Nature responds to Claudius's unnatural deeds by causing the underworld to yield up a ghost to reveal a murder 'most foul, strange and unnatural' (Act 1, Scene 5, line 28), and to demand that the murderer be punished. As a consequence of the unnatural crimes Claudius has committed, the country over which he rules is also cursed: 'Something is rotten in the state of Denmark' (Act 1, Scene 4, line 92).

Claudius used poison to murder King Hamlet. As a result, a metaphorical poison seeps through the play: rottenness, cankers and 'things rank and gross in nature' (Act 1, Scene 2, line 136) are found at every turn. The metaphorical poison becomes a literal one again when Gertrude, Claudius, Laertes and Hamlet are all poisoned in Act 5, Scene 2. As if to symbolise the greater guilt of Claudius, Hamlet forces the poisoned cup down the king's throat even though he is already dying from the poisoned rapier.

Claudius perpetuates the evil that prompted his original crime. He takes control of Laertes, initially a decent youth, and leads him to dishonour and death, making him and Hamlet colleagues in tragedy as they poison each other. He also corrupts Gertrude; this in turn threatens Hamlet's mental stability.

Another agent of the contagion identified in the play is Polonius. He befouls the love of Hamlet and Ophelia: her obedience to her corrupt father in rejecting Hamlet compounds Hamlet's distrust of women, which was caused by his mother's adulterous relationship with Claudius and her betrayal of his father. The rottenness in Denmark has corrupted love itself.

Friendship has also been spoiled. Hamlet first greets Rosencrantz and Guildenstern, his old schoolfellows, with enthusiasm. He soon discovers that Claudius is using them as agents, and his friendship quickly turns to enmity.

Eight of the nine significant characters in *Hamlet* are dead by the close of the play. Horatio is the exception. He is forcibly prevented by Hamlet from sharing in the common death. He, unlike the others, has stood outside the action, and has not been tainted by the poisonous atmosphere of the royal court.

The eight deaths can be seen as elements in a single pattern: evil, once started on its course, will attack and destroy without distinction the good as well as the bad, the evil characters such as Claudius and the virtuous ones such as Ophelia. Virtue and innocence offer no protection.

In *Hamlet*, particularly in Act 5, after Hamlet has returned from his sea-voyage, we are made to feel that God, or divine providence, is directing events. Hamlet is convinced that there is a divine purpose behind human activity: 'There's a divinity that shapes our ends, rough-hew them how we will' (Act 5, Scene 2, lines 10–11). He finds proof of this in his safe return to Denmark in the most unlikely circumstances. For example, when he found that he had the ring to seal the letter to the King of England, and so save his own life, he sensed the hand of providence in this: 'even in that was heaven ordinant' (line 48).

Hamlet faces the prospect of a fencing match with Laertes in the same frame of mind, telling Horatio that divine providence is expressed in every individual event, whether that be the fall of a sparrow or his confrontation with Claudius (lines 202–6). In other words, everything that happens is part of an eternal, divine law.

If, as Hamlet claims, providence is working in human affairs, and if the play sets out to illustrate this idea, what is the catastrophe (the conclusion of the play) telling us? The most we can say is that justice is served in some measure. Claudius used poison to become king, and he dies by poison. Laertes used his own poison to kill Hamlet, and dies by the same poison. Gertrude drinks Claudius's poison literally, as she once did metaphorically. Hamlet is killed because he could not eradicate evil in time, but he finds honour in his own death and is vindicated by Fortinbras, who affirms his worth and allows military music to proclaim his praises.

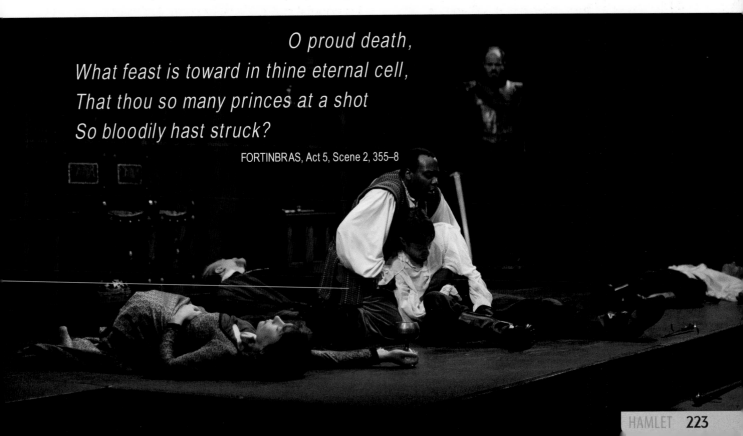

O proud death,
What feast is toward in thine eternal cell,
That thou so many princes at a shot
So bloodily hast struck?

FORTINBRAS, Act 5, Scene 2, 355–8

Characters

All accounts of dramatic characters and their relationships, including those given here, should be received with caution. It is seldom possible to give a definitive account of any character or relationship in *Hamlet* or any other Shakespearean play.

Theatre productions and film versions of *Hamlet* show us that the text of the play can be used by directors and actors to impose various interpretations of characters, motives and actions. No two productions provide us with quite the same overall impression, particularly of the characters. Those who have got to know the text of the play well, and formed their own views on its characters, will often notice that what they see on stage or screen does not match the impressions they formed from their reading.

It should be remembered that a performance of the play involves much more than Shakespeare's words. Actors use facial expressions, gestures, stage positions, accents and so forth to convey information about the character they are playing. Similarly, production decisions about casting, costumes, lighting, music, etc. often seek to influence our interpretation of a character.

Hamlet includes features such as royal processions, a dumb show and a fencing match, all of which last longer on stage than we may realise when we read the text. These action scenes provide further opportunities for revealing character traits.

Hamlet

witty
melancholy
refined
reflective
philosophical
disillusioned
popular
intelligent
cynical
sarcastic
cruel
quick-thinking
noble
scholarly
courteous

Hamlet is probably the most talked about and the most written about character in world drama. For some commentators, he is an admirable character, a noble hero. For others, his inertia or cruelty make him closer to a villain.

Hamlet offers some unfavourable commentary on his own character. He tells Ophelia: 'I am very proud, revengeful, ambitious, with more offences at my beck than I have thoughts to put them in' (Act 3, Scene 1, lines 123–5). The text of the play provides a good deal of material to justify Hamlet's derogatory account of himself.

Even those who regard Hamlet as an essentially 'good' or sympathetic character will admit that his virtues are offset by some disturbing features in his personality, outlook and behaviour. The bitterness, sarcasm and hatred that mark his dealings with some of the other characters are clear to see. His other faults include callous cruelty, cynicism and occasional coarseness.

Hamlet's cruelty to both Gertrude and Ophelia amounts to extreme mental and emotional torture. He seems to relish their suffering and misery. His interview with his mother (Act 3, Scene 4) is marked by withering sarcasm, self-righteousness and obscenity of language and ideas. This exchange is remarkable for its compulsive and obsessive emphasis on lust and the corruption of human relationships. The imagery he uses is at times repulsive and excessive, and the tone of his remarks is hysterical and violent.

He also delights in the torment he inflicts on Claudius through the insert-play, congratulating himself for causing such a reaction and calling for music to celebrate it (Act 3, Scene 2, lines 259–61, 274). When he finds Claudius at prayer, he takes an unholy pleasure in preserving him for a horrible fate at some future time. He wants to kill him when he has no chance of repenting for his sins, so 'that his soul may be as damned and black as hell, whereto it goes' (Act 3, Scene 3, lines 95–6).

Hamlet sends his old friends Rosencrantz and Guildenstern to their deaths and refuses to take moral responsibility for doing this: 'They are not near my conscience' (Act 5, Scene 2, line 58). He may believe that they, as agents of Claudius, knew that they were leading him to execution, and that his only chance of escaping that fate was to have them executed in his place. As such, Hamlet's action could be seen as self-defence.

However, his casual attitude to what he has done shows how far he has been corrupted in the course of the play. The cause of this corruption is Claudius.

When Hamlet kills Polonius, thinking he is killing Claudius, he reacts to this violent deed in a manner that does him little credit. He callously dismisses the death as an irrelevance: 'Thou wretched, rash, intruding fool, farewell!' (Act 3, Scene 4, line 31). He then proceeds to treat his dead victim as no better than an animal: 'I'll lug the guts into the neighbour room' (line 215).

Hamlet displays the more attractive side of his character to those whom he respects. He forgives Laertes with his dying breath, prevents Horatio's suicide and shows practical concern for the visiting players. He inspires the absolute devotion and loyalty of Horatio, the character who (apart from Gertrude, presumably) knows him best. This more attractive Hamlet earns Horatio's sincere epitaph:

> Now cracks a noble heart. Good night, sweet prince,
> And flights of angels sing thee to thy rest.
>
> (Act 5, Scene 2, lines 350–51)

We should also recognise Hamlet's moving devotion to the memory of his father, and his desire to know the truth, warped though these may be by the pressure of circumstances. He is an intelligent thinker, highly skilled in the use of language, and often displays good sense and refined taste.

Hamlet's tragic experience can be understood only by taking the two contradicting sides of his nature fully into account. His tragedy is that of a noble, idealistic young man, the hope and jewel of his society, whose greatness of mind and soul is overthrown by a succession of catastrophic events, and perverted to cynicism, grossness and cruelty.

His disillusionment

The ghost seeks to incite Hamlet to act against Claudius. Hamlet, however, is as much concerned with his mother's betrayal of his late father and her disgusting relationship with Claudius (as he sees it), as he is with his uncle's crime. He is so shocked that his mother could marry so unworthy a man as Claudius within a few months of his father's death that it taints his mind against all women. Hamlet's obsession with Gertrude's frailty threatens his balance and self-control. His bitterness towards her must be understood in terms of this resentment felt by a son towards a guilty mother. It is the essential emotion of the play.

It also causes him to lose whatever belief he might have had in the possibility of a virtuous, stable love between a man and a woman. He begins to see the innocent Ophelia as a mirror-image of his mother. In Act 3, Scene 1, he calls Ophelia's chastity into question. He tells her to enter a convent in order to avoid marriage. He suggests that women, including Ophelia, are more likely than not to betray their husbands by being unfaithful to them. Ophelia can only assume that Hamlet's rant means he has lost his mind.

Is it reasonable for Hamlet to find his mother's behaviour so appalling that it compromises all women: 'frailty, thy name is woman' (Act 1, Scene 2, line 146)? The most appropriate answer to such a question is that Hamlet's thoughts about his mother are seldom reasonable or balanced. It is also fair to say that many people in real life, faced with similar situations, tend to react as Hamlet does: disillusionment with one male or female can lead to disillusionment with all males or all females.

Hamlet's disillusionment extends to more than Gertrude, Ophelia, or women in general. From the beginning, we find him expressing a sense of ennui at having to endure the routine of human existence:

> How weary, stale, flat and unprofitable
> Seem to me all the uses of this world!
>
> (Act 1, Scene 2, lines 133–4)

This statement is uttered before he discovers that his mother's new husband has murdered her last husband (Hamlet's father), suggesting that his depressive state is due to the sudden death of his adored father, and the indecently hasty and incestuous marriage of his mother to an uncle he dislikes.

Hamlet is already at a low ebb, therefore, when he finds out that his father was murdered. There is the further overwhelming burden of the ghost's command that Hamlet should take speedy vengeance on Claudius, without turning against Gertrude. Since the ghost does much to convey the impression that Gertrude has been the partner of Claudius in adultery, it would be difficult for Hamlet to ignore her faults.

He also has to contend with the knowledge that he has been prevented from becoming king in succession to his father because Claudius stole the crown from King Hamlet. In this context it is significant that on his return from England, Hamlet announces himself, in the graveyard, as King of Denmark: 'This is I, Hamlet the Dane' (Act 5, Scene 1, lines 243–4).

His delay

Hamlet's slowness in taking revenge is built into the very fabric of the play. He frequently mentions his failure to act, and seems baffled, angry and frustrated when he contemplates it. Various explanations have been offered for his delay, including:

- He may be squeamish about shedding blood; able to think about the act of revenge as a duty, but reluctant to perform it.

- He may be struggling under the burden of extreme melancholy (depression), which stops him from undertaking positive planned activities.

- Like most of us, despite initial enthusiasm, he simply defers urgent duties for as long as possible.

- When he has time to reflect, he may find the ghost's vindictive commands too brutal and repulsive for a person with a sensitive nature like his to carry out.

- To satisfy his conscience, he may first need to establish the 'honesty' or good faith of the ghost, who may, after all, be a devil in disguise seeking to damn his soul.

Whatever the explanation, Hamlet never takes on the full duty of an avenger. This is not because he is incapable of ending a person's life. After all, he rashly kills Polonius in mistake for Claudius, coldly sends Rosencrantz and Guildenstern to their deaths, and murders Claudius in the closing scene. But these are acts of impulse, carried out on the spur of the moment. It is another matter to plan murderous vengeance and then carry it out with full deliberation, which he seems unable to do, as his behaviour when he spares Claudius in the prayer scene (Act 3, Scene 3) suggests.

What Hamlet actually does is to play a waiting game, remaining alert to what his enemies are planning, and matching their moves with his own. He senses towards the end that Claudius will, in good time, ensnare himself.

Shakespeare allows Hamlet to fulfil the task of vengeance without undertaking any morally revolting scheme of slaughter. Had he made Hamlet follow the brutal, undiscriminating course of the bloody avenger, it would inevitably have alienated our sympathies. As it is, Hamlet stands morally apart from his enemies, whose plans involve levels of treachery and deceit to which he cannot stoop.

His 'antic disposition'

Hamlet's state of mind remains an issue throughout the play. The word 'mad' is used by and about Hamlet fifteen times, while 'madness' is similarly used on twenty-one occasions. Hamlet's behaviour towards Ophelia, Gertrude, Claudius, Polonius, Rosencrantz and Guildenstern clearly gives them the impression that he is not in a normal frame of mind.

However, members of the audience know that Hamlet is not insane. We have heard him explain to Horatio and Marcellus that he intends to engage in odd and abnormal behaviour, 'To put an antic disposition on' (Act 1, Scene 5, line 171), whenever he considers this appropriate. He also warns them not to tell anybody that they are aware of any reason why he should behave strangely.

One might wonder why Hamlet feels the need to put on this 'antic disposition', and take on a new personality. The answer seems to lie in what the ghost has revealed to him (i.e. that his uncle has murdered his father, and that his mother has betrayed his father's memory by marrying the murderer) and the burden placed on him of avenging his father's murder. Hamlet cannot be certain whether the ghost is his father's spirit telling the truth, or is a devil tempting him to commit murder.

Hamlet's adoption of 'a crafty madness' (Act 3, Scene 1, line 8) may then be seen as a way of protecting himself while he tries to deal with the problems the ghost has left him with. If his strange behaviour leads others, especially Claudius, to think of him as a harmless madman, he will feel less threatened. The mask of madness also offers him protection as he expresses his pent-up feelings: others tend not to take seriously the rhetoric of a person they are convinced is mad.

One key to Hamlet's mental and emotional condition, and to his role in the play, is his description of himself as being 'but mad north-north-west' (Act 2, Scene 2, line 356). He qualifies this by saying that 'when the wind is southerly, I know a hawk from a handsaw' (lines 356–7). What he means here is that his 'madness' is limited, that he is only a little mad, or mad only on certain occasions: north-north-west is one of the sixteen main points on the compass. When the great majority of ideas and topics come up for discussion, he is able to deal with them perfectly reasonably and intelligently, as he shows throughout the play.

There is one topic, however, the Claudius–Gertrude relationship, that constantly threatens the balance of his mind. He cannot think of this, or discuss it, without losing control of his emotions. What Claudius and Gertrude have

I am but mad north-north-west: when the wind is southerly, I know a hawk from a handsaw.

HAMLET, Act 2, Scene 2, 356–7

done, and been, has poisoned his mind, not only against them but against women in general.

The shrewd Claudius senses that whatever is disturbing Hamlet's mind is not madness. He also rejects the theory put forward by Polonius that Hamlet has been broken by Ophelia's rejection of his love. He concludes that there must be something else 'in his soul o'er which his melancholy sits on brood' (Act 3, Scene 1, lines 162–3).

Hamlet reveals the truth behind his assumed madness when he confronts his mother, telling her in confidence, 'I essentially am not in madness, but mad in craft' (Act 3, Scene 4, lines 190–91). In other words, he is not really mad, but is cunningly pretending to be mad. There is every reason to believe what he is saying here.

Gertrude does not betray Hamlet's secret, but instead uses his 'madness' to protect him from Claudius and Laertes. She tells Claudius that her son is 'mad, as the sea and wind', having killed Polonius in a 'lawless fit' (Act 4, Scene 1, lines 7, 8). When Hamlet confronts Laertes at Ophelia's grave, Gertrude again dismisses his behaviour as 'mere madness', a 'fit' that 'will work on him' but soon pass, restoring him to the gentle side of his nature (Act 5, Scene 1, lines 270–74).

Hamlet's crafty pretence at madness persists until the final scene of the play, when he offers Laertes a deceitful apology for what he has done to Polonius and to Ophelia. He claims that everybody present knows, and Laertes must

have heard, that he has been suffering from a serious confusion of mind, a 'sore distraction' (Act 5, Scene 2, line 211). He announces that his wrongs were the result of 'madness' (line 214). He also claims that the real Hamlet cannot have wronged Laertes, because when the wrongs attributed to him were committed, he was not himself (lines 215–18).

He declares before 'this audience' (i.e. the king, queen and members of the court) that what he did to Laertes, Polonius and Ophelia was not motivated by evil intentions (lines 222–6). If he were in a court of law, Hamlet would be expecting a verdict of guilty but insane, or not guilty by reason of insanity. However, members of the theatre audience who have been paying close attention to what he has said and done might well take a different view. It can be argued that Hamlet has been the victim, not of insanity, but of an obsessive hatred of his uncle, a hatred intensified by the ghost's revelations, and a related obsession with his mother's betrayal of his father.

As if this were not enough, he has been ordered to take revenge on Claudius, a revenge that he knows cannot be publicly justified. The only firm evidence he has that Claudius murdered his father is the word of a ghost, given to him in private. This evidence would scarcely satisfy a legal judge, and if brought forward by Hamlet, would merely convince everybody that he was really insane.

Claudius

hypocritical
clever
courteous
wheedling
ruthless
immoral
wicked
capable
efficient
manipulative
self-interested
self-controlled
corrupt
dishonest
treacherous

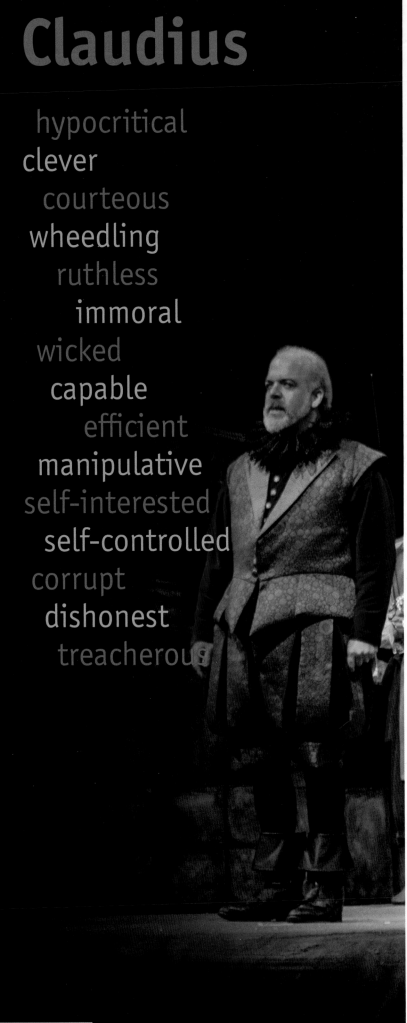

Claudius is the villain of the play, but he is much more than that. He is a complex character, with a number of qualities, both as a ruler and as an individual, that deserve admiration.

Claudius illustrates Shakespeare's understanding of the combination of good and evil in human nature. In creating Claudius, Shakespeare allows for the possibility that even the treacherous murderer of a brother and king can, at least until the final moments of the play, be loved by the murdered man's widow and (most of) his subjects.

As a king, tasked with governing Denmark, he is extremely successful. Evidence of this is found in his swift and successful settlement of the Fortinbras affair. He uses diplomacy to persuade the King of Norway to put a stop to the military activities of young Fortinbras, and thus prevents a war between Denmark and Norway.

Claudius displays considerable skill in keeping the loyalty and trust of those who serve him. He does this by showing extreme courtesy and gratitude for any service they render. These include the ambassadors he sends to Norway, and Rosencrantz and Guildenstern.

As a politician, Claudius is shrewd and efficient. He is expert at spotting danger when it confronts him. He can be suspicious when he needs to be, and his penetrating mind is quick to devise solutions to problems.

When, for example, he becomes aware of the real danger to his life posed by Hamlet's presence in Denmark (following the insert-play), he decides to send Hamlet to England. When he realises that Hamlet killed Polonius, thinking it was Claudius, he decides that Hamlet should be put to death in England.

Or perhaps that was his plan all along – we cannot be sure. The plan fails only because Hamlet is quick-witted enough to foil it.

The way in which Claudius deals with Laertes provides evidence not only of his skill in manipulating other people, and bending them to his will, but also of his courage in the face of extreme danger. The rebellious, angry Laertes, at the head of a lawless group calling for the overthrow of Claudius, confronts him with sword in hand. Claudius remains perfectly calm in the face of this serious threat, merely asking Laertes why he is behaving as he is, and reminding him that God protects kings against traitors. He then wisely lets Laertes have his say, before asking if he wants to take vengeance on him, Claudius, who is both 'guiltless' of Polonius's death and 'in grief for it' (Act 4, Scene 5, lines 149–50), or on the person responsible for that death. Laertes can only answer that his vengeance will be solely confined to enemies. Laertes is fully won over when Claudius assures him that the guilty will be punished: 'where th'offence is, let the great axe fall' (line 215).

What Claudius manages to bring off in this episode represents the triumph of his courage and willpower. One moment the angry Laertes is ready to kill him and take his throne. The next moment a more subdued Laertes is agreeing to become his collaborator. The two men have become allies, by the end of Act 4, in a plan to murder Hamlet.

Many of the more attractive features exhibited by Claudius are on the surface. He is a polished and convincing public speaker, and carries himself with dignity. Although Hamlet, a prejudiced witness, can think of him only as a slimy beast and a degenerate drunkard, Claudius enjoys the approval of most of the other characters. Those who approve of him, and defer to him, have one thing in common: they do not know that in order to become king he poisoned his predecessor.

Below the suave surface, it is a very different story. On his first appearance in the play, Claudius laments his 'dear brother's death' (Act 1, Scene 2, line 1). We soon discover that this makes him an unblushing hypocrite. He is guilty of fratricide (killing a brother) and regicide (killing a king). His foul and unnatural murder of King Hamlet is the catalyst of evil in the play. He is also responsible for the deaths of Gertrude, Laertes and Hamlet. He has a corrupting influence on Gertrude and on Laertes.

Claudius appears to be a devoted husband. However, he does not defend the interest closest to Gertrude's heart: the welfare of Hamlet. And in the final moments of the play, when Gertrude raises the poisoned cup to her lips, Claudius makes no more than a vain attempt to stop her, before he watches her drink the poison without saying the words that could save her life. He chooses to concentrate on preserving his own life. Indeed, he goes on to tell a callous lie to save himself from detection: 'She swoons to see them bleed' (Act 5, Scene 2, line 299).

The audience, whose view of Claudius is conditioned by the ghost and by Hamlet, know the terrible truth about him. Where Polonius, for example, sees a wise and efficient monarch and a friend, we, like Hamlet, see a treacherous murderer, a hypocrite who is able to 'smile, and smile, and be a villain' (Act 1, Scene 5, line 108).

The play, however, does not always show Claudius smiling. There are moments when he has a chance to reflect, and it is then that his conscience begins to trouble him. Through these moments of reflection, he comes to terms with the truth about himself and acknowledges his guilt.

Moments of reflection

Two instances of reflection are worth considering. The first is prompted by a comment Polonius makes about the tendency people have to hide extreme wickedness beneath a virtuous appearance:

'Tis too much proved — that with devotion's visage
And pious action we do sugar o'er
The devil himself.

(Act 3, Scene 1, lines 47–9)

Polonius is not referring to Claudius here, but the latter immediately recognises the relevance of this comment to himself in an aside:

How smart a lash that speech doth give my
conscience!
The harlot's check, beautified with plastering art,
Is not more ugly to the thing that helps it
Than is my deed to my most painted word.
O heavy burden!

(Act 3, Scene 1, lines 50–54)

This is one of the most significant comments made by Claudius in the course of the play. It is a vital admission of guilt on his part, and the first fully independent indication of that guilt. He is saying that his own guilt is ugly compared with the pleasant, hypocritical pose he adopts, and the plausible language he uses. He is also acknowledging that he has a conscience, a sense of right and wrong, and admitting that the evil thing he has done is a 'heavy burden' to carry.

His second reflection offers more powerful evidence of his inner torment, and of his remorse and sense of guilt. He makes a genuine attempt to pray, but is unable to. He begins his soliloquy by remarking that the offence that now torments his mind 'smells to heaven' and has 'the primal eldest curse upon't: a brother's murder' (Act 3, Scene 3, lines 37–9). These words confirm the claim made by the ghost in Act 1, Scene 5. This clear admission of murder comes as Claudius wonders if he can be forgiven:

> *What if this cursèd hand*
> *Were thicker than itself with brother's blood,*
> *Is there not rain enough in the sweet heavens*
> *To wash it white as snow?*

(Act 3, Scene 3, lines 44–7)

The Christian context in which Claudius is considering his position is obvious. He refers to the Lord's Prayer and outlines the two main reasons for praying: to seek help in avoiding evil and to seek forgiveness for doing evil (lines 49–51). The idea of looking for forgiveness through prayer raises his hopes for a moment:

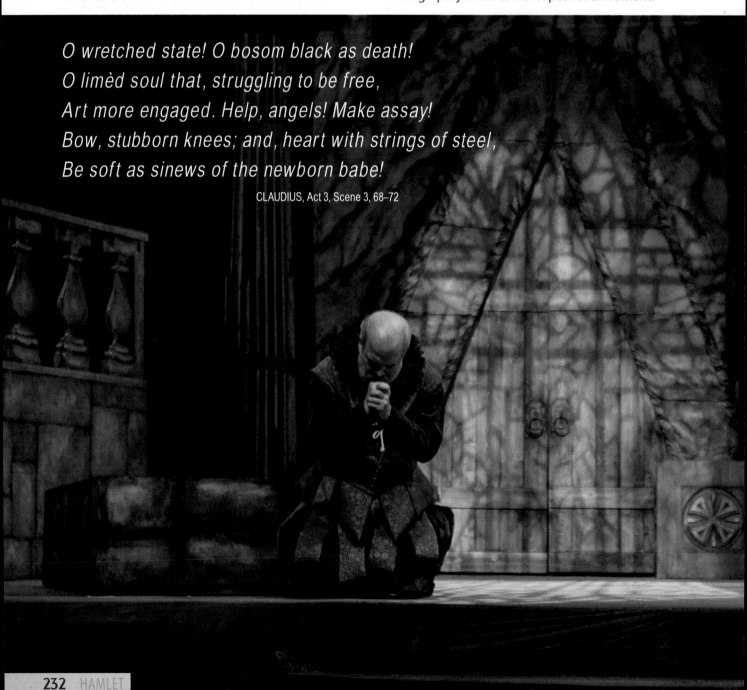

O wretched state! O bosom black as death!
O limèd soul that, struggling to be free,
Art more engaged. Help, angels! Make assay!
Bow, stubborn knees; and, heart with strings of steel,
Be soft as sinews of the newborn babe!

CLAUDIUS, Act 3, Scene 3, 68–72

'Then I'll look up. My fault is past' (lines 51–2). But hope is quickly followed by despair. Claudius knows enough about Christian teaching to realise that he cannot expect to earn forgiveness unless he gives up all he has gained as a result of committing murder. This would involve abdicating as king and losing Gertrude. He finds it impossible to do either.

The soliloquy shows that Claudius is a believer in life after death and expects all human beings to be judged on their earthly behaviour. He knows that if his crimes were to be tried before a court in this world, he might be able to avoid punishment by bribing his judges. In the next world, however, his actions will be exposed for what they are, and his evil deeds will be punished.

Claudius admits that he cannot repent. His prayer to the angels is in vain. He has failed to make his peace with God:

My words fly up, my thoughts remain below.
Words without thoughts never to heaven go.

(Act 3, Scene 3, lines 98–9)

What is said in a soliloquy must be seen as representing the truth as the character sees it. This soliloquy gives us a rare glimpse into the mind of Claudius, which is tormented by a sense of guilt at his evil deeds. He is also distressed by the knowledge that because he cannot give up the fruits of his crime (his crown and his wife), he cannot be forgiven for it and faces damnation after death.

This awful truth is later confirmed by Hamlet. As he forces poison down the throat of Claudius, Hamlet cries: 'Here, thou incestuous, murderous, damned Dane' (Act 5, Scene 2, line 316). He uses the word 'damned' to indicate that he is sending Claudius to his damnation because he will die in the midst of his crimes, with no chance to repent. It is worth noting that this is precisely how Hamlet had hoped his revenge on Claudius would be brought about (Act 3, Scene 3, lines 89–96).

It is natural to feel pity for a man who is tormented by guilt and unable to seek forgiveness. However, whatever sympathy we may feel for Claudius during his moments of reflection does not last very long. Shortly after the prayer scene, we find him arranging the killing of Hamlet in England. When that scheme fails, he devises a plan to have Hamlet murdered by Laertes during a fencing match.

An assessment of Claudius should note that the evil he has unleashed before the action of the play gets under way, which then comes to light early in the play, continues to work its corrupting way, to the detriment of every other character. In this sense he is the villain of the play.

In many productions of the play, Claudius is presented as a gracious, noble-looking monarch. This is not how Hamlet or the ghost see him. It could be argued that the physical appearance of Claudius on stage should match what Hamlet describes as he shows Gertrude a picture of him: he calls him a 'mildewed ear' (Act 3, Scene 4, line 64).

Gertrude

pleasant
unaware
protective
passive
pliant
fickle
dull

shallow
sensual
remorseful
pathetic
contrite
unwise
tragic
victim

The play gives us a number of perspectives on Gertrude. Her first and second husbands appear to be or have been devoted to her. Her son is obsessed with her. Yet, we are given little indication in the play of what makes her so appealing to them.

The first, and most significant, perspective is provided by the ghost of her late husband, who we can assume has a good understanding of her character. What the ghost reveals is entirely discreditable to Gertrude.

If we are to believe the ghost – and the play gives us no reason to doubt him – Claudius has been guilty of both adultery and incest, in addition to murder: 'that incestuous, that adulterate beast' (Act 1, Scene 5, line 42). If Claudius is guilty of incest and adultery, Gertrude must be regarded as having been complicit in both. The adultery in question must be dated to King Hamlet's lifetime, so Hamlet has to cope with the news that his mother was unfaithful to her marriage vows.

The ghost warns Hamlet: 'Taint not thy mind, nor let thy soul contrive against thy mother aught' (Act 1, Scene 5, lines 85–6). In other words, do not to feel hostile to Gertrude or plan any action against her. The problem is that the ghost

has already tainted Hamlet's mind against his mother by telling him that she allowed Claudius to win her 'to his shameful lust' and betrayed her marriage vows by transferring her affections from a virtuous husband to 'a wretch', no better than 'garbage' (lines 45, 51, 57). Angered by what he now knows about Gertrude, Hamlet condemns her in the strongest terms: 'O most pernicious woman!' (line 105).

Gertrude admits that her marriage to Claudius was 'o'erhasty' and realises that it may have distressed her son (Act 2, Scene 2, lines 56–7). However, Hamlet's dominant role in the play, both as a character and as a commentator, means that audiences and readers will tend to judge Gertrude less on how she is presented on stage than on how Hamlet presents her in his soliloquies, asides, and comments to other characters. His commentary is always unfavourable, influenced as it is by the ghost's revelation.

Hamlet's opinion of Gertrude is featured most fully in his confrontation with her in Act 3, Scene 4. His purpose is, as he tells her, to hold up a mirror 'where you may see the inmost part of you' (line 20). He wants her to explore the depths of her soul and see her true self. After he has killed Polonius, he describes what he has done as something 'almost as bad, good mother, as kill a king, and marry with his brother' (lines 28–9). He appears to be accusing her of being party to the murder of his father. However, her astonished response may be taken as evidence of her innocence. In any case, had she been guilty of murder, the ghost would surely have revealed this to Hamlet.

Hamlet goes on to depict his mother as a woman who has lost her self-control, given up the idea of preserving her virtue and allowed reason and good taste to give way to wild passion. She has abandoned her admirable, faithful husband for a wretched individual without a redeeming feature, whom she later married.

Gertrude's response shows that Hamlet's words have had the desired effect. When she looks into her soul, she sees 'black and grainèd spots' (line 90) that cannot be removed. The spots are sins, one of them being adultery. Gertrude's confession prompts Hamlet to suggest the base level to which she has fallen with Claudius, picturing the two of them as pigs 'honeying and making love over the nasty sty' (lines 93–4). He wants her to repent and to distance herself from Claudius.

Look here upon this picture, and on this,
The counterfeit presentment of two brothers.

HAMLET, Act 3, Scene 4, 53–4

Gertrude does not promise to put this advice into practice, but swears not to tell Claudius what Hamlet has been saying to her. It is natural to expect a new Gertrude to emerge after this exchange and, in Act 4, Scene 1, there is some evidence that she is a changed woman. Claudius remarks on her 'sighs' and 'profound heaves' (line 1), which implies that she is distressed.

She does her best to keep Hamlet's secret safe from Claudius, by suggesting that his killing of Polonius was the result of a 'lawless fit' of madness (line 8). Indeed, everything that Gertrude tells Claudius about the encounter is framed to protect Hamlet. She omits to mention that Polonius had cried out when she called for help. She says that Hamlet thought he was merely killing a rat, when in fact he hoped he had killed Claudius. She even suggests that Hamlet wept for what he had done, whereas his actual response was sarcastic and callous in the extreme.

When we next see her, Gertrude is refusing to grant an audience to Ophelia (Act 4, Scene 5, line 1). She has to be persuaded by Horatio to receive her, if only to protect the royal family from dangerous gossip. She appears to be weary and her aside suggests that Hamlet's words have had an effect on her conscience:

To my sick soul, as sin's true nature is,
Each toy seems prologue to some great amiss:
So full of artless jealousy is guilt,
It spills itself in fearing to be spilt.

(Act 4, Scene 5, lines 18–21)

When Ophelia enters and proceeds to sing songs and talk of her lost love and her father's death, Gertrude does little or nothing to comfort her. She may simply be astounded by Ophelia's swift decline into insanity.

When Laertes, leading a group of rebels who want to install him as king, challenges Claudius, Gertrude comes to her husband's defence. She rebukes the rebels as 'false Danish dogs' (line 109), attempts to restrain Laertes and informs him that Claudius did not kill Polonius. It may be natural for the queen to despise rebels, and it is true that Claudius did not kill Polonius, but there is a sense here that Gertrude is her husband's loyal defender against his enemies, in spite of Hamlet's revelations.

During the final scene, in the course of the duel, she displays her concern for Hamlet and her pride in him. She wants to wipe his sweaty brow and drink a toast to his good fortune. Her last words and thoughts are for Hamlet, not for Claudius: 'O my dear Hamlet! – The drink, the drink! I am poisoned' (Act 5, Scene 2, lines 300–1).

As a character, Gertrude has never attracted much favourable comment. One commentator declared that she is one of the most poorly endowed human beings Shakespeare ever drew, simply a stately defective. She has also been described as a woman with a soft animal nature, very dull and very shallow. She is seen as someone who likes to be happy and to see others happy. She is anxious to avoid trouble. Her early request to Hamlet to cast off his mourning clothes and to look on Claudius as a friend is typical of her general attitude (Act 1, Scene 2, lines 68–9). Unlike Hamlet, she prefers to live in the moment, neither reflecting on the past nor contemplating the future.

Gertrude provides a sensitive, poetic account of Ophelia's death (Act 4, Scene 7, lines 169–86), but we cannot take this as an indication that the better part of her nature is beginning to prevail. Shakespeare often uses characters as reporters or commentators on situations or events. In such cases, and this is one of them, what they say has no necessary connection with their natures.

Looked at in the overall scheme of the play, Gertrude is a tragic victim. She is the first character in the play to be corrupted by Claudius. As a consequence of her adultery, everything she values is destroyed. She has to endure seeing her son behaving as if he is mad, killing Polonius, and then denouncing her in cruel and obscene language. She sees Ophelia driven out of her senses and into her grave, and all her own hopes that Ophelia might have become her son's wife end up in ruins.

Gertrude's lapse from virtue leads eventually to a horrible death for her. She dies knowing that the cup that poisoned her had been prepared by her husband for the son she loves. Of all the deaths in the play, Gertrude's is arguably the cruellest.

Rosencrantz and Guildenstern

meddling
deceivers
subservient
fawning
untrustworthy
dupes
pushovers
inept
stupid

unfortunate
awkward
compliant
polite
deferential
ineffective

These two servants of Claudius have no interest or significance as personalities: in their case, role predominates completely over character. It is impossible to distinguish between Rosencrantz and Guildenstern. They operate as a pair, each reinforcing the efforts of the other.

Their main function in the play is to act as loyal and willing servants of the king. In fulfilling this function they illustrate the corrupting influence of Claudius on those associated with him. They will do most unpleasant things to show him their loyalty.

They cannot, for instance, find the first task he gives them very congenial. He asks them to use their longstanding friendship with Hamlet as a cloak for probing his secrets and revealing these to Claudius. Unfortunately for Claudius, the pair lack the guile or cunning needed for such a ruthless task.

Their performance in the role of concerned friends is not sufficiently skilled to deceive Hamlet, who in turn causes them considerable embarrassment by exposing their pretence: 'there is a kind of confession in your looks, which your modesties have not craft enough to colour' (Act 2, Scene 2, lines 270–71).

After this, they cannot expect to enjoy Hamlet's trust or his respect. He treats them with contemptuous indifference, ridicule and sarcasm, giving duty answers to their questions, misleading them whenever he can and pretending to misunderstand what they are saying.

Much of Hamlet's evident dislike for his former schoolfellows, whom he has come to distrust as he would 'adders fanged' (Act 3, Scene 4, line 206), springs from their association with Claudius. To his mind, such an association must inevitably contaminate.

Rosencrantz and Guildenstern die as a result of being too subservient to Claudius. They are too willing to take risks on his behalf. As Hamlet explains to Horatio after he has sent them to their deaths in England: 'they did make love to this employment' (Act 5, Scene 2, line 57). For Hamlet, what has happened to them is what always happens to fools who willingly permit themselves to be caught up in affairs too great for their capacities to cope with.

There is nothing in the text to suggest that Rosencrantz and Guildenstern knew that the commission they were carrying to England contained instructions for Hamlet's death, although Hamlet may have assumed that they did. It appears that their willingness to be the king's dedicated agents, to do the worst Claudius asks of them, is a sufficient crime in Hamlet's eyes to warrant their deaths.

The text offers some possible reasons for their absolute dedication to Claudius. When they are first summoned to the royal court, Gertrude promises them that they will 'receive such thanks as fits a king's remembrance' (Act 2, Scene 2, lines 25–6). They may, therefore, be motivated by their anticipated reward.

In reply, however, Rosencrantz and Guildenstern note that Claudius and Gertrude have the right to command their servants and they pledge to do, to the best of their ability, whatever pleases the king and queen (lines 26–32). This response suggests an unquestioning sense of duty. Later, they also point out the importance of the king and how the people depend on his safety: 'Never alone did the king sigh, but with a general groan' (Act 3, Scene 3, lines 22–3). So their motivation may be a desire to ensure the welfare of the monarch.

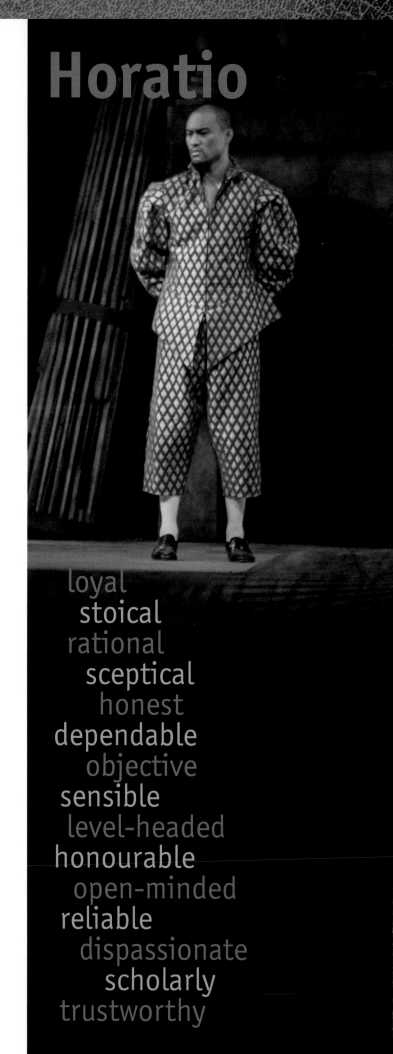

Horatio

loyal
stoical
rational
sceptical
honest
dependable
objective
sensible
level-headed
honourable
open-minded
reliable
dispassionate
scholarly
trustworthy

With Horatio, Shakespeare achieves much with remarkable economy. He gives him little to say or do, yet establishes him as a man of stature and character. For much of the play, Horatio moves about in Hamlet's shadow, echoing Hamlet's sentiments and receiving his confidences.

There are times when Horatio assumes a more important role. Indeed, in the first scene he is the dominant figure and several traits of his character emerge. He is patriotic; he is educated, able to cite Plutarch; he is not carried away by fear or superstition in his attitude to the ghost, but remains objective.

Before the appearance of the ghost, he is sceptical. This makes the audience more inclined to trust his response to the apparition. Later examples of his tact, objectivity and good sense show us that we can depend on his judgement. He is not afraid to ask difficult questions or challenge untruths.

Hamlet pays him a noble tribute of affection and admiration, highlighting the qualities that inspired him to choose Horatio as his friend:

> *Since my dear soul was mistress of her choice*
> *And could of men distinguish, her election*
> *Hath sealed thee for herself . . .*
>
> (Act 3, Scene 2, lines 57–68)

From this tribute we learn that Horatio is of a stoical temperament, and that Hamlet feels able to depend on him. Hamlet trusts him with details of his plan for the players and his hopes of catching the conscience of Claudius. Horatio assists with this task and lends moral support to Hamlet.

While he is firmly associated with Hamlet, Horatio appears to be accepted by all the characters. After Hamlet is sent to England, we see Horatio offering wise advice to Gertrude about Ophelia (Act 4, Scene 5, lines 15–16). And following the disturbance at Ophelia's funeral, Claudius asks him to keep an eye on Hamlet: 'I pray thee, good Horatio, wait upon him' (Act 5, Scene 1, line 279). Horatio manages to remain uncontaminated by the corruption that surrounds him.

Horatio is the first to hear the news that Hamlet has returned to Denmark, and throughout Act 5 he is constantly in his company, assuming a more significant part on the stage than the text can suggest, since he is not given a great deal to say. He tries to ensure Hamlet's safety by urging him not to accept the king's challenge to fence with Laertes.

Towards the close of the play, Horatio briefly becomes the dominant figure he was in the first scene; indeed, when he determines to share his master's fate by drinking from the poisoned cup, he steals attention even from the dying Hamlet. He has two final tasks: to give a true report of Hamlet and his life to those who remain, and to deal with Fortinbras.

Shakespeare's presentation of Horatio's character is not wholly consistent. A close reading of the text reveals two different Horatios, and seems to suggest that we are to take him less as a realistic portrait than as a piece of dramatic structure performing the double function of chorus or commentator on the action and of confidant to Hamlet.

In Act 1, Scene 1, he shows expert knowledge of Danish history and describes himself as a native of Denmark: he speaks of 'our state' and 'our last king' (lines 72, 83). Seeing the ghost in armour he recalls that Hamlet's father was similarly attired when he fought 'the ambitious Norway', and also mentions the dead king's encounter with 'the sledded Polacks' (lines 64, 66). He goes on to give Marcellus and Barnardo a detailed account of the past rivalry between the Danish and Norwegian sovereigns, and brings the history up to date (lines 83–110).

In the next scene, however, Hamlet treats him as though he is a foreign visitor, who needs to learn the Danish custom of drinking heavily (Act 1, Scene 2, line 176). And in Act 1, Scene 4, Hamlet feels that he has to explain Danish manners and customs to him. When, for instance, Horatio hears a flourish of trumpets, he asks, 'What does this mean, my lord?' (line 8). Later, it is clear that Horatio knows neither Laertes (Act 5, Scene 1, line 209) nor Osric (Act 5, Scene 2, line 85). These considerations suggest that Shakespeare's interest in immediate theatrical effect was sometimes greater than his desire for psychological consistency.

The following chart illustrates the interactions between the main characters in *Hamlet*.

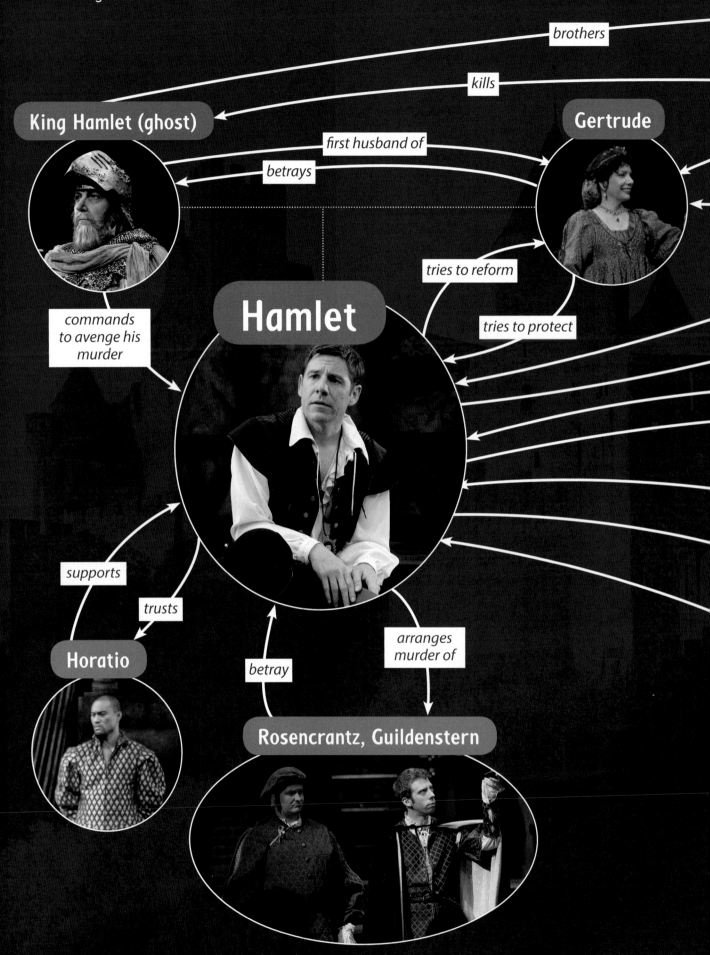

brothers

kills

King Hamlet (ghost)

first husband of

betrays

Gertrude

tries to reform

Hamlet

tries to protect

commands to avenge his murder

supports

trusts

arranges murder of

Horatio

betray

Rosencrantz, Guildenstern

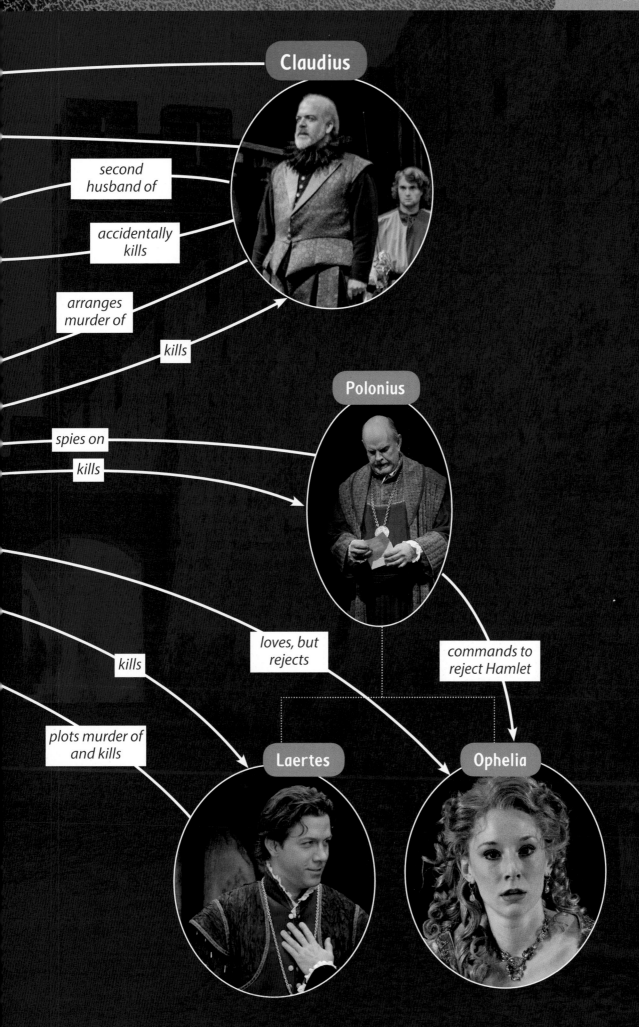

Claudius

second
husband of

accidentally
kills

arranges
murder of

kills

Polonius

spies on

kills

loves, but
rejects

kills

commands to
reject Hamlet

plots murder of
and kills

Laertes

Ophelia

Relationships

Hamlet and Claudius are at the heart of a web of relationships involving all the other characters in one way or another. But it is Hamlet who is the focus of all the main relationships in the play.

For let the world take note,
You are the most immediate to our throne

CLAUDIUS, Act 1, Scene 2, 108–9

The Hamlet–Claudius relationship is the one around which the business of the play revolves.

Hamlet recognises this in his comment to Horatio on the fate of Rosencrantz and Guildenstern, who have allowed themselves to become involved in the deadly struggle between these two powerful and fiercely angry enemies:

> 'Tis dangerous when the baser nature comes
> Between the pass and fell incensèd points
> Of mighty opposites.

(Act 5, Scene 2, lines 60–62)

Hamlet and Claudius are the two 'mighty opposites' of this play.

Hamlet instinctively dislikes his uncle even before he learns that Claudius has murdered his brother, Hamlet's beloved father. From then on, dislike turns to hatred of the man he has been ordered to kill. This hatred is compounded by the fact that Claudius had seduced Gertrude before he killed King Hamlet.

Claudius, believing that his secret murder will remain undetected, tries to win Hamlet's approval. He professes the best of intentions towards him, publicly stating that Hamlet will be his heir to the Danish throne. However, when he suspects, and then realises, that Hamlet knows his secret, he comes to regard Hamlet as a deadly enemy who must be killed. During this process he happily uses many of the other characters as his spies, decoys and agents as required.

Hamlet's relationship with his mother is poisoned by the revelations of his ghostly father that she has been unfaithful to him with Claudius. It is further compromised by the haste with which she married Claudius after the death of Hamlet's father. Hamlet is disgusted with her behaviour. His thoughts on her come fully to the surface in some of his soliloquies, and then more aggressively when he chastises her in Act 3, Scene 4. He wants her to recognise the extent of her faults and urges her to distance herself from Claudius.

There is no firm evidence that Gertrude follows Hamlet's instruction to detach herself from Claudius. There is evidence that her love for Hamlet remains sufficiently strong to make her want to protect him from Claudius after he killed Polonius. She distorts the facts surrounding that killing to make it appear that Hamlet has been grieving over what he has done. In her final moments she tries to protect Hamlet's life by warning him about the poisoned cup.

There is a sense that Gertrude is the main victim, from an emotional point of view, of the life and death struggle between Hamlet and Claudius. She is torn between loyalty to her son and loyalty to her second husband, despite all that Hamlet does to demean him in her eyes. She actively defends Claudius when Laertes leads a rebellion against him, and physically restrains Laertes as he is confronting him. Her fate is to lose her life in the war between husband and son.

The play's love-interest is supplied by Hamlet's relationship with Ophelia. On Ophelia's side, this relationship is compromised by the unwarranted intervention of Polonius, who cannot imagine that Hamlet has any interest in his daughter other than to dishonour her. She is ordered to reject Hamlet. On Hamlet's side, the evidence suggests that his professions of love for Ophelia were sincere, until Gertrude's relationship with Claudius tainted his mind against all women. Hamlet then treats Ophelia cruelly. Their lost love, followed by the murder of Polonius by Hamlet (who thought he was killing Claudius), causes Ophelia to lose her sanity and then her life.

Hamlet has grown up with Rosencrantz and Guildenstern and they were friends. This is plain during his first encounter with them: 'My excellent good friends! . . . Good lads, how do ye both?' (Act 2, Scene 2, lines 222–3). Sincere friendship immediately turns to suspicion on his part, and then to contempt when he discovers that they have been sent to spy on him. They have gone over to the enemy side and agreed to act as agents of Claudius to probe Hamlet's mind in the guise of friendship. Hamlet eventually concludes that he can trust them no more than he could trust two poisonous snakes: 'adders fanged' (Act 3, Scene 4, line 206). He later consigns them to a terrible death, making them two more victims of his war with Claudius.

As Claudius's chief counsellor, Polonius is despised by Hamlet and regarded as his natural enemy. He describes Polonius as a 'wretched, rash, intruding fool' (Act 3, Scene 4, line 31) and derives amusement from making him look ridiculous. For his part, Polonius shows little faith in Hamlet's intentions towards Ophelia,

assuming from the first that these must be dishonourable. Being an ally of Claudius means being an enemy of Hamlet, and Polonius becomes another unwitting victim in the conflict between these two men.

Laertes and Hamlet do not meet on stage until the final Act of the play. By this time Laertes and Claudius are firm allies and have devised a plot to kill Hamlet. It is clear in the graveyard scene that, although he detests the manner in which Laertes is ranting over the corpse of Ophelia, Hamlet had previously admired him and considered him a friend: 'I loved you ever' (Act 5, Scene 1, line 276). When they meet for the fencing match, Hamlet offers an apology and some excuses for killing Polonius. Laertes is unable to accept this, but in his dying moments, he and Hamlet exchange forgiveness. Laertes'

death is partly due to his own ruthless behaviour and partly because he became embroiled in the feud between Hamlet and Claudius.

One key relationship survives until Hamlet's death. Hamlet rightly admires Horatio for some of the qualities he himself lacks. In a moving speech, he pays tribute to his friend's stoicism, his even temper and his capacity to maintain a balance between reason and emotion (Act 3, Scene 2, lines 57–68). He is the only significant character Hamlet can trust. Horatio values and supports Hamlet throughout, is ready to die as Hamlet dies, but agrees to become Hamlet's apologist and the defender of his reputation into the future.

For a discussion of family relationships in *Hamlet*, see pp. 262–3.

Hero and villain

In simple terms, Hamlet is the hero of the play and Claudius is the villain. There are many times, however, when Hamlet appears to be less than a hero and Claudius less than a villain.

Shakespeare does not present us with perfect heroes or absolute villains in *Hamlet*. This does not mean that he confuses the moral issues raised by the play. The role of Claudius is seen for what it is, and he is shown to bear ultimate responsibility for the corruption that pervades the royal court and involves Hamlet in its consequences. Hamlet, on the other hand, is not immune from the effects of the immoral atmosphere created by Claudius: his response to this often involves him in acts and expressions that are cynical and cruel, and contrary to his better nature.

Hamlet: an imperfect hero

There is almost no end to the number of attractive, admirable and even lovable qualities that critics have attributed to Hamlet. When Horatio foresees a heavenly immortality for Hamlet, with flights of angels singing him to his rest (Act 5, Scene 2, line 351), he is expressing the overall attitude of the play to its chief character. However, we cannot overlook his flaws.

One of the most obvious of Hamlet's attractions is his fertile and subtle intelligence, apparent again and again in his capacity for abstract reasoning, the range of his metaphysical speculations, his quickness of perception, the mental dexterity expressed in his wit and satire, his learning and his imagination. These qualities set him apart from all the other characters in the play.

Another of his distinctive qualities is fastidiousness. He is disgusted by the drunkenness of the court and the damage that does to the reputation of Denmark (Act 1, Scene 4, lines 19–24). He is also a discriminating critic of the theatre, favouring a play that 'pleased not the million' (Act 2, Scene 2, line 411).

In spite of his royal status, Hamlet can welcome a common player as a dear friend. The relaxed ease and informality of Hamlet's manner makes an attractive contrast to the pomposity of some other characters, particularly Polonius. Hamlet is shown on terms of intimacy with several characters who would be far below him in social station.

There is much else in Hamlet to arouse admiration. For example, his devotion to the memory of his father is movingly expressed. He is, as Claudius recognises, 'most generous, and free from all contriving' (Act 4, Scene 7, line 138). He is magnanimous in describing Laertes as 'a very noble youth' (Act 5, Scene 1, line 209).

Hamlet's death is one of great nobility. In his final agony he forgives Laertes, thinks of his mother, prevents the death of Horatio and shows concern for the future of Denmark by giving his 'dying voice' (Act 5, Scene 2, line 347) to Fortinbras.

One of the most revealing passages in the play is Ophelia's soliloquy on Hamlet's apparent degeneration from an earlier, ideal self:

Poison

The imagery of disease also brings the mind back to the poisoning of Hamlet's father by Claudius. Indeed, those repulsive images may be said to derive from the horrible event described in such vivid detail by the ghost in Act 1.

The poison administered by Claudius has the effect of producing the symptoms of a disease like leprosy:

> *And a most instant tetter barked about,*
> *Most lazar-like, with vile and loathsome crust,*
> *All my smooth body.*
>
> (Act 1, Scene 5, lines 71–3)

The theme of poisoning is reintroduced at two further points in the action, emphasising its importance as a central symbol in the play. In the dumb show in Act 3, Scene 2, the poisoning of Hamlet's father is mirrored in the poisoning by Lucianus of the Player King. In Act 5, Scene 2, all the major surviving characters – Hamlet, Claudius, Gertrude and Laertes – meet their deaths by poisoning.

Taken in conjunction with the recurring images of sickness and disease, this emphasis on poisoning in the action of the play assumes a deeper significance. The events depicted on stage, along with the imagery found in the characters' words, echo and reinforce each other's meaning, and a unifying pattern emerges.

The poisoning of Hamlet's father is a major symbol of the condition of Denmark throughout the play. The 'leperous distilment' (Act 1, Scene 5, line 64) that Claudius pours into the ears of his brother spreads through his body and destroys the healthy organism from within. Similarly, the evil influence of Claudius spreads like a poison throughout Denmark, corrupting all who have contact with it.

Two of the most memorable comments in the play illustrate the above point. The first is made by Marcellus, a witness to the appearance of the ghost, who rightly senses that its visitation has to do with corruption in Denmark: 'Something is rotten in the state of Denmark' (Act 1, Scene 4, line 92). Then Hamlet uses another, more specific, disease image to convey the notion of a sick country:

> *The time is out of joint: O cursèd spite,*
> *That ever I was born to set it right!*
>
> (Act 1, Scene 5, lines 187–8)

The meaning of this image is often misunderstood. 'Time' here means 'the country' or 'the Danish state'. Hamlet is saying that Denmark is a shattered body ('out of joint'), and that a spiteful or cruel fate has given him the task of being the surgeon who must restore this sick or poisoned body to health. As he sees it, this cure will be brought about only when the poison or cause of the sickness (i.e. Claudius) has been removed.

Death

At no time during the course of *Hamlet* is the mind allowed to stray far from the thought of death: imagery and incident keep it continuously to the fore.

Death and its effects brood over the opening scenes. When we first meet Hamlet, he is in mourning and wears an 'inky cloak' and 'suits of solemn black' (Act 1, Scene 2, lines 77, 78). Shortly after this the ghost gives a graphic description of the circumstances of his death, and talks feelingly of the horrors of the world beyond the grave.

Visual images of death are provided throughout the play. Hamlet, Claudius, Gertrude, Polonius and Laertes are slain on stage. We watch Lucianus murder the Player King in the insert-play. We also witness the burial of Ophelia, and learn how Hamlet has contrived the deaths of Rosencrantz and Guildenstern. Hamlet holds Yorick's skull in the graveyard, and is obsessed with thoughts of man's mortality.

Hamlet is also fascinated by ideas of the next world and of bodily decay. The burden of his most famous soliloquy is his dread of 'the undiscovered country from whose bourn no traveller returns' (Act 3, Scene 1, lines 79–80). He speculates about the dreams that may come after death, 'when we have shuffled off this mortal coil' (line 67).

Hamlet's dialogue with the king after he has slain Polonius is full of gruesome details of the effects of death on the body. He imagines that Polonius has become a feast for an assembly of worms: 'A certain convocation of politic worms are e'en at him' (Act 4, Scene 3, lines 20–21). He returns to this theme in the graveyard, wondering if the decayed body of Alexander the Great became dust, then loam and finally the stopper in a barrel of beer (Act 5, Scene 1, lines 193–7).

Appearance versus reality

Another major theme of this play (and many of Shakespeare's plays) is the relation of reality to appearance.

The uncertainty of outward appearance becomes a problem for Hamlet as soon as he hears the ghost's revelations. At first these seem to him to bring into the light of day the grim reality behind the pleasant, glittering surface of his uncle's court. Reflection, however, gives rise to doubts, and he is faced with the possibility that the ghost may be a devil in disguise, leading him to ruin. And if this is so, then the outward appearance of Claudius and the reality beneath may be one and the same, and Hamlet's suspicions, hatred and contempt may be baseless. He decides to test the ghost's word, and finds some confirmation of its truth in the king's reaction to the insert-play.

The prayer scene provides an ironic comment on the relation of reality to appearance. To the watching Hamlet, Claudius is engrossed in his devotions, and Hamlet decides not to kill him then in case he sends him to heaven. For once, Hamlet's probing, questioning mind has failed to penetrate to the reality beneath the outward show. Behind the image of a praying man is a man who is trying, but failing, to pray: 'My words fly up, my thoughts remain below' (Act 3, Scene 3, line 98).

The theme of appearance versus reality is also kept before our minds by means of various groups of interconnected images. Three patterns deserve particular attention: those formed by recurring images of clothing, of acting and of painting. Most of these are used to suggest deliberate concealment of the true nature of things.

Polonius tells Laertes that 'the apparel oft proclaims the man' (Act 1, Scene 3, line 72), yet he knows that this is not always so, and later sends Reynaldo to Paris to pry into his son's behaviour there, instructing him to dissemble if necessary in order to discover the truth. His own concealment behind the arras in Gertrude's apartment leads to his death: the arras is a visual symbol of disguise, one of the many masking devices used throughout the play.

To Hamlet's mind, Gertrude was doing little more than acting a part when she followed her late husband's body 'like Niobe, all tears' (Act 1, Scene 2, line 149). Bitterly conscious of this, he rejects her suggestion that he should belie his true feeling by casting his 'nighted colour off' (line 68). His reply is a rebuke to hypocrisy and false seeming. Unlike his mother, he claims, his mourning apparel, his tears and his dejected countenance are not mere surface display:

> These indeed 'seem',
> For they are actions that a man might play.
> But I have that within which passeth show;
> These, but the trappings and the suits of woe.

(Act 1, Scene 2, lines 83–6)

In another angry outburst to Ophelia, Hamlet shows the same contempt for those who display a false appearance to the world. This time, he draws his images from art:

> I have heard of your paintings too, well enough. God hath given you one face and you make yourselves another, you jig, you amble, and you lisp, and nickname God's creatures, and make your wantonness your ignorance.

(Act 3, Scene 1, lines 140–43)

In this case, however, it is Polonius, rather than Ophelia, who merits Hamlet's scornful rebuke, for it is he who has contrived the encounter and prepared her for it. He has instructed her to appear engrossed in a devotional book, since by means of surface piety, as he puts it, 'we do sugar o'er the devil himself' (lines 48–9).

The visiting players and their play, particularly the ease with which the actors can simulate real passion, keep us conscious of the falsity of outward show. Hamlet berates himself that he cannot stir up similar feelings, even though he has real cause:

> Is it not monstrous that this player here,
> But in a fiction, in a dream of passion,
> Could force his soul so to his own conceit
> That from her working all his visage wanned,
> Tears in his eyes, distraction in's aspect,
> A broken voice, and his whole function suiting
> With forms to his conceit; and all for nothing!

(Act 2, Scene 2, lines 520–26)

This contradiction between outward action and inward intent is at the heart of the play. It is emphasised in the behaviour of the characters, in their spoken imagery, and in such direct comment as that of Hamlet on Claudius: 'That one may smile, and smile, and be a villain' (Act 1, Scene 5, line 108).

Although he earlier rejected the idea of false seeming and duplicity, Hamlet himself assumes his 'antic disposition', a disguise for his real feelings and intentions (Act 1, Scene 5, line 171). Claudius spends time trying to pierce this disguise, using Ophelia, Rosencrantz, Guildenstern and others to help him, while Hamlet, for his part, is busy with his own attempts to discover the reality beneath the suave, bland exterior of his enemy, Claudius.

Characterisation through imagery

Shakespeare often used imagery as one means, among others, of individualising his characters. Apart from the very minor figures in *Hamlet*, each character uses images or groups of images peculiar to himself or herself, and there is often a close conformity between the nature and frequency of those images and the mental processes, emotional life and background of the characters who use them.

Hamlet

Hamlet tends to draw his images from the real, substantial world. Although he expresses more subtle and complex ideas than any of the other characters, he illustrates them by means of similes and metaphors drawn from commonplace and familiar objects, ideas and pursuits: food, drink, clothing, gardening, domestic animals; such games and pastimes as music, theatre, hunting, bowling and dicing; and war.

Here are some examples:

- His comments on the techniques of acting are grounded in homely speech. It offends him to hear a bad actor 'tear a passion to tatters, to very rags, to split the ears of the groundlings' (Act 3, Scene 2, lines 9–10).
- His famous tribute to the glory of humanity does not begin, as one might expect, with lofty, complex ponderings, but uses a simple term: 'What a piece of work is a man!' (Act 2, Scene 2, lines 291–2).
- He declares his mother's marriage vows to be 'as false as dicers' oaths' (Act 3, Scene 4, line 45).
- He sees the king's courtiers as sponges: Claudius keeps them as an ape keeps 'an apple in the corner of his jaw; first mouthed to be last swallowed. When he needs what you have gleaned, it is but squeezing you, and, sponge, you shall be dry again.' (Act 4, Scene 2, lines 16–19).

Hamlet's stress on what is solid, commonplace and substantial, his preference for concrete vividness over cold abstraction, is a recurring feature of his speech. If it points to anything about his character, it is to his clear view of reality, and the practical, realistic bent of his mind.

But Shakespeare embellishes Hamlet's speeches with another, and quite different, thread of imagery. The prince, after all, is much more than a shrewd, penetrating observer of the humble familiar world. He is a refined man of the Renaissance.

Hamlet's scholarship, admired by Ophelia, is expressed in a wide range of learned metaphors. When he asks the actor to recite a monologue it is on a classical theme, the tale told by Aeneas to Dido. His own speeches contain references to Jove, Apollo and Hyperion, with each of whom he compares his father; he also talks of Niobe, Damon, Vulcan, the Nemean lion and Hercules. Nor is the range of his reference exhausted by his ample classical imagery: he also draws freely on images of war, nature, the theatre and the natural sciences.

Laertes

Shakespeare uses imagery to suggest a significant contrast between the personalities of Hamlet and Laertes. To turn from Hamlet's imagery to that of Laertes is to enter a different intellectual and imaginative world.

Whereas Hamlet favours directness and realism, Laertes favours euphemism and wordiness. His images are pretentious, and his style is artificial and affected. Laertes talks of 'old Pelion, or the skyish head of blue Olympus' (Act 5, Scene 1, lines 239–40), whereas Hamlet speaks of making Mount Ossa 'like a wart' (line 269).

Laertes shows the same refinement in calling flowers 'the infants of the spring' (Act 1, Scene 3, line 39) and in his description of Lamord as 'the brooch indeed and gem of all the nation' (Act 4, Scene 7, lines 96–7). Even in moments of extreme sorrow Laertes finds an outlet for his emotion in a careful and studied image: 'Too much of water hast thou, poor Ophelia, and therefore I forbid my tears' (lines 188–9).

It is significant that Laertes uses his one notably simple and realistic image as he faces death: 'as a woodcock to mine own springe . . . I am justly killed with mine own treachery' (Act 5, Scene 2, lines 297–8).

Claudius

The imagery associated with Claudius has some affinities with that of Hamlet, being largely drawn from the same homely sources. However, Claudius uses a narrower range of images, suggesting that while he may share Hamlet's practical mind-set, he lacks his intellectual vitality and breadth of vision.

Claudius's imagery is not consistent throughout all his speeches. When he is addressing a public assembly, it is formal and conventional in style and its subject matter is commonly war and the operations of justice. For example: 'where th'offence is, let the great axe fall' (Act 4, Scene 5, line 215). Alone, however, he finds a release for his mental and emotional turmoil in a sequence of images of sickness, disease, poisoning and infection.

His habit of cloaking his inward self is underlined in the imagery he draws from painting, colouring and clothing. He asks Laertes:

> Laertes, was your father dear to you?
> Or are you like the painting of a sorrow,
> A face without a heart?

(Act 4, Scene 7, lines 110–12)

Other characters

Gertrude's imagery, reflecting her character, is pallid and unremarkable. It is difficult to recall a single striking image from any of her speeches. A notable exception, however, is her poetic and sensitive account of the death of Ophelia (Act 4, Scene 7, lines 169–86), which seems somewhat out of character.

Polonius can be pompous and garrulous, but his images are as realistic and concrete as Hamlet's. They sometimes have a commercial and/or legal theme; for example, he warns Ophelia about Hamlet:

> Do not believe his vows; for they are brokers,
> Not of that dye which their investments show,
> But mere implorators of unholy suits,
> Breathing like sanctified and pious bawds,
> The better to beguile.

(Act 1, Scene 3, lines 127–31)

He seldom chooses his images from any but the most commonplace sources; it could be said that they are as limited in their scope as Polonius himself.

Ophelia's imagery is equally predictable. The images for which we remember her best are the ones derived from nature, particularly flowers. These are humble and unpretentious. She describes Hamlet as once being the 'rose of the fair state', and as someone whose vows have 'their perfume lost' (Act 3, Scene 1, lines 150, 99). She hopes that Laertes may not come to resemble the 'ungracious pastors' who tread 'the primrose path of dalliance' while advocating 'the steep and thorny way to heaven' to those to whom they preach (Act 1, Scene 3, lines 47–50).

Horatio talks of 'the most high and palmy state of Rome', of 'the mightiest Julius' and of 'Neptune's empire' (Act 1, Scene 1, lines 116, 117, 122). He sees himself as 'an antique Roman' (Act 5, Scene 2, line 332). These classical allusions, and his occasional flights of poetic fancy, make him seem a natural companion for Hamlet, and set him apart from such other minor figures as Marcellus and Barnardo, whose images are more homely.

Family

Hamlet features a number of family relationships. Most notable are the relationships between parents and their children, and in particular between fathers and sons.

Three father–son relationships are depicted in the play: the late King Hamlet and his son, Hamlet; the late King and his son, Fortinbras; and Polonius and his son, Laertes. In each case the father has recently died or dies during the play and the son feels duty-bound to avenge his father's violent death. Each son holds his father in high regard.

Laertes and Fortinbras willingly accept their roles as avengers. They see it as a natural response. It is a means of showing loyalty to, and love for, a dead father. Laertes, for example, travels immediately to Elsinore to challenge Claudius about the death of Polonius. He clearly states that he is going to avenge his father's death, regardless of the consequences:

> To this point I stand,
> That both the worlds I give to negligence,
> Let come what comes; only I'll be revenged
> Most throughly for my father.

(Act 4, Scene 5, lines 132–5)

Hamlet shares their sense of responsibility and duty. When the ghost tells Hamlet that he must 'revenge his foul and most unnatural murder', he appears eager to obey his father's command:

> Haste me to know't, that I, with wings as swift
> As meditation or the thoughts of love,
> May sweep to my revenge.

(Act 1, Scene 5, lines 25, 29–31)

Hamlet may not relish the prospect, but he accepts that he 'was born to set it right' (line 188); in other words, it is his destiny and his duty. However, it is not long before we find him doubting the ghost and seeking further proof. It can be argued, therefore, that Shakespeare included two other sets of fathers and sons in the play to indicate the typical or expected response of a son in Hamlet's situation, and to operate as contrasts to the hesitant Hamlet.

The patriarchal and authoritarian Polonius reveals another side of the father–son relationship when we see him brief Reynaldo on how to spy on Laertes. This action does not appear to be motivated by a desire to protect his son, but by a need to control his son's life.

Polonius does not trust Laertes to behave well in Paris, just as he does not trust Ophelia to behave appropriately with Hamlet. Polonius generally seems more concerned about how his children's behaviour affects him than about any negative impact it might have on them. Likewise, the ghost of King Hamlet is prepared to use Hamlet and jeopardise Hamlet's future in order to get revenge for his own murder.

Act 1, Scene 2 provides us with a glimpse of Hamlet's new and dysfunctional family set-up. His recently widowed mother has just married Hamlet's uncle, Claudius. Gertrude's marriage to her brother-in-law is presented as hasty, unseemly and incestuous. Hamlet is disgusted by it. If the other characters in the play also find it inappropriate, they simply defer to royalty and do not comment on it.

Hamlet detests his mother's marriage to Claudius, and feels betrayed by her failure to grieve properly over the death of his father. He expected his mother to at least share his intense sense of loss and his emotional pain, and perhaps also to comfort and console him.

Early in the play, Hamlet tells Gertrude, 'I shall in all my best obey you, madam' (Act 1, Scene 2, line 120). A few scenes later, he agrees to do what the ghost of his father asks. In between, we meet Polonius and his family and hear Ophelia tell her father, 'I shall obey, my lord' (Act 1, Scene 3, line 136), when he orders her to refuse to see Hamlet. These exchanges imply that children will obey their parents without question.

Ophelia's role in the play bears this out. She obeys Polonius's instructions to the letter and even allows herself to be used as a decoy against Hamlet. Polonius instructs his daughter on how to behave to test or trap Hamlet, with no regard for her feelings or interests. It might be claimed that Ophelia's docile nature reflects appropriate female behaviour in Shakespeare's day, but this argument is unsatisfactory as other female Shakespearean characters, such as Juliet and Desdemona, are prepared to put the man they love ahead of their obligations to their parents.

Ophelia's sense of unquestioning duty and obedience is shown to be a weakness, which leads to her eventual demise. Her dependence on her family is so absolute that she cannot survive for long on her own. If she had been less submissive, the play may have had a very different outcome.

As the play progresses, Hamlet's obedience falters and he challenges Gertrude. He tells her: 'You are the queen, your husband's brother's wife, and, would it were not so, you are my mother' (Act 3, Scene 4, lines 15–16). He proceeds to berate her, confront her with her failings, highlight the truth of her situation and command her to change. He tells her to 'assume a virtue, if you have it not' (line 163) and to stay away from Claudius. This represents a reversal of the traditional parent–child relationship modelled by Polonius and Ophelia.

Gertrude's love and loyalty seem torn between her son and her second husband for much of the play, but when she realises that she is about to die, her instinct is to protect her son and warn him of the poisoned drink (Act 5, Scene 2, lines 300–1). In the end it seems that the blood tie is the strongest.

We also get a glimpse of sibling relationships in the play. Claudius has killed his brother, King Hamlet, who in turn has ordered Claudius's death. One bloody and unnatural act leads to another. Such family feuds are not new, as Claudius himself points out:

> *O my offence is rank, it smells to heaven.*
> *It hath the primal eldest curse upon't:*
> *A brother's murder!*

(Act 3, Scene 3, lines 37–9)

A more caring sibling relationship is portrayed by Laertes and Ophelia. Laertes is concerned about Ophelia's encouragement of Hamlet's love. He assumes that Hamlet intends to seduce Ophelia and destroy her reputation. He is, perhaps, unfair in reaching that conclusion, and somewhat controlling in his attitude to his sister, but he clearly wants to protect her. He is distraught later when he sees evidence of her mental breakdown and then learns of her death.

The play shows the difficulties and power struggles within families, particularly between a corrupt and controlling older generation and a more idealistic and innocent younger generation. It questions, and at times undermines, the traditions of loyalty, duty and obedience within the family. Yet its resolution seems to highlight the importance of family and the enduring strength of family bonds.

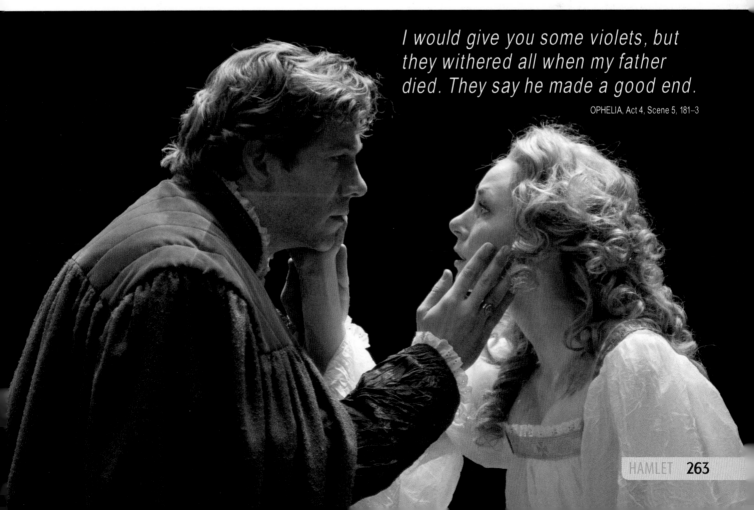

I would give you some violets, but they withered all when my father died. They say he made a good end.

OPHELIA, Act 4, Scene 5, 181–3

Exam tips

Read all the questions carefully, making sure that you understand what is being asked in each, then choose the one that you are best prepared to answer. Underline the key words in the question.

Prepare a brief list of the points you want to make and determine the structure of your answer. Make sure that you deal equally with all the elements in the question.

It is essential that you support your answer with suitable reference to the play. In order to do this you must be thoroughly familiar with the details of the plot, as well as with the characters and their actions.

Good answers include brief, relevant quotations to enhance your analysis of the play. There is no need for lengthy quotations; short ones can make the point just as well and leave more space and time for making further points.

From the beginning to the end of your answer it is essential to stay with the exact terms of the question you are dealing with. Remember that marks are awarded for making relevant points clearly and economically, with the support of reference and quotation.

A good way to ensure that you stick to the question is to mention the key term(s) of the question in your introduction, conclusion and at suitable intervals throughout your answer. This reminds the examiner, and yourself, that you are dealing consistently with the issue you have been asked to address.

Students occasionally provide long summaries of the plot or accounts of characters that may, or may not, touch on the issues raised in the question. Other students write lengthy introductions dealing with matters that they are not being asked to discuss. Such ramblings will not earn marks.

Know in advance how much time you will give to each question and stick to this plan.

It is desirable to devote a separate paragraph to each new point you make. This makes it easier for you to structure your answer properly and for the examiner to follow your argument.

Bring your answer to a clear conclusion, perhaps referring back to the question and summarising your main argument.

Ordinary Level exam questions on *Hamlet* comprise three shorter and one longer question (see examples below). Questions may deal with:

- Significant scenes and what happens in these.
- The motives of characters for behaving as they do.
- Your opinion of individual characters.
- Reasons for what happens to the characters.
- Choosing a character you would like to play and giving reasons for your choice.
- Assessing the play's merits as an exciting, moving drama, or its drawbacks as a painful, agonising experience for audiences and readers.
- How a particular scene might be staged.
- Imagining yourself interviewing one of the characters on his or her conduct at some moment in the play.

Suppose you are asked to choose a character you would like to play and you choose Hamlet. All you have to do is give a number of reasons for wanting to play Hamlet. What you must not do is simply summarise Hamlet's character. That is not what the examiner wants to know. Instead, what he or she wants to know is why you have chosen to play Hamlet.

Start your answer by giving your first reason for wanting to play Hamlet. For example: My first reason for wanting to play Hamlet is that this is the most challenging role for an actor, being full of variety, action and excitement.

You might then point out that the role would give you an opportunity to test your skill at comedy as well as tragedy; it would allow you to interact with most of the other characters; and you would enjoy the physical challenge involved in fencing with Laertes.

Higher Level exam questions on *Hamlet* may:

- Deal with a major theme or issue in the play, such as madness or revenge.

- Involve discussion of one character or a particular scene.

- Require a discussion of imagery and/or symbolism, such as disease or poison.

- Ask for your response to the play and reasons for enjoying or not enjoying it.

Two topics will appear on the paper and you will be asked to deal with one of them.

> **Remember that the highest marks are obtained by students who deal directly with the question asked and who make their points in a logical sequence. They make a series of relevant points, clearly, and back them up with suitable references to the text and with brief and appropriate quotations.**

Past papers

It is worth looking at past exam papers to familiarise yourself with the types of question asked. The following questions on *Hamlet* were part of the 2005, 2011 and 2012 Leaving Certificate exams.

Ordinary Level Paper 2, 2005

Answer **all** of the questions.

1 (a) What does Hamlet learn about his uncle Claudius when the Ghost speaks to him at the start of the play?

(b) Do you think that Hamlet treats his mother, Gertrude, fairly? Give one example to support your opinion.

(c) With whom did you have the greater sympathy, Claudius or Hamlet? Give a reason for your opinion.

2 Answer **ONE** of the following:

(i) Hamlet's father told him to take revenge on Claudius for his murder. Which of the following statements is closest to your view of how he carried out the revenge?

— *I think Hamlet did his best*

— *I think Hamlet took too long*

— *I think Hamlet failed*

Explain your view, supporting your answer by reference to the text.

OR

(ii) The play, *Hamlet*, has many exciting scenes. Briefly describe one scene that had a strong effect on you and explain why it had such an effect.

OR

(iii) Imagine that you are Ophelia. Write a letter to your brother, Laertes, telling him about the way Hamlet treats you and how you feel about the situation. Refer to events from the play in your answer.

Ordinary Level Paper 2, 2012

Answer **all** of the questions.

1 (a) What does the ghost of Hamlet's father tell Hamlet when he appears to him on the battlements of Elsinore Castle?

  (b) What is your opinion of Gertrude? Support your answer with reference to the text.

2 Explain what you find most interesting about Claudius.

3 Answer **ONE** of the following:

  (i) 'Ophelia is treated cruelly by those around her.'

   Do you agree with this statement regarding the treatment of Ophelia by either Hamlet **or** Polonius? Base your answer on your knowledge of the play.

OR

  (ii) Imagine your school is staging a version of this play. Which character would you most or least like to play on stage? Explain your choice with detailed reference to the text.

OR

  (iii) Write a piece beginning with one of the following statements:

   — I would find it exciting to live in Elsinore in Hamlet's time because . . .

   — I would find it frightening to live in Elsinore in Hamlet's time because . . .

   Your response should be based on your knowledge of the play.

Higher Level Paper 2, 2011

Answer **one** of these questions:

  (i) 'Revenge and justice are finely balanced themes in the play, *Hamlet.*'

   Discuss this statement, supporting your answer with suitable reference to the text.

OR

  (ii) 'Claudius can be seen as both a heartless villain and a character with some redeeming qualities in the play, *Hamlet.*'

   Discuss both aspects of this statement, supporting your answer with suitable reference to the text.

Higher Level Paper 2, 2012

Answer **one** of these questions:

  (i) 'Hamlet's madness, whether genuine or not, adds to the fascination of his character for the audience.'

   Discuss this statement, supporting your answer with suitable reference to the play, *Hamlet*.

OR

  (ii) 'Shakespeare uses a variety of techniques to convey a world of corruption in the play, *Hamlet*.

   Write your response to this statement, supporting your answer with suitable reference to the text.

Note: If you are asked to discuss a statement of opinion, as in the 2011 and 2012 Higher Level questions above, you are not necessarily expected to agree with the opinion quoted. You may, for example, decide that, in answering question (i), 2011, revenge and justice are not finely balanced. Matters are different in question (ii), 2011 and in question (ii), 2012, because the statements made in them are true. In answering such questions, you must demonstrate the truth of the statements by referring to relevant parts of the text and, if appropriate, referring to a stage or screen production of the play that you have seen.

Examination-based questions

The following lists give examples of the types of question that could be asked about *Hamlet* in the Leaving Certificate exam.

Suitable for Ordinary Level

1 His father's ghost appears to Hamlet on the battlements of Elsinore Castle. Basing your answer on the text of the play, explain why he appears.

2 Describe the episode in which Hamlet kills Polonius. Why does he do this?

3 Why is Hamlet deeply unhappy even before he encounters the ghost?

4 Give your opinion on the behaviour of Polonius. Refer to the text in support of the points you make.

5 Based on your reading of the play, do you think Ophelia loves Hamlet? Explain your answer.

6 In the second scene of the play, Hamlet wants to leave Elsinore. Why does he want to do this?

7 Describe Hamlet's reaction to what the ghost has to tell him. Did he expect to hear the kind of story the ghost has to tell? Explain.

8 Suggest why Hamlet decides not to tell his friends what the ghost has revealed to him.

9 Describe the problems Claudius has to deal with in the second scene of the play. Give an account of how he deals with these problems.

10 Do you think Claudius makes a good impression on his courtiers in the second scene? Has he good reason to be pleased with himself at the end of the scene?

11 Describe Hamlet's behaviour to Ophelia. Suggest why he behaves to her as he does. Refer to the text in support of your answer.

12 Imagine your school is staging a version of *Hamlet*. Which character would you most or least like to play on stage? Explain your choice with detailed reference to the text.

13 Write a piece beginning: 'I would find it exciting to live in Hamlet's time in Elsinore because . . .'. Your response should be based on your knowledge of the play.

14 Write an article for your school magazine about *Hamlet* in which you consider whether the play is relevant to young people today.

15 Imagine you are a newspaper reporter for *The Elsinore Times*. Write a piece describing what happens in *Hamlet* based on an interview with Horatio. Your article should use information drawn from the play.

16 Accidents play a large part in the development of the plot in *Hamlet*. Choose *two* examples of accidental happenings, and explain how they influence later events in the play.

17 Relationships between parents and their children are important in *Hamlet*. Write a piece about *one* of the following relationships: (a) the relationship between Claudius and Hamlet, or (b) the relationship between Gertrude and Claudius.

18 Do you think that Hamlet treats his mother, Gertrude, fairly? Support your opinion by referring to the text.

19 For which of the characters in the play do you feel the most sympathy? Give reasons for your opinion.

20 The ghost of Hamlet's father tells Hamlet to take revenge on Claudius for his murder. Which of the following statements is closest to your view of how he carries out the revenge? (a) I think Hamlet does his best. (b) I think Hamlet could have done better. (c) I think Hamlet fails. Explain your view, supporting your answer by reference to the text.

21 The play has many exciting scenes. Give a brief description of one scene that you found particularly exciting and explain why you found it so.

22 Imagine that you are Ophelia. Write a letter to your brother, Laertes, telling him about the way Hamlet has been treating you, and how you feel about this. You might also tell him why you refused to see Hamlet or to accept his letters.

23 Why does Hamlet cease his friendship with Rosencrantz and Guildenstern, and become their enemy instead? Base your answer on evidence from the text.

24 Explain how Hamlet brings about the deaths of Rosencrantz and Guildenstern. Why does he do this?

25 Can you find any evidence in the play that Rosencrantz and Guildenstern know that, on their way to England, they are carrying Hamlet's death sentence?

26 It is often remarked that, following his sea-voyage, Hamlet has a much different outlook than he had before. What evidence of this can you find in the play?

27 Give your opinion of Gertrude. Do you think she deserves sympathy? Explain your answer.

28 Gertrude has to deal with a number of problems during the play. Mention these problems, and give a brief account of how she deals with them.

29 What, do you think, is the most evil deed in the play? Give reasons for your answer.

30 'Hamlet does not like Polonius.' Mention three pieces of evidence for this statement. Do you think Hamlet is justified in disliking Polonius? Explain your answer.

31 How does Claudius turn Laertes against Hamlet? What is his motive for doing this? Base your answers on evidence from the play.

32 Do you feel sympathy for Claudius at any time in the play? Give reasons for your answer.

33 At the end of Act 1 Hamlet decides to pretend to be insane. Suggest why he takes this decision. Does it prove to be of any benefit to him? Support your answers by referring to the text.

34 Why does Hamlet stage the dumb show and The Murder of Gonzago? Is the production a success from his point of view? What consequences does it have?

35 Claudius tries to pray and seek forgiveness, but does not succeed. Why is this? How do you feel about this episode?

36 Hamlet can easily kill Claudius while the latter is praying. Why does he not do this?

37 Write a summary of what Hamlet says to his mother as he confronts her in her apartment. What, do you think, is his motive in speaking to her as he does? Do his words have any effect on Gertrude? Explain your answers by referring to the text.

38 There are comic elements in the graveyard scene (Act 5, Scene 1). Mention some of these. Do you think comedy is out of place in a graveyard? Explain your answer.

39 Describe the behaviour of Hamlet and Laertes as Ophelia is being buried. What does this tell us about Hamlet and Laertes?

40 Comment on Claudius's behaviour during the final moments of his life. What does this behaviour tell us about his attitude to Gertrude?

Suitable for Higher Level

1 Discuss the use of poisoning, literal and metaphorical, in *Hamlet*.

2 'The basic emotion in the play is the bitter feeling of a son towards his mother.' Examine this idea with reference to the text of the play.

3 'Claudius works through others; those he uses are either corrupt or corrupted.' Discuss this statement with reference to the text of the play.

4 'Death hovers over the play from beginning to end.' Develop this idea, referring to the text as you do so.

5 'The two female characters in *Hamlet* are victims of the crimes and follies of husbands, fathers and sons.' Do you think this a fair comment on Gertrude and Ophelia? Base your answer on the text of the play.

6 'In *Hamlet*, Shakespeare shows human relationships corrupted by treachery, hypocrisy and gross deception.' Give your response to this statement, based on your study of the play.

7 What, in your opinion, is the most important moment or event in *Hamlet*? Give reasons for your choice.

8 'Claudius can be seen as both a heartless villain and a character with some redeeming qualities.' Discuss both aspects of this statement, supporting your answer with suitable reference to the text.

9 'Gertrude is a pathetic character caught between the conflicting forces represented by Hamlet and Claudius respectively.' Write a response to this statement, supporting your answer with suitable reference to the text.

10 'Shakespeare uses a variety of techniques to convey a world of corruption in *Hamlet*.' Write a response to this statement, supporting your answer with suitable reference to the text.

11 'Polonius is the ideal counsellor to Claudius.' Write a response to this statement, supporting your views with suitable reference to the text.

12 '*Hamlet* is a play in which some of the major characters make serious errors or do evil things that combine to bring about fatal results.' Making reference to at least *three* characters, respond to this statement.

13 Do you think Hamlet is right to take on the role of avenger, as the ghost asks him to do? Refer to the text in support of your answer.

14 'A part of Hamlet's experience, over the course of the play, is to pass from one extreme position to another: from being at the centre of things at the beginning, "the observed of all observers", to being isolated and surrounded by enemies at the end.' Discuss this view, supporting your answer with suitable reference to the text.

15 Which character in the play do you find most interesting? Explain your choice with appropriate reference to the text.

16 'No character in *Hamlet* is completely in control of his or her own destiny.' Discuss this statement, supporting the points you make by referring to the text.

17 'The ghost has a major influence on the events of the play, for good as well as for evil.' Write a response to this comment, supporting your arguments by reference to the text.

18 'Suffering of various kinds is experienced by almost every character in *Hamlet*.' Explore this idea, referring to the text in support of your answer.

19 Write an account of the events of the play from the point of view of Claudius, explaining the actions and outlook of this character. Your account might begin: 'As King of Denmark, I would like to explain how I achieved the position I now occupy, and the difficulties now facing me . . . '.

20 Suppose Gertrude has been keeping a diary. Compose an entry, setting out her motives for sending for Hamlet to rebuke him, and describing what occurs during their meeting, and the results of these occurrences.

21 Select one theme from *Hamlet* that caused you to think deeply, and explain why. Support your answer with reference to the text.

22 Do you think Polonius should be played as a comic character, or as a dangerous, sinister individual? Support your answer by reference to the text.

23 'Hamlet has all the elements of an exciting drama: ghostly appearance, love, intrigue and murder.' Consider the play from this point of view.

24 'In Hamlet we get the impression that everybody is being constantly watched.' Do you agree with this comment? Discuss its validity in the light of the text.

25 'A significant theme in Hamlet is the relation of reality to outward appearance.' Discuss the ways in which Shakespeare develops this theme, drawing examples from the text of the play.

26 What evidence does the play contain to support a statement that Hamlet delays in seeking his revenge? How much of this evidence consists of utterances made by Hamlet himself in soliloquy? How much weight should we attach to such utterances?

27 Hamlet has been told by the ghost to avenge his father's death. Are there external obstacles to his achievement of this revenge? If so, what are these?

28 Ophelia says of Hamlet, 'O what a noble mind is here o'erthrown!' Would Hamlet's nobility have been evident without Ophelia's comment? Refer to the text in support of your answer.

29 Discuss the evidence offered by the text of the play in relation to the following three questions about Gertrude: (a) Was she unfaithful to her first husband, King Hamlet, while he lived? (b) Was she aware of the murder of her first husband, either before or after Claudius committed it? (c) Does she follow Hamlet's instructions to break off her relationship with Claudius, given during their encounter in her apartment?

30 Does Hamlet believe that he has the right to carry out the ghost's command to kill Claudius? Base your answer on the text of the play.

31 Hamlet says that the deaths of Rosencrantz and Guildenstern 'are not near my conscience'. Do you agree that Hamlet is not morally responsible for sending them to certain death? Do they deserve instant death on arrival in England? Is it reasonable to speak of their murder? Answer these questions, supporting your comments with evidence from the text.

32 'Hamlet is corrupted by the events in which he is caught up.' Respond to this view with the aid of suitable reference to the play.

33 'Hamlet offers a number of contrasting versions of human nature, ranging from nobility and idealism at one extreme, to baseness and profound evil at another.' Discuss this statement, with suitable reference to the text.

34 'Reading or seeing Hamlet is an exciting, but at the same time horrifying, experience.' Discuss this interpretation, supporting your comments by reference to the text.

35 'In many works of fiction, the villains are much more interesting than the heroes and heroines.' Discuss this statement in relation to Hamlet, supporting your arguments by reference to the text.

36 'Hamlet is a play in which many of the characters' actions bring about fatal results.' Explore this view of the play, using the text to support your points.

37 'Chance, accident and coincidence play an important part in the development of events in Hamlet.' Discuss this statement with the aid of suitable reference to the text.

38 'In Hamlet, the wicked are punished and die a deserved death, but apart from that, justice is not done.' Give your views on this verdict, supporting your arguments by reference to the play.

39 'Hamlet accepts the ghost's demand for revenge as a moral duty, but he is a reluctant avenger: a conscript, not a volunteer, in a war he has to wage against his uncle.' Does this interpretation of Hamlet's role in the play make sense? Does the text of the play provide evidence to back it up?

40 'Our experience of Hamlet is greatly enriched by a variety of recurring images.' Write your response to this statement, based on your study of the text and/or a performance of the play you have seen on stage or screen.

Sample answers

Suitable for Ordinary Level

> **1** (a) What does the ghost of Hamlet's father tell Hamlet when he appears to him on the battlements of Elsinore Castle?
>
> (b) What is your opinion of Gertrude? Support your answer with reference to the text.

(a) There are two main aspects to what the ghost of Hamlet's father tells him.

The first applies to the circumstances of his death and the nature of his present existence in purgatory. He is doomed to spend his days fasting in fires, and his nights roaming the earth until the sins he committed while he lived burn away. His sufferings are so great that he knows Hamlet would not be able to endure a description of them. He moves on to tell Hamlet how he met his death. While he was sleeping in his orchard, his brother, Claudius, now King of Denmark, poured deadly poison into his ear, which disfigured his body as it killed him. He also reveals that his wife, Gertrude, was unfaithful to him before he died.

The second aspect of the ghost's communication with Hamlet deals with his command that Hamlet punish Claudius for his crime. Hamlet is to take revenge on his uncle by doing to Claudius what Claudius did to his father. In other words, Hamlet must kill Claudius. The ghost also instructs Hamlet not to become hostile to his mother, and not to take any action against her.

(b) My opinion of Gertrude changed several times over the course of the play.

On her first appearance, I felt a lot of sympathy for her as she tried to convince Hamlet that it would be better for him to give up mourning for his father and to try to adjust to life at court. She seemed disappointed, like her husband, that Hamlet wanted to go back to Wittenberg to resume his studies, and begged him to remain at home in Elsinore. I was impressed by this, and felt that it showed how much she valued her son and appreciated his company. When Hamlet denounced her in his soliloquy for marrying so soon after her husband's death, I felt he was being harsh. It also seemed unfair to describe her tears for her late husband as insincere, and I wondered how Hamlet could know this.

The ghost's revelations to Hamlet changed my mind about Gertrude. She was not the kind of person she had first appeared to be. It was a shock to discover that she had been unfaithful to her first husband and to hear the ghost describe her second marriage as incestuous. I could see why Hamlet called her a 'most pernicious woman'.

I found Gertrude to be a very passive character. I noticed that she seemed very anxious to please Claudius, and to restore Hamlet to his old self. In general, however, she made very little impression on me until the scene in her closet, during which Hamlet reprimands her and tries to save her soul. It was then that the character of Gertrude appeared to come to life. It became clear that she did not know that her new husband had murdered her first husband. Hamlet's method of making her face up to her faults seemed to me to be cruel and extreme, and I began to feel pity for her. I found her admission of guilt very moving.

Afterwards, I admired Gertrude for protecting Hamlet by doing her best to convince Claudius that her son regretted the death of Polonius and wept over it. I was also moved by her regret that Claudius was sending Hamlet to England. However, I was surprised that she rallied to the side of Claudius when Laertes confronted him. Given everything Hamlet had told her,

I expected her to be less protective of Claudius.

Gertrude's final moments partly redeemed her character in my eyes. She supports Hamlet in the fencing match and seems totally unaware of her husband's plans to have her son killed. However, realisation dawns on her when she lies dying and her response is admirable: she saves Hamlet from drinking from the poisoned cup, and in doing so alerts him to her husband's guilt.

2 Explain what you find most interesting about Claudius.

The most interesting thing about Claudius is that he appears attractive on the outside, but is evil deep down. When I first encountered him in the play I thought he was a reasonable, friendly and sincere man, doing his best to get over his grief for his 'dear' dead brother. Thus, when he married his brother's widow, he did so with one eye happy and the other shedding tears. I noticed that he dealt efficiently with state business, spoke kindly to Laertes and tried to please Hamlet by calling him his son, begging him to think of him as a father, and naming him as the heir to the throne. He also pleaded with Hamlet to remain in Denmark as his most favoured guest. I now realise that this was mostly for show and that Claudius is skilled at adopting a pleasant and appealing mask.

A few scenes later, the ghost shows us a different Claudius. This is a man who poisoned his brother after he had gained the love of that brother's wife and begun an adulterous affair with her. Nobody, even Gertrude, knows about the murder until Hamlet learns about it from the ghost. Claudius does not know that Hamlet knows, so he feels sure that his crime will never be detected. It is still most interesting that he is able to act as though nothing has happened. I would expect someone who had committed one of the worst crimes of all, the murder of his brother, to be plagued by guilt and give himself away.

Halfway through the play we learn that Claudius does feel guilty, but he keeps this to himself and seems to be able to live with it. When Hamlet arranges for him to see an enactment of a murder similar to the one he has committed, he is startled enough to leave the room in haste, but shortly after he regains his self-control and keeps it to the end.

Claudius is a fascinating individual: the most interesting aspect of his character is his ability to separate his two selves, the attractive outward one and the repulsive evil one, for so long, and to convince everybody except Hamlet that the outward one is the only one. Claudius is the perfect hypocrite.

3 'Ophelia is treated cruelly, by those around her.'

Do you agree with this statement regarding the treatment of Ophelia by either Hamlet **or** Polonius? Base your answer on your knowledge of the play.

In agreeing with this statement, I have chosen to discuss the treatment of Ophelia by Polonius. We cannot say for certain that Polonius means to be cruel to Ophelia. Indeed, the directions and advice he gives her may be well-intentioned. However, it seems to me that her obedience to his instructions causes her to suffer cruelly.

Polonius cannot be unaware that Ophelia is strongly attracted to Hamlet and he to her. He admits that he knows that Hamlet has been giving a good deal of his time to her, and that she has taken seriously what Hamlet has been saying to her. She tells Polonius that Hamlet has

given many indications of his affection for her. More than that, she says that Hamlet has been making urgent and persistent declarations of his love for her. There is nothing to indicate that there is anything improper in the relationship described here. Most fathers would be pleased to know that the heir to the throne was making honourable declarations of love to their only daughter.

Polonius insists that Hamlet's attentions to Ophelia cannot be honourable, and that he is trying to win her affection in order to seduce her and ruin her reputation. He takes no account

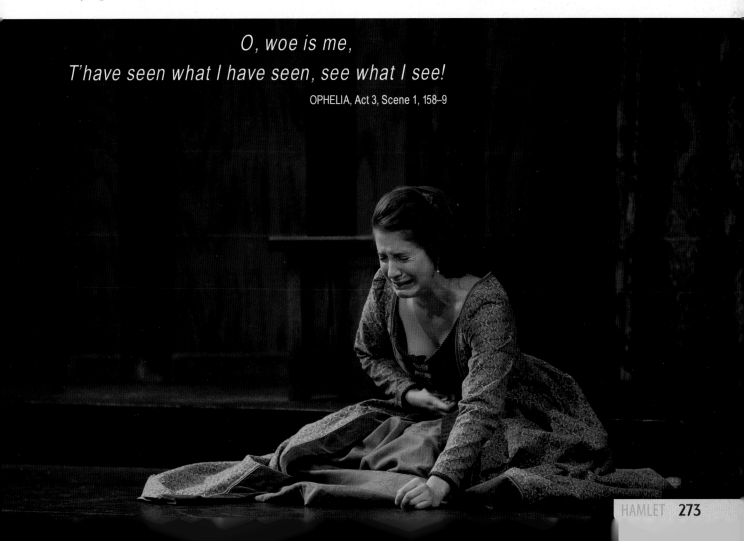

O, woe is me,
T'have seen what I have seen, see what I see!

OPHELIA, Act 3, Scene 1, 158–9

of Ophelia's feelings, and orders her to break off all contact with Hamlet. His interference in the lives of Hamlet and Ophelia leads to serious emotional suffering for her.

When a distracted Hamlet enters her apartment in a state of physical and mental distress, and leaves without speaking, Ophelia reports it to her father. Polonius thinks that Hamlet has lost his reason because Ophelia did what he had ordered her to do, and refused to see Hamlet or accept his letters. His first instinct is to inform the king of this event, rather than to comfort his daughter and check that she is all right.

Another decision by Polonius, to 'loose' Ophelia to Hamlet and spy on their meeting, causes even greater distress to his daughter. When she offers to return keepsakes Hamlet once gave her, he launches a ferocious attack on her, on women in general, on marriage and on the character

of Polonius. Ophelia, believing that Hamlet has completely lost his reason, is reduced to a state of despair and wretchedness at the thought that the most wonderful of human beings, who had made her life happy by declaring his love for her, is now afflicted with madness.

The awful experiment Polonius has involved her in has made her the victim of mental torture. Instead of offering to console her, Polonius merely says that what Ophelia has just suffered had its origin in her rejection of Hamlet, which Polonius himself had forced on her.

The cruel effects of her father's control over Ophelia do not cease with this episode. It can be argued that the absence of Hamlet from her life, which Polonius has brought about, is one of the factors contributing to her eventual collapse into insanity and to her cruel death.

---

4 (a) Why does Claudius send Hamlet to England?

   (b) Do you think Laertes deserves to be killed by Hamlet at the end of the play? Give one reason for your answer.

   (c) What is your opinion of Horatio? Explain your answer.

   (d) Write a piece about the relationship between Polonius and Ophelia.

(a) Claudius has been considering sending Hamlet to England ever since he decided that Hamlet was a threat. However, it is only when Hamlet kills Polonius that Claudius takes immediate steps to send him to England. Claudius realises that had he been behind the arras when Polonius was, he would have been killed by Hamlet.

Claudius tells Gertrude that Hamlet is a danger to everybody, and the Danish people will blame him for allowing 'this mad young man', who should have been controlled and kept away from people, to become a public danger. The only way to avoid such blame in the future is to ship Hamlet abroad with all possible speed.

A final reason for Claudius's decision emerges after his guards have arrested Hamlet. Claudius has come to the conclusion that he will never feel contented while Hamlet remains alive. He has decided to order the King of England to have

Hamlet put to death as soon as he arrives, under guard, in England. Claudius would not have been able to do this in Denmark, where Gertrude and public opinion would have intervened to save Hamlet.

(b) To answer this question, it is necessary to look closely at what happens in the course of the fencing match between Hamlet and Laertes in the final scene. During this duel, each man is fatally wounded by the other with the same poison-tipped rapier with which Laertes had planned to kill Hamlet. Laertes wounds Hamlet with the poisoned rapier when he catches Hamlet off guard, and then, in the scuffle that follows, they exchange rapiers and Hamlet wounds Laertes.

There is nothing to show that Hamlet deliberately seizes this weapon, or that he knows that its point is unbated and treated with a deadly poison. In other words, there is no evidence that when he fatally wounds Laertes, Hamlet knows that he is doing so.

In his dying remarks to Hamlet, Laertes makes this clear. Pointing to the poisoned weapon in Hamlet's hand, he confesses that he and Claudius have been involved in a plot to make use of this weapon to kill Hamlet.

Moreover, Laertes admits to Osric that he is dying because of his own treachery. His last and most significant words are spoken to Hamlet. Here he makes it clear that Hamlet is not to blame for his death. When he asks Hamlet to exchange forgiveness with him, Hamlet prays that heaven will forgive Laertes for what he has done.

Based on the above points, I would argue that the question needs to be reframed. It is true that Laertes is killed by Hamlet, but with a weapon poisoned by Laertes himself, which Hamlet does not know is poisoned. The real question should be: Does Laertes deserve to be killed by a deadly weapon made deadly by himself, and innocently used by Hamlet who has

no intention of killing him with it? Laertes answers this question for us when he says: 'I am justly killed by my own treachery.' If I were to devise a lethal weapon with the purpose of killing someone else, and that person unintentionally killed me with it, it is clear that I would have deserved my fate. Laertes, who should know best, comes to the same conclusion in his case.

(c) I admire Horatio. My opinion of him is influenced by what Hamlet thinks of him. Hamlet has known Horatio for a long time. He has chosen Horatio as a friend because of his qualities as a human being. He makes it clear that when he praises Horatio for being well balanced, he is not trying to flatter him, but to tell him the truth about himself. What Hamlet most admires about Horatio is that he keeps his emotions and his reason in harmony. If Horatio meets with good fortune, he is grateful, and if bad fortune strikes, he does not complain. He is not at the mercy of his emotions, or a slave to passion; he is a well-balanced human being, fully in control of himself.

It is clear that Horatio is a man to be trusted, someone in whom Hamlet can confide and be sure that his secrets will remain safe. For example, when Hamlet wants to reveal what he has done to Rosencrantz and Guildenstern, it is Horatio he tells. He knows that revealing it to anybody else would put his own life in danger.

Horatio is at his best in the final moments of the play. When he realises that Hamlet is dying, life appears to have no further meaning for the loyal Horatio, and he is ready, as an ancient Roman might have been, to end his own life, by drinking what is left of the poison and joining Hamlet in death. Hamlet prevents this tragic outcome, and gives Horatio a new role: to defend his character and to inform the people properly about his story.

To sum up, I admire Horatio for his integrity, his self-control, his trustworthy nature and, above all, his loyalty.

(d) In his dealings with Ophelia, I think that Polonius means well. He is concerned for her welfare, especially when it comes to her relationship with Hamlet. When he advises her to keep Hamlet at a distance, and then to break off her relationship with him, he is genuinely fearful that Hamlet is merely toying with her, and has no intention of marrying her. In addition, he knows that Hamlet is not entirely a free agent where marriage is concerned: his wife will probably be chosen for him.

However, Polonius misjudges the nature of the Hamlet–Ophelia relationship and later has to acknowledge that Hamlet's intentions towards his daughter were honourable and that he loved her. On her father's instructions, Ophelia has denied Hamlet access to her, the relationship has broken down and Ophelia is deeply distressed as a result.

It has to be noted that Polonius intrudes into Ophelia's private life to an undue extent, and interferes with her freedom. Their relationship is an unequal one. He commands, and she obeys. This situation was regarded as acceptable in Shakespeare's day, but is much less common today. Sometimes, when he is exercising his control over Ophelia, Polonius strikes a jarring note, as when he talks of 'loosing' his daughter to Hamlet in order to spy on their encounter.

It is clear from the text that Ophelia loves her father, and is prepared to obey his commands no matter what they mean for her. The extent of her love is demonstrated in her response to his death. His loss is the main cause of her insanity. She cannot cope with life without him. In her madness, she demands an audience with the queen. She speaks mainly of her father, and she is thinking of him as she sings of a dead man buried in the 'grass-green turf' with a stone at his heels. She would like to distribute violets, symbols of fidelity, but says 'they withered all when my father died.' Then she sings a lament for Polonius: 'His beard was as white as snow, all flaxen was his poll: he is gone'.

I hope all will be well. We must be patient, but I cannot choose but weep to think they should lay him in the cold ground. My brother shall know of it.

OPHELIA, Act 4, Scene 5, 67–9

Suitable for Higher Level

> **1** 'The main action of *Hamlet* may be described as the attempt to find, and deal with, the hidden danger threatening the welfare of Claudius's Denmark.'
>
> Discuss this statement, supporting your answer with suitable reference to the text.

In the opening scene we see Marcellus, Barnardo and Horatio on guard, watching for the hidden danger facing the regime of King Claudius. It may be war (threatened by Fortinbras of Norway). Or it may be the unspeaking ghost, resembling the late King Hamlet and dressed in armour. The key comment is Horatio's: 'This bodes some strange eruption to our state.'

We then see the threatened danger from the point of view of Claudius. He concentrates on three restless young men as possible threats to the security of his throne: Hamlet, Laertes and Fortinbras. Laertes seems the least threatening: all he wants is permission to travel. Fortinbras wants to go to war to recover lands lost to Denmark, but Claudius can deal with that threat by means of diplomacy. There remains Hamlet, moody and sullen, who has not accepted the new king with good grace. Claudius may assume that Hamlet's hostility is the result of his father's death, but he must also regard Hamlet as the most obvious danger to his rule as King of Denmark.

When Hamlet is left alone on stage, we hear about another disease that threatens the health of Denmark. As Hamlet sees it, the source of the disease is Claudius, under whose rule, Denmark, and Hamlet's whole world, have been transformed into 'an unweeded garden that grows to seed' and that is filled with 'things rank and gross in nature'. Gertrude is also part of the disease, having married the beastly Claudius and betrayed the memory of his father.

The revelations of the ghost about Claudius as a murderer seem to confirm what Hamlet already suspected. When the ghost tells him that 'the serpent that did sting thy father's life now wears his crown', Hamlet answers, 'O my prophetic soul! My uncle.' Hamlet's suspicion has now hardened into something much stronger, although he is not yet ready to place absolute faith in the ghost's words.

In Act 2 Polonius thinks he can diagnose the malady threatening Claudius's reign in Denmark. Hamlet has visited Ophelia in a state of distraction, behaving irrationally. Polonius, having already ordered Ophelia to return Hamlet's love letters and deny his access to her, concludes that this 'hath made him mad', and fears that his madness or 'ecstasy' may lead him to 'desperate undertakings'. Satisfied that he has identified the cause of the disease that makes Hamlet a danger to Claudius, he takes this news to Claudius.

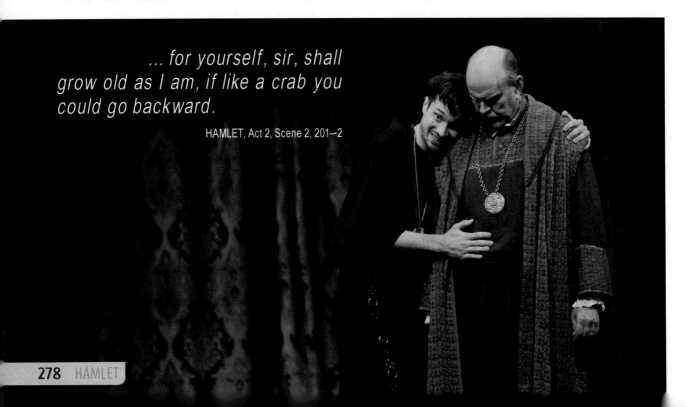

... for yourself, sir, shall grow old as I am, if like a crab you could go backward.

HAMLET, Act 2, Scene 2, 201–2

Claudius has also been exploring the cause of Hamlet's disturbed state, having satisfied himself that the latter is the real and only threat to his security. He makes use of Rosencrantz and Guildenstern to see if they can discover what the real cause of Hamlet's transformation is: 'to gather so much as from occasion you may glean whether aught, to us unknown, afflicts him thus'. Claudius, in other words, wants to find out if more is troubling Hamlet than his father's death. Hamlet sees through this attempt to discover his secret.

Claudius is not convinced by Polonius's crude diagnosis, 'Your noble son is mad', and his belief that Hamlet's rejected love for Ophelia is the cause. Claudius wants to test this theory of unrequited love further. Polonius contrives an opportunity for them to secretly observe Hamlet and Ophelia. Claudius is then convinced that neither love nor madness can account for Hamlet's menacing behaviour, concluding that there is 'something in his soul o'er which his melancholy sits on brood', and that whatever plans he is hatching will prove dangerous to the health of Denmark and of its king.

When the players arrive at Elsinore, Hamlet plans to get firmer evidence than the word of a ghost that Claudius poisoned King Hamlet. He will arrange for the players to enact a play similar to the murder of his father in the hope that it will force Claudius to betray his evil nature in public. Hamlet's play is decisive in his effort to identify

the hidden disease that threatens the moral health of Denmark. It finally locates this disease in Claudius. It justifies Hamlet's earliest intuitions and the story told by the ghost.

Having failed with his attempt to use Rosencrantz and Guildenstern to find the cause of Hamlet's disorder, Claudius next, on the advice of Polonius, uses Gertrude. The interview between Hamlet and Gertrude goes badly wrong when Hamlet kills Polonius, who is concealed behind a curtain, thinking that he is Claudius. Hamlet then reveals to Gertrude how she herself has become involved in the contagious evil that Claudius is spreading. She, like Claudius, is part of the hidden disease that is poisoning Denmark.

An image of disease is appropriate to the way in which Hamlet warns his mother to confess her sinful state, and not to try to evade it by pretending it is a figment of his supposed madness. To ignore the evil Claudius has involved her in 'will but skin and film the ulcerous place, whiles rank corruption, mining all within, infects unseen'. Hamlet is telling Gertrude that trying to conceal the moral infection spreading from her association with Claudius is like applying a remedy to the surface of an ulcer that only covers it up but does not heal it, and which allows the hidden corruption to work through the body unchecked. The body here is a metaphor for Denmark.

Hamlet also uses a metaphor for the corruption in both Poland and Norway, comparing it to an abscess or 'imposthume' that threatens to destroy them. This image can also be applied to Denmark: when Hamlet exposes Claudius in all his guilt, and destroys Polonius, he has opened the abscess. As a result, forces of social disorder are unleashed: Laertes starts a rebellion, Ophelia loses her reason, and Claudius corrupts Laertes.

Just as Hamlet freely uses disease imagery when talking about Claudius, the latter does the same in referring to the threat posed by Hamlet. For example, when Claudius reflects on the death of Polonius, and blames himself for not having dealt with Hamlet sooner, he thinks of Hamlet as a disease from which he, Claudius, has been suffering and neglecting at his peril: 'But, like the owner of a foul disease, to keep it from divulging, let it feed even on the pith of life'. The disease Hamlet represents has been silently undermining the very life of Claudius.

Again, Claudius imagines that if he sends Hamlet to England, it will be like ridding himself of an illness. When he instructs the King of England to arrange for the immediate death of Hamlet, the image he uses extends the disease-pattern: 'For like the hectic in my blood he rages, and thou must cure me.' In other words, the King of England must cure Claudius of the disease that Hamlet's continued existence represents, by killing Hamlet.

In Hamlet's eyes, Denmark under Claudius is like a human body that looks healthy on the outside but is thoroughly diseased within. In the eyes of Claudius, it is Hamlet who represents the deadly disease that will have to be cured if Denmark (and his own throne) is to be safe.

Shakespeare makes us see the characters and events of the play mainly through Hamlet's eyes, so that we tend to share his point of view. Hamlet becomes the privileged interpreter of the source of the disease, which spreads from the primary guilt of Claudius to ruin all the lives within his circle of power.

It should be remembered that both Gertrude and Ophelia are defined almost exclusively in reference to men. This makes their exposure to the poisonous atmosphere generated by Claudius more extreme than is the case with other characters. Gertrude has a stake in Claudius and equally in Hamlet. Ophelia has a stake in the regime of Claudius because her father is the king's chief minister, but equally in Hamlet, the man she loves.

In the final catastrophe, Gertrude, Claudius, Hamlet and Laertes all die of poison on stage. These four poisonings are literal enactments of the metaphorical poison that has been working itself out through the course of the play. This poison is the danger that threatened Denmark, and it was introduced by Claudius himself.

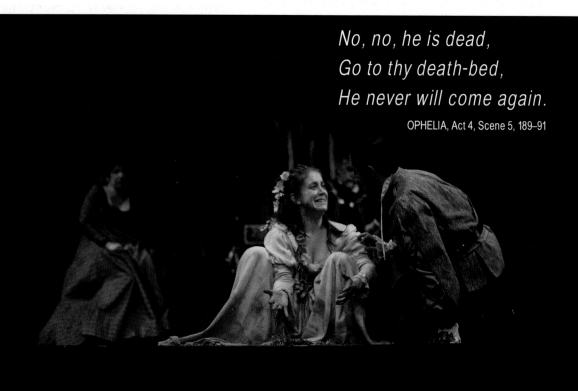

No, no, he is dead,
Go to thy death-bed,
He never will come again.

OPHELIA, Act 4, Scene 5, 189–91

2 'The ghost is the real villain in Shakespeare's *Hamlet*.'

Discuss this statement, referring to the text in support of the points you make.

For the purposes of this discussion, I define the term 'villain' as the character in the play who is important to the plot because of his or her evil motives or actions. There are only two characters in the play to whom this definition can apply: Claudius and the ghost. When we speak of the 'real villain' we are suggesting that one villain in particular is a greater villain than any other. I believe that this greater villain is the ghost, in particular in terms of the harm done to others.

I would first like to consider the harm, or evil, that the ghost does to Hamlet. Even before the ghost intrudes into his life, Hamlet is not a happy, carefree, contented man. He dislikes his uncle/stepfather Claudius, and finds it hard to be civil to him. His mother's sudden marriage to Claudius after his father's death has come as a shock to him, and left him disillusioned with women. The father he worshipped has been replaced, as he sees it, by a man his mother should never have married. He is so depressed that he does not seem to care whether he lives or dies, and is obsessed with his mother's betrayal of his father's memory. He wants to escape Denmark and return to his studies in Germany. In spite of all of this, Hamlet's situation is not impossible. Time might have helped heal his emotional wounds. As Claudius reminds him, his situation as a bereaved son is not unique.

The ghost's first encounter with Hamlet makes the latter's situation a great deal worse, as well as changing his character and outlook for the worse. Once the ghost tells him about Claudius's crime, orders him to avenge this, and reveals Gertrude's adultery, Hamlet is placed at the centre of a cobweb of evil, so that his life is caught in the net, and there is to be no escape.

As the ghost approaches him, Hamlet wonders whether he is 'a spirit of health or a goblin damned', or from heaven or hell. The ghost is none of these things. He is a spirit suffering in purgatory for unconfessed sins committed during his life and hoping to reach heaven eventually. Given his status, the commands he gives Hamlet are difficult to explain or justify. Having told Hamlet to 'revenge his foul and most unnatural murder', he goes on to describe any kind of murder as 'most foul'. If murder is most foul, and if the ghost is suffering unspeakable torments for lesser crimes, what right can he have to demand that Hamlet burden his soul with murder, which he will have to if he obeys the ghost?

The ghost is ordering Hamlet to commit an evil act of the very same kind as he is asking him to punish: murder, particularly the murder of a king. He is asking him to do this on no more evidence than the word of a ghost. He has not considered what might happen to Hamlet if he kills Claudius, and then seeks to defend his action by saying that a ghost ordered him to do so. But this is only part of the evil set in motion by the ghost.

Hamlet already resents what Gertrude has done by marrying Claudius. By the time the ghost has finished talking about Gertrude and Claudius, Hamlet's resentment has turned to intense hatred for Claudius, and extreme contempt for Gertrude. What the ghost says about Gertrude has a damaging effect on Hamlet's character and outlook: he is convinced that all women are liable to betray men as Gertrude betrayed his father.

There can be no doubt that the ghost has corrupted and coarsened Hamlet's character. This becomes evident in various ways. As he comes upon Claudius praying or trying to pray, Hamlet is provided with an excellent opportunity to kill Claudius. But killing his uncle would not be enough for him. He has grown to hate him so much that he wants to damn him as well as kill him. Hamlet's personal hatred of Claudius, undoubtedly reinforced by the ghost's story, contaminates his desire for justice.

It is impossible to miss the cynicism, bitterness and hatred that mark Hamlet's dealings with others, especially in the middle scenes of the play. His extreme cruelty to Ophelia is an example. Another is the brutal sarcasm with which he addresses Gertrude, and his threatening attitude to her. These two women are bullied and degraded by him: Ophelia is the target of obscenities and Gertrude the victim of his obsessive emphasis on lust. It is significant that the ghost, in his comments on the Claudius–Gertrude relationship, displays the same obsessive interest: 'So lust, though to a radiant angel linked, will sate itself in a celestial bed and prey on garbage.'

The ghost's habit of degrading those he condemns by dehumanising them is taken up by Hamlet as he echoes the imagery of human degradation, imagining Gertrude and Claudius 'in the rank sweat of an enseamèd bed, stewed in corruption, honeying and making love over the nasty sty'. Hamlet's comment on the dead body of Polonius is in the same vein: 'I'll lug the guts into the neighbour room.'

It is remarkable that the ghost commands Hamlet not to turn against Gertrude, but to leave her to heaven, and at the same time reveals details about her that are bound to taint Hamlet's mind against her, for example her adultery and incestuous relationship with Claudius, and her hypocrisy ('my most seeming-virtuous queen'). Had the ghost not revealed Gertrude's adultery, Hamlet's attitude towards male–female relationships would not be as warped as it has become.

At the end of the play, as the bodies of Hamlet, Claudius, Gertrude and Laertes lie on the stage, Horatio outlines for Fortinbras the

circumstances leading to these four deaths and the other deaths that preceded them. Horatio talks of 'carnal, bloody and unnatural acts' of 'casual slaughters' and 'deaths put on by cunning'. It is common to blame all of this on Claudius, the source of poison and murder, but what happens in the play strongly suggests that the ghost, employing and manipulating his avenging agent Hamlet, is still more to blame than Claudius is for turning the royal court into a slaughterhouse.

Eight people die in the course of the play. The entire royal family is wiped out as Claudius, Gertrude and Hamlet die violently. Polonius

and Laertes suffer similar deaths, and Ophelia is drowned having lapsed into insanity. Rosencrantz and Guildenstern are executed in England. The primary engine of this cycle of death is undoubtedly the ghost. Without his intervention in the affairs of Denmark, it seems unlikely that these eight violent deaths would have come about.

Had the ghost taken the advice he gives to Hamlet in the case of Gertrude, and been content to leave her, as well as Claudius, to heaven and their own consciences, most of the evil that occurs in the play would have been avoided. Hamlet's adoption of the role of avenger when commanded to do so by the ghost precipitates the deadly sequence of events that follows.

To test his right to perform this role, Hamlet stages a play depicting a murder similar to the one the ghost wants him to avenge. Claudius panics, thinking, correctly, that Hamlet knows his secret. As a result, Gertrude, disturbed by the offence offered to Claudius in the insert-play, sends for Hamlet in order to chastise him, while Polonius hides behind a tapestry to spy on what transpires between them. When Hamlet becomes aggressive, Gertrude calls for help, Polonius repeats her call, and Hamlet kills him, thinking he must be Claudius. Hamlet the avenger kills the wrong man. Claudius then sends Hamlet to England, escorted by Rosencrantz and Guildenstern, who carry sealed orders for the King of England to have Hamlet executed on arrival there. Hamlet changes these orders at sea, and his two escorts are executed instead of him. Meanwhile, the death of Polonius leads to Ophelia's insanity, and then to her death by drowning. These two deaths in his family provoke Laertes first to blame Claudius, then to blame Hamlet, and finally to collaborate with Claudius in a plan that will lead to four more deaths: those of Claudius, Gertrude, Hamlet and Laertes.

It is clear that the appearance and command of the ghost act as the catalyst that sets this train of events in motion. For that reason, I agree that the ghost is the real villain of the play.